REWILDING THE WAY

ADVANCE PRAISE

"Once more, Wynward offers wild hope for a tame world. If you are yearning for an earth-honoring, despair-crushing, culture-resisting, Jesus-following response to the crises of our times, look no further: make this book a part of your life."
—*Richard Rohr, founder of Center for Action and Contemplation*

"For those who think Christianity should run counter to the dominant culture, this book offers a wild and exhilarating idea about how lives might be lived!"
—*Bill McKibben, author and activist*

"*Rewilding the Way* is a clarion call not to the 'good life' but to a better life, a life based on God's dream rather than the American dream, the Jesus Way rather than culture's mores. Wynward invites us to make the leap from a mild faith to a wild faith based on the countercultural gospel message of less *me* and more *we*."
—*Nancy Sleeth, cofounder of Blessed Earth and author of*
  Almost Amish

"*Rewilding the Way* calls us to be dangerously alive to the ultimate source of life and the critical challenges of our time. Todd Wynward is a voice crying out in the wilderness with surprising playfulness, practicality, and hope."
—*Mark Scandrette, author of* Free: Practicing the Way of Jesus *and* Soul Graffiti

"Here is a primer for a First World Christian faith seeking to respond to the interlocking social and ecological crises stalking our history with discipleship rather than denial. Wynward knows his way around wilderness—as landscape and religious tradition—and is a reliable guide for exploring both. I commend this readable, engaging introduction to following Jesus and de-domesticating our churches in this demanding and discouraging historical moment."
—*Ched Myers, Mennonite activist theologian*

"I met Todd Wynward in a group of folks committed to the risk of smuggling refugees safely across the Southwest border. A lot of lives were saved. Now, Todd has written a text that will save a lot of souls. Read this book, rewild your spirit, and join with the Jesus Way to save the sacred earth."
—*John Fife, human rights activist and cofounder of the Sanctuary Movement*

REWILDING THE WAY

BREAK FREE TO FOLLOW
AN UNTAMED GOD

TODD WYNWARD

Herald Press

Harrisonburg, Virginia
Kitchener, Ontario

Library of Congress Cataloging-in-Publication Data
Wynward, Todd, 1967-
  Rewilding the way : break free to follow an untamed God / Todd Wynward.
    pages cm
  Includes bibliographical references.
  ISBN 978-0-8361-9948-2 (pbk. : alk. paper) 1. Christian life.
2. Human ecology--Religious aspects--Christianity. I. Title.
  BV4501.3.W96 2015
  248.4--dc23
                                2015012888

REWILDING THE WAY
© 2015 by Herald Press, Harrisonburg, Virginia 22802
    Released simultaneously in Canada by Herald Press,
    Kitchener, Ontario N2G 3R1. All rights reserved.
Library of Congress Control Number: 2015012888
International Standard Book Number: 978-0-8361-9948-2
Printed in Canada
Cover and interior design by Merrill Miller
Cover photo by Tashka/iStockphoto/Thinkstock

All Scripture quotations, unless otherwise indicated, are taken from the
Holy Bible, New International Version®, *NIV*®. Copyright ©1973, 1978, 1984,
2011 by Biblica, Inc.™ Used by permission of Zondervan. All rights reserved
worldwide. www.zondervan.com The "NIV" and "New International
Version" are trademarks registered in the United States Patent and
Trademark Office by Biblica, Inc.™

William Stafford, excerpt from "A Message from the Wanderer" from *Ask
Me: 100 Essential Poems*. Copyright © 1977 by William Stafford. Reprinted
with the permission of The Permissions Company, Inc. on behalf of
Graywolf Press, Minneapolis, Minnesota, www.graywolfpress.org.

To order or request information, please call 1-800-245-7894, or visit
www.heraldpress.com.

19 18 17 16 15   10 9 8 7 6 5 4 3 2 1

Today outside your prison I stand
and rattle my walking stick: Prisoners, listen;
you have relatives outside. And there are
thousands of ways to escape.

—William Stafford,
"A Message from the Wanderer"

To Peg and Nico—two traveling companions with whom I forever want to share the journey.

TABLE OF CONTENTS

PART III: OUR WORK AHEAD

PROLOGUE

WANT TO HEAR A SECRET most of us know but rarely admit? The good life in modern society really isn't so good. In fact, these days it often feels exhausting. Frantic. Broken. Headed for a cliff. Actually, why is it called "the good life" when it's so often a stress-inducing, resource-hogging, soul-deadening, never-ending pursuit of *more*? What once was good—personal advancement, increased consumer choices, and technological progress—has gone haywire. For all its glittering perks, the current version of "the good life" often feels suffocating: to ourselves, other people, and the planet.

Millions of us know we are shackled to Earth-ruining, life-sucking systems we don't want to engage with—like an economy based on producing plastics, burning coal, driving cars, and ripping resources out of the ground—causing us to act in ways we know are not best for ourselves or the wondrous planet we depend upon. Fast food, cheap oil, chronic debt, and constant pressure are only some of the cultural cages that hold us captive. Bottom line: We've been constrained and colonized by corporations. We've become their tamed and well-fed pets. And we willingly let it happen, every day, through the choices we continue to make. I know I do. We let our very identities be domesticated by a dominant and destructive consumer culture.

Enough is enough. Our authentic selves, our awaiting children, and our aching planet need us to find a better path. It's time to break from the destructive systems of dominant culture so we can become the free and untamed people God has always wanted us to be. I'm not going to lie: we've got some creative and courageous work ahead of us. For modern affluent Christians, our task is clear: It's time to reinvent our current American way so we can better follow the Jesus Way. It is time to rewild our Way.

REWILDING BIOLOGY, REWILDING SPIRITUALITY

Rewilding is a concept I've borrowed from conservation biology to name the system-changing, ecologically grounded spirituality Christians need to embody in our times. Caroline Fraser's book *Rewilding the World* provided me with some language and concepts I've found extremely useful in my attempt to connect ecology with Christianity. In biological terms, rewilding means just what it sounds like: a scientific vision to bring our ecosystems back to a wilder state, at a scale previously unimagined. Ecological rewilding—as a guiding vision—has become the ultimate weapon in the fight against fragmentation over the last two decades, as a coherent way to design, connect, and revitalize protected areas.[1] Since the late 1990s, extraordinary steps to "rewild the world" have been taken across the globe. Countries have rallied to place vast amounts of land under protection. Geographical "megalinkages" have been restored, throughout and in between vast continents. These restored megalinkages— massive international land corridors linking core wilderness areas—once again allow apex predators and keystone species to migrate and flourish, which then improves health for the entire bioregion.[2]

REWILDING THE JESUS WAY

So how can rewilding inform the Jesus Way? Ecological rewilding resurrects natural vitality within ecosystems that have been overly controlled, manipulated, and domesticated. I want spiritual rewilding to do the same for the Way of Jesus: resurrect its original vitality after being, for far too long, alienated from Earth and manipulated by corporate industrial culture. Many Christians like me live too easily in this time of unprecedented environmental and economic precariousness. We've become like domestic house pets, tamed by the twin masters of nonstop technology and comfy consumerism. How we who follow the Way of Jesus choose to act right now—in this "watershed moment" of history—matters more than ever. We need to rewild our way and restore our own "megalinkages" between a God-filled heaven and a God-filled earth, between following Jesus and doing justice, between sacred belief and transformative praxis.

A LOOK AT THE WHOLE BOOK

Do you love Jesus, but you're leery of what institutional Christianity has become? Me too. Are you eager to redirect a consumer-frenzied culture gone terribly awry? So am I. Ready to become the Earth-honoring, untamed people God yearns for us to be? Then let's get going.

This book is an unapologetic rallying cry to rewild a Christianity that has become terribly tame. Can today's cozy Christians become the countercultural prophets God aches for us to be? Will we repent—turn around to God—and be able to vitally embody the subversive, transformative life way that

Jesus practiced and offered? Raised in our overcivilized and ecocidal society, what traits must we rediscover to be partners in God's plan so that instead of being anxious foot-draggers and bland bystanders we can be salt, light, and leaven in a future where God mightily uses our gifts?

Part 1 of *Rewilding the Way* describes both our current predicament and our incredible potential as children of God, and the wilderness testing that has always been God's way to craft a transformed people. Part 2 explores seven pathways we can pursue to become deeper allies of God: more love-spreading, culture-defying, fear-abolishing, Earth-honoring followers of the Jesus Way. Part 3 outlines our work ahead: highlighting some of the Spirit-filled cultural initiatives and social movements that are already shifting our society toward a positive future in an uncertain time. Finally, the book's epilogue reminds us that we follow a ferociously loving and fantastically living God, whose wild Spirit is always present and active, ready to lead us even in the most troubling of times.

Read on, if you are willing to be transformed and become one who transforms. The road is long and there are no maps. Together we have a journey of doing and undoing to begin.

May the wild return.

Todd Wynward
Taos, New Mexico

PART I

OUR PREDICAMENT, OUR POTENTIAL

1

TAME CHRISTIANITY

MANY OF US are waking up to realize that our current version of the American way—a path of strength, superiority, and self-centeredness—is often opposed to the Jesus Way. We're also seeing that what has become the modern "American dream"—ensuring personal privilege by raiding the commonwealth of the planet—is not nearly as satisfying or significant as God's dream. Millions of folks seeking to follow the way of Jesus in the shadow of dominant culture are—in ways both small and large—defecting from business as usual. We're beginning to ask: What kind of a better "good life" can we embody in today's times—one that is better for us *and* our world?

MAKING A BREAK
Fifteen years ago, my wife and I acted on that question. We moved from Albuquerque, New Mexico, into a little adobe house heated by a wood-burning stove, high up in the Sangre de Cristo Mountains near Taos. There we raised our son, ran a summer camp, and started an innovative public school that uses the surrounding farm and wilderness as its classroom. We

dove headlong into transformative work with youth and the task of reinventing public education. It was an amazing life, full of close friendships, meaningful labor, inspiring break-throughs, and incredible natural settings. It was also exhaust-ing. For those ten years we worked extremely hard, with little time for anything else, which meant we were fully engaged in the American way, purchasing and consuming and throwing away far more stuff than any generation before us.

Five years ago, we made a significant shift. We decided to engage more deeply with our watershed in our search for a bet-ter practice of the good life. We reduced our work demands a bit and relocated into a yurt we built in our backyard. With some like-minded friends we milk goats, shear sheep, plant trees, catch water, and try to grow a lot of our food in the high desert. More than once we have been called "feral." Once a citi-fied visitor from Philadelphia giggled in awe when she entered our thirty-foot-diameter yurt, and she immediately started snapping photos. She simply couldn't believe we use a compost-ing toilet and carry water by hand in buckets, like millions of people across the world.

If you're daunted by our example, don't be. We're pretend-ers. Yes, we've cultivated a slightly parallel existence, but don't be fooled: we're still solidly embedded in American consumer culture. My family has a laptop per person, too many cars, a cappuccino maker, cell phones, and a voracious appetite for Netflix. We daily take our son to soccer practice in a Prius and monthly drive a hundred miles to shop at the nearest Trader Joe's. Though we dabble with homesteading in the high des-ert, we're still enmeshed in the economy of empire, deeply con-forming to the system.

Lucky for us, we follow a God of mercy who ever invites us to take another step deeper into the Way. As the poet Rumi invites: "Come, come, whoever you are. Wanderer, worshiper, lover of leaving. It doesn't matter. Ours is not a caravan of despair. Come, even if you have broken your vows a thousand times. Come, yet again, come, come."[1]

DEMANDS TOO DAUNTING

The larger-than-life British explorer Ernest Shackleton accomplished many things, but he is most famous for what he did *not* do: traverse the Antarctic continent in 1914. His infamous exploratory voyage aboard the *Endurance* is one of history's most inspiring failures: rather than crossing the vast Antarctic, the *Endurance* became trapped in polar ice, and the expedition turned into a heroic struggle for survival, creatively and courageously endured by twenty-eight crewmen over a span of nearly two years. But Shackleton seemed to know what he was getting into. Legend tells us that in preparation for the epic voyage, he posted the following want ad in a London newspaper:

> Men wanted for hazardous journey.
> Low wages. Bitter cold.
> Long months of complete darkness.
> Constant danger. Safe return doubtful.
> Honour and recognition in event of success.

Authentically following the Way of Jesus can seem equally daunting sometimes: hazardous, foolish, impossible in our modern society. Like many residents of the United States and Canada today, I grew up middle class. We had our own house, had a decent family car, and college was an assumed right. We never experienced malnutrition, displacement, or the terror and chaos of living in a war zone. We were blessed with security. Globally speaking, I was born into privilege. I also grew up in a Christian home. As a teenager, I made my own decision to follow Jesus.

Raised both privileged and Christian did not seem odd in afflu-ent America; in fact, it seemed the norm. Therefore, I felt am-bushed when I encountered the story of Jesus and the rich young man in the gospel of Mark. In this dialogue, Jesus tells this man of privilege who has "done all the right things" that he still needs to do one thing: "Go, sell everything you have and give to the poor." The story continues: "At this the man's face fell. He went away sad, because he had great wealth" (Mark 10:17-30).

The man went away sad because Jesus' demand was just too daunting. *Give away everything, right now? Not gonna do it*, thought the rich man. How about you? If you're like me, the challenge is too daunting, as well. I've got a family to feed, bills to pay, my kid's college education to plan for. Jesus' challenge has been too daunting for most Christians. It seems that most Christians throughout history have somehow sidestepped or explained away this daunting demand. In doing so, we sidestep full participation in the kingdom of God, as well.

The challenge to the rich man is not the only extreme expec-tation Jesus throws down, of course. Andrew and Simon may have jumped at Jesus' invitation alongside the Sea of Galilee. But if I'd been there with my brother, hip-deep in our fishing work, I might have responded, "Leave our nets, right now? Are you serious?" Even though I'm wild about Jesus, I probably would have said, "Let me catch some food for my family, then I'll be right there."

If I'm honest, the needs and wants of my family come first. Because of this, I don't meet a lot of Jesus' other qualifications for hard-core discipleship, either; in the Bible, Jesus asks those who follow him to drop our careers, love our enemies, hate our families, share our resources, turn the other cheek, and be pre-pared to lay down our lives nonviolently for our friends.

I must say, I'm not doing any of these very well.

Looking across the last two thousand years, I find many other daunting examples of discipleship I'm not ready to emulate. Look at the fourth century, when Constantine created an unholy alliance of moneyed church and military state—am I ready to leave empire behind and live the rest of my life in a desert cave like the desert fathers did? Hardly. Am I prepared to dive into a life of strict voluntary poverty like Clare and Francis did in Assisi in the 1200s? I like a simple life, but not that simple. How about devoting my entire life to lepers like Mother Teresa did in Calcutta? No again.

As I contemplate my inability to follow these examples, I realize something obvious: my spiritual tradition overwhelmingly emphasizes the single, childless life. The landscape of Judeo-Christianity is packed with stories of single people who seem to have no families to provide for, no debts to pay back, no homes to keep up, no crops to cultivate, no diapers to clean. Nowhere in the New Testament do I read: "John slept through the morning prayers because his baby kept him up all night." Or: "Paul stayed longer than expected with the church in Corinth, because his teenager was on the track team." Or: "After supper, Jesus and the twelve took some time to wash dishes, and Peter stayed behind to deal with the crusty soup pots." The most memorable time kitchen chores are mentioned is in the story of Martha, who is shown to represent the worst of two choices (Luke 10:40-41).

Give away everything. Dwell in the desert the rest of your years. Embrace poverty as a way of life. Renounce family. As a parent with kids to feed, these daunting demands of renunciation seem so unrealistic that, if you're like me, you reject them before you even begin. As G. K. Chesterton famously said, "The Christian ideal has not been tried and found wanting; it has been found difficult, and left untried."[2]

So here's our modern dilemma: we avoid absolute renunciation for good reasons, but then we completely cave to dominant culture. We may have deep relationships and wonderful worship experiences within our church communities, but we still cozily conform to consumerism. Our souls, and our habits, are allegiant to corporation culture, unconverted. Along with everyone else around us in modern society, we settle for practicing a comfortable, market-approved version of Christianity. We focus on our families and jobs, surrounding ourselves with other middle-class families, and together we live lives of isolated busyness and unexamined privilege. We are a staid and stale shadow of something that should be full-bodied and transformative. Søren Kierkegaard may have felt much the same in a very different time and a very different place. More than 150 years ago in Denmark, he determined his country's Christianity—both domesticated and desiccated—to be about as genuine and flavorful "as tea made from a bit of paper which once lay in a drawer beside another bit of paper which had been used to wrap up a few dried tea leaves from which tea had already been made three times."[3]

A THIRD WAY?

Between the options of absolute renunciation and unexamined affluence, could there be a third way? Our precious planet, God's gift, is imperiled, largely by the actions of affluent industrial societies like ours. Could there be a transitional path that might help privileged people like us unshackle from consumer culture to wade ever deeper into the kingdom of God?

I think there is. My mind turns to some biblical examples of life change that seem a touch more possible for people like me. I don't normally think of a locust-eating wilderness prophet in a camel's-hair cloak as a guide for families, but listen to this straightforward advice from John the Baptist: to be part of God's ideal society, those who have two shirts should share with those who lack; those who are blessed with surplus food should do the same (Luke 3:11). And then there's the life example of the tax collector Zacchaeus, who—after experiencing radical acceptance by Jesus—feels so forgiven and blessed that he immediately gives half of his possessions to the poor and pays back those he cheated at 400 percent interest (Luke 19:8).

These two examples are not about absolute renunciation; they encourage us *to give away half and keep living in the world.* Now this kind of mandate seems both powerful *and* possible— countercultural and life changing, yes, yet doable, even when raising a family. Are we, as modern disciples with surplus possessions, called to a path of significant relinquishment? Looking at the inequity in the world, how could we not be?

My family is part of the massive silent body of modern Christians who live in two worlds, striving to follow the radical Jesus while still being shackled to Caesar. Maybe you are, too. We are the tribe of the semi-transformed, the halfway-there, the partially free. We want to live more transformatively, but we've made important life commitments—meaningful vocations, good marriages, growing families, home mortgages, community involvements—that we don't intend to break.

Is there any hope for sorry half-disciples like us? Luckily, yes. Remember what Jesus said as the rich young man turned away sad, unwilling to give away his possessions? "With man, this is impossible, but not with God; all things are possible with God." I pin my hopes on the fact that God is extravagant, mercy within mercy within mercy. God knows our hearts. He created us, inconsistent and imperfect, to be just as we are. I have to trust that God expects us to love our families *and* seek to walk the Jesus Way.

And so we come to the key questions of this book: How can we nurture families *and* practice radical discipleship? How can we be *in* today's consumer culture but not tamed *by* it? How shall we imagine and then embody a better, wilder "good life" in this watershed moment of history—one that is better for ourselves *and* our aching planet?

These are daunting questions for those of us captive to corporation-controlled thinking. We've been trained to think small and ask permission from the authorities. We've been conditioned to believe this is the only kind of life there is. So the first thing we need to do is clear the cobwebs and reclaim our incredible, wild potential as beloved children of God.

WE'RE THE PEOPLE GOD'S BEEN WAITING FOR

We're the people God's been waiting for. If this sentiment seems heretical to you, I understand. Like me, perhaps you've been raised to believe in Christendom, a kind of institutional religion initiated by the Roman emperor Constantine that replaces the liberating Way of Jesus with a way that encourages its own accumulation of wealth, control, military might, and political power. Christendom is a control-oriented corruption of authentic Christianity, for it teaches a distant and judgmental God lording it over a miserable human race, holding out the hope of an otherworldly heaven as a carrot. Under this model, humans aren't supposed to do much but worship and obey, avoiding sin as best they can. One of the greatest tragedies of Christendom over the centuries is that it has domesticated our God-given human potential.

No matter what you've been taught, know this: God has always desired for us to be conspirators in God's dream, collaborators in redemption. What is this God project? Heaven on earth. From the beginning, God has dreamed of an ideal society, something that Jesus called "the kingdom of God": human community embodying covenanted right relationship with each other and all creation. So why hasn't God's dream been fulfilled yet? The wild truth is that God needs us, and we humans have yet to do our part.

In our sacred stories, God originally walked and talked daily with humanity along the riverbanks and among the trees. Moses also regularly encountered God face-to-face. During the exodus, Yahweh was so often present for personal consultations that Moses had a conference room set up in the desert, something he called "the tent of meeting." Anyone inquiring of the Lord would go there (Exodus 33:7). This was no distant interaction: "The Lord would speak to Moses face to face, as one speaks to a friend" (Exodus 33:11). God showed up to discuss strategy and imagine next steps, like a coach working with a team. Israel was to be God's pilot project, a priesthood of all believers, a light to the nations, an example of how societies should live. The Israelite people would have no king; they would be content with enough and not covet too much; they would not mimic the social and economic class systems of the empires around them; and they would live in covenanted right relationship with God, with one another, and with the Earth. This would be no kingdom of humanity, but a kingdom of God. In order for the Israelites to fulfill such high expectations, Yahweh breathed on their leaders, giving them spiritual resilience for the long haul.

JESUS' HIGH EXPECTATION FOR HUMANITY

Do you recall Jesus' first public words upon return from the desert? "Change your life!" he exhorts in the first chapter of Mark (1:14-15 *The Message*). "The kingdom of God has come near" (1:15 NIV). From the first moment of his public ministry, Jesus promises that God's dream of covenanted right relationship is near enough to touch; what we need to do is grasp it, get on board, and live it out day by day. This expectation is at the heart of the Lord's Prayer: "your kingdom come, your will be done, on earth as it is in heaven" (Matthew 6:10). As John Dominic Crossan emphasizes, Jesus' vision of the kingdom of God "is about the transformation of this world into holiness, not the evacuation of this world into heaven."[4] And soon Jesus boldly declares something even more immediate and empowering: God's kingdom is not only at hand, it's *within* you, *among* you (Luke 7:21).[5]

Sometimes we forget: God's dream of *heaven on earth* is a partnership requiring our full engagement. It's at hand, but it's not being done for us; we need to grab on. In this light, look again at an incident when Jesus could not do his healing, transformative work: Jesus could not heal in his hometown because the people did not believe it was possible (Mark 6:5). But right before that, in the preceding chapter, a woman reaches out in trust and finds true healing (Mark 5:25-34). The uncomfortable but exciting message: unless humans do their part, the kingdom of God cannot be realized. John Dominic Crossan emphasizes this need for our total involvement: "Jesus announced the presence of the kingdom of God by inviting all to come and see how he *and his companions* had already accepted it, had already entered it, and were already living in it. To experience the kingdom, he asserted, come, see how *we* live, and then live like us."[6] Jesus was providing not just a vision but a living laboratory of transformation, a community of practice.

I'm guessing some of the early disciples were as taken aback as we are about Jesus' expectations. *Join you, now? To be collaborators and allies in God's project? Can't God just rescue us and fix everything?* Jesus corrects this notion by sharing some expectations that remain mind-blowing even two thousand years later: in John, he says that his disciples have the capacity to do even greater things than he has done (14:12). I'm sure that shocked more than a few of his followers, and a few more probably fell out of their seats when he added, "I no longer call you servants. . . . I have called you friends" (15:15-17). Jesus makes it clear the divine project of *heaven on earth* needs friends, allies, partners. To empower his disciples as collaborators in this God-project, he breathes on them, giving them *pneuma*, Spirit, filling them with his own liberating power and an electrifying mandate to forgive sins and release economic debt and free people from oppression.

Talk about high potential! Jesus expects nothing less than social transformation out of his cell groups. Filling them with spiritual power, he expects his highly imperfect followers to be capable of incredible things, to go viral with the community-based kingdom of God, sharing the vision and practice of covenanted right relationship that will spread like leaven in the loaf.

THE EARLY CHURCH PASSED IT ON

The early church faithfully carried Jesus' message: divinely revolutionized humans are to be conspirators with God's dream of heaven on earth. Saint Irenaeus, a second-century father of the church, taught that human existence is a process of "soul-making." He asserted that humanity was created immature, and that humans needed both free will *and* a difficult world in order to develop into the divine likeness.[7] If this concept sounds different or dangerous, it might just show how influenced by Christendom we are, as it was a central tenet of the early church before Constantine. We can trust Irenaeus as a mainstream source: his best-known work was entitled *Against Heresies*, and he was a key player in defining "correct belief" as early Christianity evolved.

Reclaiming our potential reclaims our role in the partnership God has always desired with us. God *needs us* to realize his dream. Saint Augustine, during the fifth century in Rome, expressed this divine-human interdependent partnership in a memorable maxim: "Without God we cannot; without us He will not."[8] It's a strange and wonderful realization: God chooses to conspire with us and in us. Thomas Merton, the best-known Catholic monk of the past century, echoes this same sentiment in a way that makes me think it might actually be true:

> God seeks Himself in us, and the aridity and sorrow of our heart is the sorrow of God who is not known to us, who cannot yet find Himself in us because we do not dare to believe or trust the incredible truth that He could live in us, and live there out of choice, out of preference. But indeed we exist solely for this. . . . But we make all this dark and inglorious because we fail to believe it, we refuse to believe it. It is not that we hate God, rather that we hate ourselves, despair of ourselves.
>
> If we once began to recognize, humbly but truly, the real value of our own self, we would see that this value was the sign of God in our being, the signature of God upon our being.[9]

We are the people God's been waiting for. Why is this so hard for modern Christians to believe and embrace? Because God's amazing expectations, and our divine potential, have been hijacked by empire-based Christendom and subverted by the framing stories of dominant culture.

YOU'VE BEEN OCCUPIED

Try this on: Your native, indigenous character as a child of God has been distorted by dominant culture. If you're a privileged North American like me, your mental and spiritual environments have been colonized by the captains of conspicuous consumption. You've been tamed and domesticated, shackled and stuffed. Despite professing values of love and justice and sharing, you often make choices that are unfair, unjust, and unhealthy for the rest of the world. You hoard too much, spend too much, work too much, worry too much, consume too much, attack too much, protect too much, waste too much. You love too little, share too little, forgive too little, risk too little, enjoy too little. You've become devoted to gadgets and diversions. You've become enthralled by the tempting titillations, frenetic compulsions, and enticing attachments of the world-ruling corporate economy.

Any of this resonate? If not, put this book down, pat yourself on the back, and keep living as you are. But if these words ring true, then like me, you may suffer from the addictive disease known as *affluenza*.

AFFLUENZA, THE PANDEMIC OF OUR TIME

See how you do on this quiz:

1) Which of the following is comparable in size to today's typical three-car garage?

   a. A basketball court

   b. A McDonald's restaurant

   c. An RV (recreational vehicle)

   d. The average home in the 1950s

2) Since 1950, Americans alone have used more resources than:

   a. Everyone who ever lived before them

   b. The combined third-world populations

   c. The Romans at the height of the Roman Empire

   d. All of the above

In case you're interested, the correct answer to both is d.[10]

PBS raised these not-so-trivial questions in the late 1990s to promote its television special *Affluenza*, which opened people's eyes to the effects of the dangerous and rampant consumerism plaguing modern America. Affluenza is a disease of affluent overconsumption, and like its inspiration, influenza, it is a highly transmittable disease of epidemic proportions that has dire consequences.

The term *affluenza* originated less than twenty years ago and, as a new word in our lexicon, still retains some fluidity in its precise meaning. The best definition I have found, from 2001, describes affluenza as "a painful, contagious, socially transmitted condition of overload, debt, anxiety, and waste resulting from the dogged pursuit of more."[11] Affluenza is the motivator that drives our modern technocratic society, and as such is responsible for creating unimagined levels of both global personal privilege and global planetary peril. Both blessing and curse, Joanna Macy and Chris Johnstone describe our affluenza-riddled culture this way: "Our technologically advanced society has achieved wonders our ancestors could never have envisioned. We've put people on the moon, decoded DNA, and cured diseases. The problem is this collective level of power is also destroying our world. Countless seemingly innocent activities and choices are acting together to bring about the sixth mass extinction in our planet's history."[12]

What a mixed bag we've been born into! Racing after the good life, we become unwitting agents of death. In recent years affluenza has taken on ever more foreboding shades of meaning. It now also describes a deeper disease: a sociopathic inability to understand the consequences of our actions because of a life steeped in entitlement, disconnection, and financial privilege.

AFFLUENZA UP CLOSE: THE CASE OF ETHAN COUCH

The power of affluenza reared up into America's headlights in a different way in 2013, during a dark and disturbing series of events that unfolded in Texas. The deaths themselves were tragic enough: a sixteen-year-old teen carelessly killed four people while driving drunk. But it was the court decision a few months later that sent chills of terror down my spine.

The details I can piece together are these: on June 15, 2013, Ethan Couch stole beer from Walmart with his pals, drank a large amount of alcohol while zooming around in his pickup truck, and during the reckless driving spree slammed into a woman whose car had broken down on a road in Burleson, Texas. He had been driving seventy miles per hour in a forty-miles-per-hour zone. Couch's careless actions behind the wheel of his Ford F-150 truck killed not only the woman but also two people living nearby who had come to help get her car started, as well as a youth pastor who had also stopped to assist. Two pals riding in the back of Couch's truck were seriously injured due to the impact, one so much so that he could not move or talk after the incident. During later questioning at the scene by police officers, Couch allegedly said, "I'm outta here" and walked away.[13]

Court records reveal that Couch's blood alcohol level was three times the legal limit.

During the court proceedings six months later in December 2013, Couch confessed to his actions. He admitted to being drunk while driving and losing control of his vehicle; he pleaded guilty to four counts of manslaughter by intoxication; he pleaded guilty to two counts of assault by intoxication causing bodily injury.[14]

RICHIE RICH

Now comes the disturbing part. His defense, justifying this cold-blooded carelessness, was bold, inventive—and utterly terrifying. His wealthy parents hired an elite trial attorney and an expert psychologist to shape what has been called the "Richie Rich defense." Couch was a victim of affluenza, the attorney argued. The teenage murderer was to be excused from responsibility because he grew up never experiencing limits and never learning consequences; his entire upbringing made him hardwired to be uncaring and irresponsible.[15] "He never learned that sometimes you don't get your way," stated psychologist Gary Miller during the court proceedings. "He had the cars and he had the money. He had freedoms that no young man would be able to handle."[16]

State district judge Jean Boyd bought Couch's defense. The teen walked away from court with no jail time. Texas sentencing guidelines for crimes like this suggest fines of up to $10,000 and between two and twenty years confinement in the state penitentiary.[17] Instead, Couch received no jail time whatsoever—just ten years of probation and court-mandated therapy at a residential treatment center chosen and paid for by his family. Prosecutors reminded the judge that there were drug and alcohol treatment programs in prison, but Judge Boyd decided that the facility chosen by the family—a Southern California institution offering equine sports, yoga, and massages—would be a better fit.[18]

I'm not sure what horrifies me most about the Ethan Couch case. An entire upbringing of entitlement without consequences? Couch's utter lack of remorse? The lawyer's gall to suggest affluenza as an illness justifying a legal defense? The judge's complicity with it all?

Actually, I know what horrifies me most: the fact that *I am just like Ethan*. The fact that we North Americans *are just like*

Ethan. North Americans are hardly the only ones, of course, but we've been leading the charge for a long time. Here we are as a society, on a petroleum-fueled joyride with our friends, high on affluenza behind the wheel of life, blissfully destroying precious life systems, aware of—but not really caring—about the permanent devastation we leave in our wake. And the biggest horror of it all? The likelihood that, when the time comes to face up to the consequences of our actions, many of us will survey the damage, not like what we see, invest in the latest space station technology, and say, "I'm outta here."

2

BETTER LIVING THROUGH TESTING

THE CATCHPHRASE "Better living through chemistry" permeated the spirit of progress-oriented modern America throughout the twentieth century. DuPont adopted a version of this saying as its corporate slogan in 1935, and kept it as their official company motto for nearly fifty years.[1]

The company used the slogan not to directly endorse their particular products but rather to modify Americans' opinions about the role of large corporations in society. It was a meta-message, a culture shift. Charles Hackett, DuPont's advertising director, designed the advertisements to dispel Americans' fears of big business and huge corporations, fears that DuPont believed had "an emotional rather than a rational foundation."[2]

For better and for worse, DuPont's corporate strategy worked. They and others masterminded a brilliant occupation of the consumer mind. Massive multinational corporations no longer were objects of suspicion but became welcome fixtures of modern life. "Better living through chemistry" became a national mantra far larger than DuPont could have ever imagined. For the last eight decades, this sentiment—now morphed into

"Better living through technology"—has infiltrated every corner of our national psyche. This slogan—now an unexamined doctrine—has been the continual rationale by corporations to promote endless lines of petroleum and plastic products, create new prescription and recreational drugs, encourage the use of fertilizers, reengineer foods and environments, fund medical and military advances, justify new policies and laws, and manufacture and market a never-ending supply of electronic life-enhancing devices. "Better living through technology" became the rallying cry for our entire industrial civilization.

Here we are—with the unalterable demise of our very air, water, and soil waiting in the wings—and "Better living through technology" continues to be the mantra we follow with religious zeal. Through the clamor about how greener technologies will save us, and amid the applause confirming that the newest iGadget will make life so much better, I keep hearing a still, small voice saying that it is our *character* that must change, not just our consumer choices.

If Yahweh has a slogan for human advancement, I suggest it might be this: Better living through *testing*. God has always taught his people to unshackle from systems that dominate and control. And God's process is clear, even if old school: we need to go *cimarron* to become the wild people God wants us to be.

MOSES IS THE MAN

The path of Moses is a powerful model of rewilding for us today. The ancient stories tell us he was an Israelite orphan adopted as a baby into Pharaoh's household. As a youth, he was raised in the luxurious lap of affluenza, as part of the royal elite whose opulent lifestyle depended upon the backbreaking labor of Israelite slaves. Do you see any parallels to our situation today? As a grown man, Moses sees the suffering of his own people and wakes up to his own complicity with an oppressive system. He rejects entitled court life, and in a rage against Egyptian injustice, strikes down a cruel overseer who was mistreating an Israelite slave (Exodus 2:12).

Uh-oh.

Moses kills a man and commits class treason, and is suddenly on empire's most-wanted list. Confused, alone, pursued by power, he flees the only home he knows and goes *cimarron.*

Cimarron?

In his amazing book *Goatwalking*, Jim Corbett tells us *cimarron* is a Spanish word describing a slave or domesticated animal gone free. In the southwestern United States, where I live, the term has been used for escaped stallions that run loose in wild herds, hardy and feral mustangs originally derived from Spanish stock. The antonym of *cimarron* is *reducido*, "reduced one," used by the Spanish conquerors as a category to describe Native Americans who had been tamed and domesticated.[3] Moses goes *cimarron* from the household of Pharaoh. What happens next? As a stranger in a strange land, on the run, trying to embody a new set of values, he defends some vulnerable women, covenants to a new family, and leads a far humbler existence close to the land. He learns to live as a herder, and for many years he wanders the wilderness, mission-less, learning land-based skills to thrive far from empire (Exodus 2:15-22).

One day he ventures to the *far side* of the desert, and there—deep in uncolonized, undomesticated space—he finds an elemental and untamed God roaring in the burning bush (Exodus 3:1-4). This desert encounter transforms Moses utterly. His long-standing desire for justice melds with God's own and kindles to a white-hot heat. God's passion burns away Moses's insecurities, and God's presence fills him with clarity and purpose.

In the desert, Moses is reborn, refashioned, reanimated to become the wild prophet God needs him to be. He gains the strength and conviction to return to Egypt, face Pharaoh, and speak truth to power. One intriguing detail of the exodus story is that, after the first four plagues, Pharaoh tries to make Moses a deal: he will let the Israelites worship their God, as long as they worship in his land, *within the boundaries of the Egyptian Empire.* Domesticate the divine, Pharaoh suggests. Moses, agent of an untamed God, responds bluntly: "That would not be right." Instead, he insists that the God of Israel is to be worshiped in the deep desert, not in civilized cities (Exodus 8:25-27).

It would be more comfortable for us today if we could write Moses off as an aberration, as the only figure in our tradition who left privilege and went *cimarron* to find his true self in a wild God. But he isn't. As Matthew Colwell writes, "it is a recurring biblical theme that the wilderness is the space in which human beings find liberation, identity, and new life. Leaving domesticated space for the 'wild' is the age-old narrative of God's people and God's prophets." Breaking free of dependence upon a dominating culture—whether it be Egyptian, Babylonian, Roman, or American—is a necessary first step for anyone serious about following an untamed God.[4]

How to break free? As William Stafford says in his poem "A Message from the Wanderer," "there are thousands of ways to escape." I have to agree. Some of us might spend years in the desert, like Moses. Others may spend forty days, like Jesus. Others, like the traveler Ruth in the Old Testament, may sojourn through wild lands, moving from one place to another. The important thing, our tradition shows us time and time again, is to simply get out into uncolonized space *whatever way you can.*

But what of people tied to city lives? Delores Williams tells us that even Africans enslaved in America prior to the Civil War found it both possible and necessary to get out into *some kind* of wild space; they knew that, without conversion in an uncolonized place, you were a kept creature, both in body and in soul. A powerful slave song from that era urges the "half-done Christian" to "go in de wilderness, go in de wilderness, go in de wilderness."[5] These slaves knew that an environment away from the crowded and coercive plantation was necessary to gain a full connection with God, transform the interior spirit, and strengthen the Christ-consciousness needed to face life's challenges and tribulations.[6]

REWILDING PUNCTUATION

It's amazing how much difference a little punctuation can make. Grammarian and author Lynn Truss points out how different a sentence can become simply by adding a comma.[7] Check out the two sentences below. Each refers to the actions of an adult panda bear:

a) Eats shoots and leaves.

b) Eats, shoots and leaves.

One comma, a world of difference. Now look at these two:

a) There is a voice calling in the wilderness: prepare a way for the Lord.

b) There is a voice calling: in the wilderness, prepare a way for the Lord.

See how the placement of the colon changes everything? The first sentence provides information, reporting about a lone herald who makes an important announcement. We may find it interesting, but we are not moved to action. We're not urged to *do* anything.

The second sentence, however, is not information but a mandate, charging us to leave society to change our lives. This is the original, actual intent of the well-known passage found in the book of Isaiah, calling the Jewish people to life change and preparation so they may be able to embody God's ideal society. The full text is this: "A voice of one calling: 'In the wilderness prepare the way for the Lord; make straight in the desert a highway for our God'" (Isaiah 40:3).

Enter the wilderness and there prepare a way for the Lord. This is one of the deepest threads running through our four-thousand-year-old tradition. Fleeing dominant culture, Moses did it. Escaping from bondage, the ancient Hebrews did it. Bereft of security and identity, Ruth did it. Inside the whale, Jonah did it. Confronting kings and cults and coin, Elijah did it. Organizing a radical life-change movement, John the Baptist did it. Prior to exploding on the scene, Jesus did it. Reeling from a devastating new awareness on the Damascus road, Paul did it. Resisting a state-endorsed Christianity aligned with militarism and wealth, the desert fathers did it. Finding deep sustenance in God away from their taskmasters, Africans enslaved in America did it.

Encountering God and changing one's life in the wilderness has been a continuous thread. However, it has never been particularly popular, nor easy. That's because it's not a spectator sport; it requires deep engagement, causes significant disruption, and results in untold transformation. It may take you where you do not want to go.

AT RISK: THAT'S US

Have you heard the phrase "hoods in the woods"? It's shorthand for taking "at-risk" individuals on long wilderness trips to kick-start character change. After thirty years working as a wilderness guide, I've realized something: my friends, we're *all* at-risk individuals in need of character change.

All of us immersed in modern culture are "at risk." I've led hundreds of people on wilderness trips: the troubled, the spoiled, the entitled, the insecure, the bored. I've led people addicted to cocaine, and I've led people addicted to capitalism, comfort, and career. I've led people hooked on Valium, volume shopping, and video games. Most people are hardwired about their habits; even with fascinating folk and scenic mountains surrounding them, it takes days for some people to stop fantasizing about home and longing for what they *don't* have. For decades I've offered tough love to spoiled people on my wilderness treks, watching them struggle, helping them grow, seeing them change. So I can imagine a little of what Moses, the original wilderness guide, might have felt as he and God provided tough love to his ragtag band deep into the wild.

Exodus is the "charter myth" of Israel, the grounding story that gives meaning and direction to the culture. The ancient story tells us that the Israelites were enslaved in body by Egypt to be the backbone of the labor force, yet they were bound in other ways, too: captured in mind, soul, and tongue. They had become habituated to the expectations of empire and to the creature comforts they received from a domination system, few as they were—perks such as imported foods, stable housing, and meat stew bubbling in cooking pots (Exodus 16:3). They had become tame—*reducidos*, reduced ones—and their view of their God's power and their own human potential had diminished greatly.

Returning to Egypt after encountering the untamed God in the burning bush, Moses saw this captive character of his people—this half-living—and was appalled. *This is the best God's people can be?* Moses's social critique, driven by Yahweh, was unsparing: my people need to be transformed. God's ideal society was to be a royal priesthood of all believers: no king, no royalty, no enslavement, no domination, no inequity, no small and petty living. To embody this society—to become the God-filled people Yahweh yearned for them to become—the Israelites needed to experience some tough love, gained through wilderness detoxification, adaptation, and purification.

TOUGH LOVE

Moses, the primordial wilderness trip leader, explained to his flock of *reducidos* why God plunged them into the crucible of the wilderness: "to humble you and test you in order to know what was in your heart" (Deuteronomy 8:2). Like Outward Bound founder Kurt Hahn, God and Moses were avid practitioners of experiential wilderness education. God and Moses both needed to know: Did the people have what it takes? Were they willing *and* able to embody God's ideal society? The only way to know was to come to the proving grounds.[8]

The tough love experience of exodus was so foundational for the Israelite culture that it's referred to in many other books of the Bible written hundreds of years later. It was a wild ride of transformation, and its drama can match any TV reality show. The complaining happened regularly—in fact, it is one of the constant threads of the exodus experience. God's enoughness in the desert was not enough for the Israelites, who remembered the imported foods Egypt procured by dominating other nations. Cravings were common. The Israelites' grumbling seems scripted by Hollywood: "If only we had meat to eat! We remember the fish we ate in Egypt at no cost—also the cucumbers, melons, leeks, onions, and garlic. But now we have lost our appetite; we never see anything but this manna!" (Numbers 11:4-6). Faced with drab rations, the ex-slaves remembered the wide variety of food they ate at no cost—no cost, that is, except their freedom. Having to fend for themselves was a harsh reality. "Why did you bring us up out of Egypt to this terrible place? It has no grain or figs, grapevines or pomegranates" (Numbers 20:5). Freedom, it appears, was a lot less palatable than captivity.

The drama doesn't stop there, nor does the comedy. Moses, called to lead these grumblers through the purifying desert, gets fed up. He grieves to God about the hassle. "What have I done to displease you," he rants, "that you put the burden of all these people on me?" The dripping sarcasm of his cantankerous rapport with the Almighty shouts out from the text even today. "Did I conceive all these people?" he queries acidly. "Did I give them birth? Why do you tell me to carry them in my arms, as a nurse carries an infant?" As a wilderness guide myself, I get his frustration. Indignant at needing to be parent, camp counselor, and nursemaid, he vents to God like a drama queen: "If this is how you are going to treat me, please go ahead and kill me" (Numbers 11:11-15).

GRUMBLING AND GRATITUDE

Grumbling was the opposite of the gratitude God was hoping for. In fact, if the desert testing in Exodus is an example for us to learn from, then we see that grumblers don't get to be part of God's ideal society. After forty years wandering the desert, who was allowed to enter the Promised Land? Only the children born in the desert, the "non-grumblers" raised to appreciate enoughness, seemed to have the right character. God makes it clear that only those of an *appreciative spirit* will be able to enter the land. "No one who has treated me with contempt will ever see it. But because my servant Caleb has a *different spirit* and *follows me wholeheartedly*, I will bring him into the land" (Numbers 14:23b-24).

Caleb, he of the appreciative spirit. Who was Caleb? Why did he get to enter the new country, but not the other elders? He was one of the older men by this time—one of the original gang who fled Egypt, presumably, not some young whipper-snapper—but while his peers pointed out what was wrong with God's plan and what was unsuitable about the land they were entering, Caleb cut through their complaints with an apprecia-tive stance and a humble heart: "The land we passed through and explored is exceedingly good. If the Lord is pleased with us, he will lead us into that land" (Numbers 14:7-8). Caleb was ap-proved by God, pleasing to God, because he'd been tested, and came through on the other side a different man.

ARE WE PLEASING?

Moses's repeated face-to-face encounters with God in the des-ert—figuring out on the fly what he should do and how he should lead—provide uncanny similarities to Jesus' later experience in the desert. To Moses—right in the middle of deep uncertainty, discernment, and questioning—God says, "I am pleased with you and I know you by name" (Exodus 33:17). Both Moses and Jesus were tested in the desert; both gained a radical awareness of their own worth and acceptance by God; both returned to lead their people into God's vision of an ideal society.

Paul, recalling the ancient Israelites wandering in the desert, is blunt in his assessment: "God was not pleased with most of them" (1 Corinthians 10:5). Paul uses the story of exodus—the archetypal "hoods in the woods" wilderness trip—as a caution-ary tale for his own community, perhaps a thousand years later, "to keep us from setting our hearts on evil things as they did" (1 Corinthians 10:6).

What wisdom might we gain from these examples to guide us today? Moses and Jesus, seeking with their whole hearts to serve God's will and guide people into a new life, are radically pleasing to God. Caleb, he of the appreciative and humble spirit, is welcomed by God into the new land. In contrast, most of the wandering Israelites—holding on to the appetites of empire—had their hearts set on the wrong things, and God wasn't pleased with them.

It makes me wonder: Are we, today, pleasing to God? Many Christians today aren't used to asking this question. Maybe it's because we've been steeped in the amazing, unconditional love that Jesus offers. Or maybe we think that because Jesus saved us *personally*, we don't need to become a new person *economically*. Remember, however, that Zacchaeus—in response to such love and acceptance—transformed his life and gave away half of his belongings to those who had less. This, I would venture, was an abundant act very pleasing to God.

Being loved and being pleasing are two very different things. I love my teenage son unconditionally, and always will, but I am not always pleased by his actions. Sometimes his actions cause me deep pain and frustration. (He's not always pleased by what I do either!) Yet we stay in an unbreakable bond of love. I'm guessing this is how God relates to humanity—always loving, always in relationship, but not always pleased by what we do.

And so we come back to the question: Are we pleasing to God? Have we been tested with tough love and come through on the other side as better beings? Have we learned restraint and enoughness, or do we remain addicted to the appetites of empire? Do we each have an appreciative spirit, or do we grasp for more? Like Caleb, are we humble enough to inherit the land on God's terms?

This era of severe global inequity and radical climate devastation is our own proving ground, the time for our characters—and our pocketbooks—to be tested and transformed.

We remain shackled to the comforts of empire, yet an encounter with God in uncolonized wilderness lies waiting at the edges of our culture.

Will we, like Moses, heed the call? Like us, he was unprepared and full of excuses. At Mount Sinai, God offers Moses a vision of new possibility for his people: compassion, solidarity, liberation, empowerment, and the opportunity to be citizens of a good and spacious land. But leading people into this new possibility would require Moses to be an utterly different person. So of course Moses passes on the opportunity: "Please send someone else" (Exodus 4:13). I love how polite Moses is as he declines the Almighty, as if he was turning down a dance request. God's response? *You're the person I've been waiting for*, Yahweh seems to say. He doesn't take no for an answer. Instead, God offers what Moses needs: human support, a little speech coaching, and most importantly, Yahweh tells Moses, "I will . . . teach you what to do" (Exodus 4:13-15).

Are we not today, in our own watershed moment, tasked to do the same in the face of our own version of empire: resist a dominant culture that is based upon inequality of people and devastation of the planet? Can we, too, trust that God will teach us what to do? Like Moses, we'll need to cultivate new traits. We've got a long journey ahead of us if we seek to follow the Jesus Way in a society obsessed with the American way. To be free to follow an untamed God, we must begin to live untamed lives. We must step out of business as usual, step into the wild, and become a different kind of human.

WANTED: A NEW SPECIES

Charles Darwin once predicted a species that would only be seen forty years later. Darwin encountered an extraordinary night-blooming orchid that is only found in Madagascar. He noted three important facts about this flower: (1) it bloomed only at night; (2) pollination was key to its existence; and (3) its pollen was hidden improbably deep down a tubular opening. Synthesizing these three facts, Darwin predicted the existence of something yet unseen by biologists: he hypothesized that there must be a nocturnal pollinator, probably a moth, endowed with an incredibly long and narrow proboscis.

Forty years later, a night-flying subspecies of moth equipped with a proboscis nearly a foot long was witnessed feeding from the flower. Scientists named it *Xanthopan morganii praedicta*, the Predicta moth.[9]

Darwin examined a mystery found in nature that was unsolvable based upon *what currently was known to exist*. His solution was to suggest—predict—a species not yet identified, something that could fill a needed niche.

Moses—in a very different time and place, with a very different purpose—also imagined a species not yet known. The tame *reducidos* who had been captive in Egypt were not the unfettered *cimarrons* who could enter the Promised Land—they had to be humbled, tested, and transformed. So, too, our task is to free ourselves to become the people God wants us to be. In our fragile place, in our fragile time, we need to be a species not yet identified: followers of the living God who can manifest God's dream of heaven on earth, and who can learn to coexist with the rest of creation.

3

THE DEAL WITH THE DESERT

HAT REALLY HAPPENED OUT THERE? When I read Luke's report that Jesus "was led by the Spirit into the wilderness" (Luke 4:1), that's the question I'm left with. The accounts in the Gospels differ a bit, but all the stories of Jesus' testing leave me with more questions than answers. As far as we know, no one was following Jesus around during his forty days of solitude to record the actual events. So what really happened?

One thing that feels unsatisfying about the telling of Jesus' wilderness event is that none of the temptations seem to have perturbed him much. *Temptation, schmemptation*, Jesus seems to say with a yawn, refusing each enticement with a quick, wise response. It's as if he overcomes all trials without any effort, is changed not one bit from the testing, says hasta la vista to the evil one trying to corrupt him, and then clocks back into society to get busy. Without breaking a sweat.

If his temptations weren't a big deal, why did Jesus even go to the wilderness? Why would it matter? I want to offer a suggestion: *the temptations had to have been a big deal.*

WHAT REALLY HAPPENED OUT THERE?

As Jim Douglass asks in the phenomenal little book *Lightning East to West*, what did Jesus find in the desert?[1] I'm not sure, but I can make some guesses. Out in the wild lands, alone, I'm guessing Jesus experienced radical emptying—*kenosis*—prior to being filled with an incredibly deep assurance of identity, purpose, abundance, and radical grace. Could it be that Jesus *lived into* his divine potential *because* of his testing in the desert? Could it be that—in the midst of his desert sojourn—Jesus experienced such profoundly deep union with God that it was there where his oneness with God was revealed?

My gut tells me yes. The Scriptures resonate. It was only after his baptism in the desert by John that Jesus understood himself as an utterly beloved child of God. It was only after the wilderness that Jesus dared to name the Creator "Abba"—an intimate word we would translate as "Daddy"—his one and only provider, source, guide, and caretaker. Only after the wilderness did he call the universe abundant. Only after the wilderness did Jesus start his public ministry of personal and social transformation, daring people to repent, to turn over their lives from empire to an all-embracing, extravagant God, just as he had.

Now let's turn the question on us: How can wilderness strip away pieces of our small selves to release our God-given potential?

A WAY OPENS IN THE WILD

When Isaiah proclaimed, "In the wilderness prepare the way for the Lord," he was saying we need to be remodeled. Clean up your act, he urged. In the wilderness, change your head, change your allegiance, change your life.

We moderns tend to spiritualize Isaiah's challenging words. We like seeing wilderness as a metaphor. Yet wilderness is a necessary crucible for people attached to empire. When we avoid a literal refashioning, we're left with what we've already had: two thousand years of earnest people who want to follow a wild God, but can't because they keep getting distracted by baubles and busyness. It's awfully hard to be divinely transformed when we're protected by, provided for, and utterly entranced by mother culture.

Safe within our cradle of consumption, we remain untested, entitled, fearful, and wholly dependent upon the teat of technocratic society. In this state, we can't begin to embody the kingdom of God in our lives. Defined by corporations and Christendom, we can't begin to imagine the society Jesus envisioned: a place where violence does not have dominion over human interaction, where money does not have dominion over human exchange, and where humanity does not have dominion over nature's cycles and limits. This kind of place can only be occupied by *cimarrons*—those who have broken free of empire's value system.

How deep do you think you're trapped? Not so deep?

Try this on: the degree to which you are addicted to empire is the degree to which you depend upon money, technology, and mother culture to meet your demands for food, shelter, security, entertainment, and identity.

The *cimarron* desert fathers and mothers who escaped the rise of Christendom in the fourth century knew they were in danger of being trapped, so they took Isaiah's words seriously. Thomas Merton describes the earliest desert monks as true anarchists—individuals who refused to let their lives be led "by a decadent state." Rather, in the desert they devoted themselves to crafting lives of conscious integrity, refusing "slavish dependence on ... conventional values."[2] Merton asserts that the desert fathers' flight to the desert was "a flight toward experience."[3]

What kind of experience were the monks seeking, so removed from civilization?

An experience of limits. For modern people addicted to affluenza, time in wilderness can become a form of fasting. When I dwell in wild places, living apart from civilization, I can't have it all; my needs must be met by what I can carry on my back and what I can find in my immediate environment. Kurt Hahn, the inspiring figure behind Outward Bound, knew that traveling in wilderness caused groups of people to undergo two powerful experiences: reasonable self-denial and crucial interdependence. This may seem mundane enough until you realize how countercultural such a situation is to the affluent modern person. To not have anything I want, just a click or a phone call away? To need other people to meet my basic needs? To be unable to buy my way out of boredom or hunger or discomfort? In the American empire, such a situation is considered primitive, backward, undesirable. Wilderness sets us right with God by setting healthy limits—limits on our individual ego, power, activity, and greed.

An experience of Sabbath communion. Rainstorms. Mountains. Seasons. The time the sun rises. The temperature in the deep of night. In the wilderness, there is so much we cannot control. We must simply adapt and say thank you for the blessings we get. We cannot influence our surroundings through our reputation, power, or wealth. In nature, a cash economy is absurd. Wilderness becomes a *shabbat*—sabbath, a time apart—for those of us addicted to our modern cult of busyness and control. Time in the wild gives us an enforced holy rest, exposing our restlessness. For many of us who consider ourselves important, the idleness of wilderness time is a shock—no big events to plan, no conference calls to make, no big product deadlines to meet, no house to maintain, no Internet to check up on. The Sabbath that comes from wilderness sojourn reminds us that we are human *beings*, not human *doings*. We can love the world just as it is. But an attitude like this is scandalous to empire-based thinking. As Ched Myers notes in *The Biblical Vision of Sabbath Economics*, our culture of affluenza is built around controlling, harnessing, and taming the natural environment, breaking nature into priced commodities to serve our purposes.[4] Spending time in wilderness, however, can be an antidote, and can show us how to fit into untamed communities of plants and animals as members of this community.

An experience of identity formation. "What the Fathers sought most of all was their true self, in Christ," Merton writes of those early monks who fled Christendom for the wild places. The desert was the place where they could "reject completely the false, formal self," fabricated amid social compulsion under the Roman Empire, and find true self in God. "They accepted and clung to the primal assertions of the Christian tradition," Merton explains, "yet sought a way to God that was uncharted and freely chosen, not inherited from others who had mapped it out beforehand. They sought a God whom they alone could find."[5] In wilderness, we can become new creatures. Civilized labels no longer stick. Questions of identity and purpose abound. Why do I spend so much time performing an unfulfilling job? Why do I worry so much about a future I can't control? Do I really need so much stuff? Who am I beyond my job, my friends, my family, my nationality? Not just *who* am I, but *whose* am I? To paraphrase a line from Mary Oliver's poem "Wild Geese": What shall I do with my "one wild and precious life?" In wilderness, distractions disappear, busyness recedes, social pressures diminish. We're left with one of the Bible's core instructions: "Be still, and know that I am God."

In my life, I've spent more than a thousand nights sleeping out in wild places. I know from experience that the wilderness exposes the false self: obsessions with self-importance, addictions to comfort, illusions of independence and control. There are many places in our lives we can learn these lessons, of course. But once you learn to thrive in the wilds for weeks at a time with just what you can carry and find, you can become a little more fearless, a little less demanding, and a little more grace-filled. Spending time in wilderness can build our trust in the abundance of God and the untamed gift economy that creation provides. Empire starts to have less of a hold on you. Wilderness can help us claim the radical stance of the prophet, based upon undomesticated communion with God. Unplugged and unpressured, we can gain the clarity to cut through confusion, experience communion, find our true identity, and practice creative cultural resistance.

A WANDERER FINDS THE WILDERNESS

Tim DeChristopher became a modern folk hero overnight when he staged an unprecedented kind of environmental defense protest in 2008. His actions were so provocative that *Rolling Stone* magazine called him "America's most creative climate criminal."[6] Why? Instead of waving a sign or chaining himself to a tree in an effort to stop relentless corporate eco-destruction, this young man acted in ways both courageous and outrageous. Knowing he would go to jail, he fraudulently posed as a corporate bidder at an illegal government auction, and—before being taken into custody—successfully acquired millions of dollars' worth of oil-and-gas drilling leases on federal land in Utah's red rock country (I'll be discussing Tim's conviction more in chapter 8).

Tim was not always a wild man: God and the wilderness did it to him. In his late teens, about the same time he was beginning to find his own faith, Tim struggled with angst and anxiety.

In his own words, he felt "overwhelmed with the world." He describes it this way: "I had this feeling that I just wanted things to stop for a while so that I could catch up. And I told my mom at one point that I was going to pretend that I was crazy and get myself checked into a mental institution so that I could spend a few weeks where people wouldn't expect me to do anything other than just stare out the window and drool."[7]

Her response: "You need to go to the wilderness."

The DeChristophers were living in Pittsburgh at the time. His mother directed him to the Otter Creek Wilderness in West Virginia, a spot Tim had been before. He remembers his eight days alone in the woods: "It was a really powerful experience that led to my formation as an individual. I mean, it was the first time that I ever experienced myself without any other influences. Without any cultural influences, any influences from other people. And it was terrifying to experience that—I mean I really thought I was actually going crazy at that point. But it allowed me to develop that individual identity of who I was without anyone else around."

The wilderness played an even bigger role in Tim's life once he went to college. He started an outdoor recreation and conservation group during his first year and spent most weekends somewhere out in the Arizona desert. After two years, Tim dropped out of college to work with kids in the wilderness, in the Ozarks. After three years of that, Tim plunged deeper into the wilds, moving to Utah to work for an intense wilderness therapy program for troubled teens. During these years, Tim was deeply immersed in the wilderness, especially in Utah. "I was out there all the time," Tim remembers. "That was where I lived."

How did these experiences of going *cimarron* affect him as a young man? "It put me in perspective," Tim reflects. Living as a part of those vast western landscapes was particularly powerful because of their sheer enormity, he says. "When you spend all your time in a little room, you feel very big and very important . . . and everything that happens to you is a big deal. And when you're out in the desert, you see that you're really small. And that's a very liberating sense—of being very small. Every little thing that happens to you isn't that big a deal. Going to prison for a few years—it's not that big a deal."

Wilderness also changed Tim's views on *how* to live. He came to see that wandering in the wild allows us to live the way we actually *want* to live, at least for a while. In wilderness, we discover all kinds of authentic truths: what actually makes one happy, how to form a tight and trusting community with just a few people, and how humans authentically interact when a dominant culture isn't constantly telling us what to do.

A BUMPER STICKER FROM THE BAPTIST

There's a bumper sticker I see around Taos that feels like the voice of John the Baptist: *If you're not outraged, you're not paying attention.* Tim gets the sentiment. In today's troubled times, he finds deep resonance in the story of Jesus and John going out to the wilderness for a long time and then returning to engage deeply with a corrupt society in a transformative manner. Years of wilderness immersion helped Tim see our current consumer-mad society as what it is: outrageous and unacceptable. "So many things about our society, I just kept looking at them after being in the wilderness for so long and saying, 'How the hell could people accept this? This is outrageous.'"

Going *cimarron* puts modern "civilization" in perspective and makes us realize what a strange, recent, human-made construct it is. Being in nature, surrounded by natural systems, reminds us that the current human system is not inevitable, that reality doesn't actually *have* to be this way. Wilderness living gives us the strength to look at something in contemporary so-ciety and say, this is not how I want to live, this is unacceptable. "I think activism at its best is refusing to accept things," remarks Tim. "I felt that so strongly sitting there at the auction, watching parcels go for eight or ten dollars an acre. I mean that's why I first started bidding—just to drive up the prices—because I had this overwhelming sense that this is not acceptable."

AN OUTDOOR TRAINING SCHOOL FOR THE AGES

The most powerful and subversive characteristic of wild lands, says Tim, is that—from the time of Moses to Isaiah to Jesus to now—they remain places where people can think freely and experience the untamed God. Ponder upon this powerful state-ment from Tim: "Tyranny can never be complete as long as there's wilderness."

Nowhere is this more evident for Christians than in the story of John the Baptist. Already dwelling in a wild place, not depending upon empire for shelter or food, security or iden-tity, Jesus' cousin John encouraged thousands of city dwellers to leave civilization behind for a while and be transformed by God in undomesticated space (Mark 1:1-8).

Through the lens of recent archaeological findings, it seems the man we've come to call "the Baptizer" was not acting alone but rather was part of a much older wilderness tradition. In 1991, James Tabor and colleagues uncovered a cavern com-plex near Suba, Israel, which they called "The Cave of John the Baptist." This cave complex—remote from civilization—ap-pears to have been used for water-purification rituals, and the underground pools contain baptismal pottery artifacts dating back to the Bronze Age: 700 BC, the time of Isaiah.[8]

Wait a minute. *Baptism in the desert, in 700 BC?* A complex of caves, underground pools, water-purification rituals, hundreds of years of continued use—archaeology may be telling us there was a *direct wilderness teaching tradition* passed down from the prophet Isaiah through John the Baptist through Jesus to his followers, a tradition we have lost today. It's not certain, but it's intriguing to think about. Whether formal or not, I'm guessing that Judeo-Christianity has had a tradition of wilderness transformation for thousands of years. Why? Because empire-addicted people have always needed to undergo some kind of testing in the wild in order to become God's people.

4

STAYING AWAKE

'VE ALWAYS THOUGHT it odd that the Lord's Prayer includes the line "Lead us not into temptation." In some translations, the phrase reads: "Save us from the time of trial." The Greek word translated as temptation is *peirasmos*, which can mean temptation, test, or trial.

Wait a minute—we're supposed to ask God to keep us from the time of trial? It doesn't make sense. The Israelites were tested for forty years in the wilderness. Jesus was tested for forty days in the wilderness. Both were transformed by the experience. Testing seems to be God's favorite tool for transformation. So why would the Lord's Prayer end with a plea *not* to be tested? Considering God's penchant for wilderness challenge and experiential education, wouldn't it be more likely that Jesus would teach us to pray, "Lord, lead us *into* temptation"?

LEAD US INTO TEMPTATION (NOT)

I've traveled in Greece twice—once for six months during an academic program in college, and once for a winter investigation into the lives of monks on Mount Athos (more on that in a later chapter). Both times, whenever I asked locals for a favor, the usual response was a broad smile, followed by the words *den peirazei*: "it's no problem."

Peirasmos is ancient Greek for a test or a problem. *Peirasmos* can mean lots of things, depending on the context. On the positive side, it can mean the trial and refinement of one's character, a necessary testing that strengthens. In this light, the word is related to refining metal or forging a people in the desert, as happened to the Israelites. On the negative side, *peirasmos* can also mean a temptation or a distraction that weakens a person or draws them off course, or a grueling event that causes suffering, loss, or unhealthiness.

Considering how unreceptive most of us are to tough love, I can see why we humans want to avoid necessary but painful transformation. We naturally want to pray to God for a pass: Lord, lead us not into temptation. Please do not toss us into times of testing, into trials that transform. We like ourselves just as we are, thank you very much.

But why would *Jesus* teach his disciples to pray "Lead us not into *peirasmos*"? As I pondered this question, I realized something fascinating: Jesus uses *peirasmos* in this case to mean the temptation of *self-absorbed sedation*—unconscious distraction that leads us off course. Look at this fascinating story at the Mount of Olives. In it we see Jesus remaining painfully and poignantly awake, while his trusted allies fall into self-centered unconsciousness:

> Jesus went out as usual to the Mount of Olives, and his disciples followed him. On reaching the place, he said to them, "Pray that you will not fall into *peirasmos*." He withdrew about a stone's throw beyond them, knelt down and prayed, "Father, if you are willing, take this cup from me; yet not my will, but yours be done." . . . In anguish, he prayed more earnestly, and his sweat was like drops

of blood falling to the ground. When he rose from prayer and went back to the disciples, he found them asleep. . . . "Why are you sleeping?" he asked them. "Get up and pray so that you will not fall into *peirasmos*." (Luke 22:39-46)

There are two tests going on in this scene: one of Jesus and one of the disciples. Jesus, eventually, surrenders unto God; the disciples, on the other hand, simply surrender to sleep. This kind of self-absorbed sedation is the *peirasmos* that Jesus warns us about, the *peirasmos* he rejects and asks God to help us avoid. Here's Jesus, in the middle of the night, struggling to do this thing he must, perhaps wishing he could have an easier life, yet he resists the temptation to stay small. Ultimately, he surrenders to God's larger call.

In his dark hour of need, with empire breathing down his neck, Jesus needed support. He needed allies. How much more so do we, in our time and in our place? The prayer he taught his disciples to pray is needed today in our culture of afflu-enza more than ever: Lord, keep us from self-absorbed seda-tion. And his query of his disciples at the Mount of Olives is the same question he asks of us today: *Why are you sleeping?* Why are we slumbering and sedated in this time of great need? Lives are transforming, the climate is changing, the planet is groaning, storms are gathering, history is altering, the Spirit is moving, and we are . . . comfortably dozing? Jesus, through his actions at Gethsemane, shows us to do the exact opposite: stay vigilant for a transformative calling, stay ready for an im-possible opening, stay awake for a personal revolution.

DON'T SLEEP THROUGH A REVOLUTION

"Remaining Awake through a Great Revolution" was a sermon Martin Luther King Jr. preached numerous times, in numerous places, encouraging privileged Christians to remain awake and engaged during this era of great social transformation. Some of the words would change, depending on the sociopolitical events of the day, but invariably King would launch into this sermon by recalling Washington Irving's "Rip Van Winkle."

The major thing that usually sticks with us, King would say, is that Rip Van Winkle slept twenty years. But there's another crucial detail we often forget: a changed sign on the side of the road, which Rip passed by during his travels. King reminded his audience that when Rip went *up* into the mountain for his long sleep, he walked through a town on the Hudson River and passed an inn with a sign bearing an image of King George III of England. When Rip came *down*, years later, the inn's sign had changed and now bore an image of George Washington, the first president of the United States. When the recently awoken Rip gazed at the picture of Washington, he was confused, for he knew not who the new leader was. In his sermon, King's big punchline was this: "the most striking thing about the story of Rip Van Winkle is not merely that he slept twenty years, but that he slept through a revolution."[1] While he snored away up on the mountain, great changes were happening in his world.

Dr. King would sometimes change the title of this sermon, or certain details, depending on his audience. Yet time and time again, he would return to his core message: far too many people, during periods of great social change, fail to make the engaged mental and spiritual leaps the new situation demands. They underestimate the power of the moment—considering something a fad rather than fundamental—or they remain in denial, holding on to a dream of a bygone status quo.

Channeling Christ, channeling King, we must ask ourselves: How awake are we during this watershed moment in history? Our human fate is inextricably tied to the rest of God's creation:

the fate of the rainforest, the aquifer, and the honeybee. Our health is inextricably bound to the health of our water, air, and soil. Though half a century old, King's words from his "Remaining Awake" sermon ring with truth today:

> Modern man, through his scientific genius, has been able to dwarf distance, and place time in chains. Yes, we've been able to carve highways through the stratosphere, and our jet planes have compressed into minutes distances that once took weeks and months. And so this is a small world from a geographical point of view. What we are facing today is the fact that through our scientific and technological genius we've made of this world a neighborhood. And now through our moral and ethical commitment we must make of it a brotherhood. We must all learn to live together as brothers and sisters—or we will all perish together as fools. This is the great issue facing us today. No individual can live alone; no nation can live alone. We are tied together.[2]

DISTURBED SLUMBER

Our ancient stories tell us that Abraham thought a lot about his unborn descendants, and imagined them as numerous as the stars in the sky and the grains of sand on the seashore (Genesis 22:17). Modern poet Drew Dellinger also imagines his unborn descendants, but in a very different way. They disturb his sleep, and in his dreams they ask him: "What did you do while the planet was plundered? / What did you do when the earth was unraveling? / Surely you did something when the seasons started failing?"[3]

What did you do once you knew? Baldly put, even as I write, the modern civilization we live in is devouring the planet we love. Our expanding industrial systems—not just power plants but also the production of our shiny new gadgets and the transport of our organic vegetables—are daily reducing God's gifts of clean air, pure water, and good earth. This precious Earth is not transferable, returnable, or disposable, and it is under attack. By us. This is not an opinion to debate or a conspiracy to debunk. It is a fact with which we must deal, something that can no longer be ignored or slept through. As Ched Myers says, for Christians there are two options: active discipleship, or active denial.

So what did you do once you knew? Martin Luther King Jr. jumped into the spirit of his times and became a center-point in a revolutionary period of great change. In his "Remaining Awake" sermon, there was one great question he would always ask his Christian listeners: What is the church called to do, and be, in times of great change?

"There are some things in our nation and in our world to which I'm proud to be maladjusted," cried King. He then issued this call to his listeners: "All people of goodwill need to be maladjusted to these things until the good society is realized." King, both silly and serious, proposed a new global organization: the International Association for the Advancement of Creative Maladjustment. He imagined the organization's poster child would be the maladjusted prophet Amos from the Old Testament, who in the midst of the injustices of his day cried out in words that echo across the centuries: "Let justice roll down like waters and righteousness like a mighty stream" (5:24).[4]

What will we of the church do in our watershed moment? The church has a great responsibility, King said, because when the church is true to its nature, it stands as a moral guardian, confronting power and standing in solidarity with the vulnerable, and always, always crying out for justice. It has always been the role of the authentic church to expand possibilities, challenge the status quo with imaginative alternatives, and break up business as usual whenever necessary.

REWILDING THE LORD'S PRAYER

Martin Luther King Jr. ached to birth a new world. Jesus did too. So why does the Lord's Prayer come across as so . . . passive? The way the words have been handed down to us through layers of tradition—the "received words," called *textus receptus* in Latin—have always seemed a little tame to me. Could the original prayer, articulated two thousand years ago by Jesus in his native Aramaic, have been a little wilder?

Tradition teaches that, when Jesus taught his disciples to pray, he instructed them to pray these words:

Our Father who art in heaven,
hallowed be thy name.
Thy kingdom come,
thy will be done, on earth as it is in heaven.
Give us this day our daily bread, and forgive us our debts as we
forgive our debtors.
Lead us not into temptation, but deliver us from evil.
For thine is the kingdom, the power and the glory forever. Amen.

Christian tradition calls this the Lord's Prayer. For more than a thousand years, millions upon millions of Christians worldwide have recited this prayer—or something very similar—every week. It is, by far, the prayer most spoken in the entire Western world.

So why does it seem so passive? I've often been muddled about the prayer's purpose. Why did Jesus teach his followers this particular prayer? Was it meant to lead his disciples to do anything, be anything? Or was it simply meant to be comforting?

The phrasing of the Lord's Prayer makes things a bit unclear to me. For example, when Jesus says "thy kingdom come," is he saying that the kingdom *has* come already, that it *will* come sometime in the future, that he *wishes* it to come, or that it's coming *right now*? When he says, "thy will be done," is he commanding God to get busy, or is he reminding his followers to do God's will?

And why all the requests? In Matthew, in the sentences preceding this prayer, Jesus tells his disciples that "your Father knows what you need before you ask him" (6:8). If God knows what we need, then why do we *ask* God for bread, forgiveness, protection, and deliverance? Is this prayer really meant to remind God about *our* needs—or, more importantly, to remind *us* about what God provides?

Millions of churchgoers recite this prayer every day, but rarely does reciting lead to changed behavior. Too often, God's will still takes a backseat to our own will—usually focused on personal advancement, entertainment, and security. Business as usual continues unabated. Debts still stand and grudges still remain, even though we ask God to forgive us just as we forgive. For most of institutional Christianity, the prayer has become rote. Comforting, but not particularly transforming.

Was that Jesus' intent as he taught this prayer—to conform, but not transform? Hardly. So what *was* its original intent? This is a sacred and murky question that must only be entered with a prayer-filled heart. We'd all like to believe that we have access to the original words of Jesus, yet many versions of the Lord's Prayer have existed across Christian history. Even the versions found in Matthew and Luke have substantial differences in wording. Any version extant today in our language has been passed down across the centuries through many tongues—from Aramaic to Greek to Latin to English, at least—and words have changed across cultures, denominations, and regimes. Layers of additions over time have turned the basic, elemental prayer of Jesus into something more elaborate and inscrutable.

I'd like to offer a possibility. Imagine the Lord's Prayer sounded more like this:

> Father of Everything,
> Your presence fills all of Creation.
> Again today, your kingdom has come.
> Again today, I join my will to your will to make earth as heaven.
> Again today, you'll give us the bread we need for your daily work, and you'll show mercy to us just as much as we show mercy to others.
> Again today, as we face times of testing, you'll be with us in our trials.

I offer this version not as a scholarly or literal translation, but as a meditation to dwell on. I offer this because I'm pretty sure that, for Jesus, this prayer was meant to incite a daily revolution in the hearts of his followers. It was not meant to be rote, nor passive, nor confusing, nor tame. It was to be wild, immediate, and transformational. I think it was intended to be said daily by Jesus' followers in order to enlarge their hearts, direct their actions, and alter the way they saw reality. It was meant to be the philosophical foundation of the kingdom of God emerging within them, standing starkly in contrast to the kingdom of Caesar surrounding them.

Seen in this light, is it likely that Jesus taught this prayer to his disciples just once, making sure they were taking notes to write it down later? Unlikely. More probable, the prayer was part of the disciples' daily rhythms as they walked through daily life with their master. Remember, the earliest followers of Jesus traveled as a migratory band. They traveled light. They didn't write, and I'm guessing they didn't carry burdensome scrolls; they were talking, listening, doing, walking, praying. This daily prayer taught by Jesus would have been said hundreds of mornings as the group rose to greet the sun and break their fast; it would have been said regularly around coastal campfires, as the hungry group roasted fish and baked loaves in coals.

Jesus taught this prayer to remind his disciples of the bountiful, unbelievable partnership they had with their abundant God. In the earliest years after Jesus died—before gospels were written, before Paul's writings were collated and codified, before the New Testament even existed—this prayer may have been called the Hesed Prayer. *Hesed* is best translated as "covenanted loving-kindness." The prayer certainly embodied covenanted loving-kindness: in it, Jesus reminds followers of the Way of their cooperative, everyday, two-way relationship with their God. Could this prayer have been a daily contract, a renewable covenant between partners? It certainly echoes back to the Old Testament promise Yahweh made several times to the Israelites: "you will be my people, and I will be your God."[5] The mutual covenant—the daily promise to embody God's will, trusting in turn that God will provide for the day—shines forth as the authentic message of the Master we follow. Its bold promise of partnership fits the one who dared to proclaim, "But seek his kingdom, and these things will be given to you as well" (Luke 12:31).

5

LIVING ON THE LOOSE

THE OLD TESTAMENT, like an immense quilt, covers an impressive scope of time and thought—thousands of years, and perhaps as many perspectives. Scores of voices emerge from its pages, many of which seem in conflict: we hear different voices saying that God supports peace but also war, equality but also favoritism, mercy as well as vengeance, rooted humble living and manifest colonial destiny, free anarchic association as well as classist monarchy. Similar to the conflicting voices we hear in our culture today, the Old Testament holds contrasting views of what is God's will and what makes God's ideal society. Some opinions enter the fabric of Scripture for a single moment, while other themes connect deep through the cloth like a recurrent thread.

One of the strands that recurs most often is the concept of *enoughness*—enough sustenance in the desert, enough shelter for the storm, enough bread for the day, enough grace to redeem all of creation.

This theme of enoughness is captured by the prophet Nehemiah, as he recalls what God provided to the Israelites during the exodus: "You gave your good Spirit to instruct them. You did not withhold your manna from their mouths, and you gave them water for their thirst. For forty years you sustained them in the wilderness; they lacked nothing; their clothes did not wear out nor did their feet become swollen" (Nehemiah 9:20-21).

Having done a little wilderness wandering myself, I appreciate the details Nehemiah chooses to note. Others might have complained about the conditions, but Nehemiah reminds his hearers that what God provided was enough: the wanderers could bank on the basics, they could count on their clothes, and their feet weren't too worn out after a long day's journey. This is the long and rich story of God's people in the Old Testament: when they follow faithfully, they experience enoughness. So where did we moderns—who search and grasp after far too many things—get off track?

REWILDING THE PENTATEUCH

I wonder how long ago we got off track and missed the major themes of the first five books of the Bible. These first five books are a set—in Greek, the *Pentateuch*, which means "five-volume book." These writings emerged from Moses and his cohorts from their desert experiences, and in Jewish tradition they are considered five-fifths of the Law.

These five books are the ages-long story of God's people traveling, tenting, being tested, and turning out all right. They are the primeval core of our tradition—full of deep stories, divine encounters, risky situations, key teachings, and exciting exploits. If we are modern followers of the Way, situated in Jesus' tradition, they are must-reads. So why did we make their titles so boring?

We did a superb job naming the first book. Its Hebrew title is *bereshith*—"in [the] beginning." This was later translated into

Greek as *geneseos*, meaning "birth" or "history of origin." Our English title, Genesis, seems to be a faithful translation of the original intent, as it is primarily a book of beginnings.

We did pretty well with the second book, too: our title Exodus and the Greek title *exodos* both mean massive exit or departure, and that's what the book is about.

It's in the translation of the third book that we started to stumble. Why did our cultural forefathers choose the title Leviticus, meaning "of or relating to the Levites"? Its Hebrew title is *wayyiqra'*, which means "he called." Sure, the book deals with special duties of the Levite priests and with many ceremonial laws and social regulations that we find alien to modern life. Yet I think the title *He Called* is not only more in the spirit of the original Hebrew but also far more compelling than the title Leviticus. I wonder how many of us never wade into Leviticus because we think it is a catalogue of irrelevant and archaic priestly laws. By avoiding Leviticus as a whole we miss nuggets of explosive social wisdom, such as that found in chapter 25. Check this out: through Moses, God says *the land itself must observe a sabbath.* "The land is to have a year of rest," declares the Lord. God, through Moses, goes on to decree that whatever the land produces on its own, the people may eat— but the community *may not manage* the land, sow seeds, or even harvest the grapes of untended vines.

Do you understand the rewilding of this mandate? God is telling a settled agricultural people that they are to *give the land a break* every seven years. God is laying out his ideal social structure, and it is a shock: a society habituated to farming *must stop land management* every seventh year and learn to be hunter-gatherers again, living off the enoughness of what the land provides. Just imagine! What skills would need to be honed? What place-based knowledge would need to be cultivated and remembered? What entrenched power hierarchies would be disrupted? What greedy ambitions would be put in check?

Let's move to the fourth book of the Pentateuch, which we've given another zippy title: Numbers. *Numbers*—really? That's the best we could do? It sounds like a statistics course in college. It's not really our culture's fault, since early English translators just copied the Greek title. But why did the Greek scribes choose Numbers for a title? Did they decide that the major theme of the book were the two lengthy census lists found at the beginning and end? Did they skip over the middle? It seems so, because they missed the main point of the work. Why didn't they follow the Hebrew title *bammidbar*, which means "in the desert"?

In the Desert. Now that's a title I would pick up in a bookstore. *In the Desert* is also much more descriptive of its actual contents, since struggling in the wilderness is the dominant theme of the book, far more prevalent and meaningful than a few census lists.

In Numbers, we see Moses, in the desert both literally and metaphorically, struggling to find a path for his people, listening to his God, trusting his own instincts in the dark, crafting a religion never seen before. More than 150 times, in over twenty ways, the Lord speaks to Moses, and through Moses to Israel. The title *In the Desert* makes me imagine where these impossible wanderers were and how they felt; the title Numbers simply makes me yawn.

Finally, we come to the title of the last book of the Pentateuch: Deuteronomy. Come on. Have you ever used that word in normal conversation? "That dress looks so deuteronomy on you." Or how about: "I read through the legal proceedings and all I could find was deuteronomy after deuteronomy." That last one is pretty close. It turns out that Deuteronomy means "repetition of the law." Scholars report that the term accidentally became a title owing to a long-ago mistranslation passed along via the Greek Septuagint and the Latin Vulgate. Again, I wonder, why didn't our cultural forebears follow the book's Hebrew title? Instead of "repetition of the law," the Hebrews called it *'elleh haddebarim*, meaning "these are the words."

These Are the Words—that's a far more fitting title for a book consumed with articulating the covenanted right relationship between a people and their God. This book's call to total, unreserved commitment to the Lord became a deep inspiration to later prophets throughout Scripture, and it was a massive influence on Jesus himself.

The period that these five books emerge from—the period of desert exodus—was a watershed moment in history for the Israelites, an utterly defining time that solidified who they were and who they would become. As a captive people entering into a new era ourselves, we would be wise to dust off Deuteronomy and the other books of the Pentateuch, honoring their wildness and desert wisdom by remembering their original names: *Birth. Departure. He Called. In the Desert. These Are the Words.* These are the kinds of names that would be given to sacred texts by a tenting people, fierce and free, a people who knew their God walked with them.

Reading about rewilding in our modern, insulated houses with weather-clad windows, we need to remember that the ancient Israelites *chose* to be a tenting people. They did not have to be; they did so because they knew God was easier to connect with in the wild. It was no accident that Moses found God in a burning bush on the far side of the desert, in uncolonized space.

Since their untamed God was at home in wild lands, you can bet the ancient Israelites took camping seriously. Their leave-no-trace ethics would make Outward Bound proud: "Designate a place outside the camp where you can go to relieve yourself. As part of your equipment have something to dig with, and when you relieve yourself, dig a hole and cover up your excrement" (Deuteronomy 23:12-13). Camping was both covenant and communion. Camp itself was sacred space, holy ground, "for the Lord your God moves about in your camp" (23:14). God traveled with his people as they traveled.

God's vision of ideal society, from ancient times, has been camping communion with his people on Earth. I mean this literally: God is a big fan of tent camping. Civilized society tends to forget this elemental truth, and as we continue to shield ourselves from nature and distance ourselves from living with the land, it becomes harder and harder to see the original meaning of ancient, earthy Scripture. For example, in most modern translations of Leviticus, God tells the ancient Israelites, "I will put my dwelling place among you" (Leviticus 26:11). Yahweh is making a promise to walk among his people and journey with them. *Dwelling place* is rather abstract and displaced, isn't it? A more literal translation is both more accurate and more intimate: "I will pitch my tent among you." God wants to camp with his people, on the ground, in the dust. This ancient vision from the earliest days of the Israelites is later invoked at the opposite end of the Bible in Revelation, when the author paints a future picture of creation redeemed. The writer is describing a band of God's people (like the ancient Israelites) who have suffered and journeyed. In our civilized English translations, we read that God "will shelter them with his presence." This is a beautiful image, but an even richer dimension of companionship and caring emerges when we read a more elemental rendering: God will literally "spread his tent over them." The Lord will be their shepherd, their trip leader. He will care for their needs and bring them to springs of fresh living water (Revelation 7:15-16).

We see, then, that camping communion was at the heart of the Israelite experience of the divine. Tent traveling was how they experienced life and encountered God, not in metaphor but in fact. In truth, tenting was such a pervasive part of daily living and sacred ceremony in Biblical times that the word *tent* shows up 333 times in Scripture. That's right: not 3, not 33, but 333 times. They lived in them, slept in them, ate in them, worshiped in them, died in them, gave birth in them. Who else, thousands of years later, was a huge fan of tents? Why, Paul, of course.

A TENT-MAKING GUILD OF *CIMARRONS*

Paul's tent making is well-known. But modern Christians dwelling in houses have a tendency to think of Paul's tent making as a generic example of self-funding; they seem to think that *any* revenue-generating trade, such as being a carpenter or a lawyer, a translator or a teacher, would be the same.

Not so.

Paul's tent making was a tool for living liberation that allowed him to go places few could go. Paul lived tents, patched tents, carried tents, breathed tents. There can be no doubt he used tents and slept in them, over and over. Like the ancient Israelites, Paul didn't *have* to be all about tents. He *chose* to be, so he could live wild and follow an untamed God, free of empire. And he wasn't alone, I think. The facts are a little hidden, but I've come to believe that Paul was part of a posse of tent-making *cimarrons*.

Check it out: Acts 18 tells us that Paul left Athens and went to Corinth. There he connects with Aquila and Priscilla, a couple recently arrived in Corinth, who are traveling—on the loose and on the lam—because Emperor Claudius had ordered all Jews to leave Rome, on the double. Scripture says: "Paul went to see them, and because he was a tentmaker as they were, he stayed and worked with them" (18:2b-3). He stayed in Corinth a year and a half (18:11).

This brief factual account seems straightforward, yes? Actually, it poses more questions than it answers. Were Paul, Aquila, and Priscilla already tent-making collaborators? Seems so, since Paul went to see them and somehow he knew they'd arrived in Corinth, on the run from empire. "He was a tent-maker as they were," the passage says. Could it be that he knew of their sudden deportation because they *were of the same guild*? Biblical commentaries describe the composition of a Jewish synagogue at Alexandria in this way: People did not sit in a mixed manner, but according to guilds. Goldsmiths sat in one area, silversmiths in another, and the same with iron-workers, miners, and weavers.[1] Paul likely had a history with Priscilla and Aquila already, or knew friends of friends in his tent-making guild who could vouch for their trustworthiness. Finally, since no conversion is mentioned and Paul quickly arranges a work partnership that lasts quite a while, I'm guessing they were already Christians, already trusted members of Paul's growing network.

What does all this questioning reveal? I don't know about you, but it sounds to me like Paul and his pals were part of an underground *cimarron* network of God-filled, anti-empire, simple-living, on-the-road, self-reliant tentmakers.

REWILDING PAUL

Sometimes we forget how hard-core Paul was. Because he is sometimes hoisted up as the poster child of tame, institution-alized Christianity, we forget how deeply counterculturally he acted, how fearlessly he spoke, and how wildly he wandered.

Check out this example: the whole city of Ephesus was furious because Paul and his pals were criticizing the city's cash cow, the purchase-oriented worship of Artemis (Acts 19:29). The crowd seized Paul's traveling companions, causing a mass riot. When the uproar ended, Paul parted from his companions, traveled through Macedonia, and eventually arrived in Greece, where he stayed for three months (20:2-3).

Again: straightforward, yes? Hardly. Paul left Ephesus to travel through *Macedonia*? That's some craggy country. Trust me, I've hiked there. Probably Paul was alone and on foot, staying where he could and tenting as he went. Paul keeps it fast and loose, a guerilla ministry, running afoul of the establishment and willingly making wild journeys, just him and his tent. After three months in Greece, he decides to hike *back* through Macedonia again, but this time with a posse of companions (20:6). From Philippi, they take a five-day sail to Troas, where they meet up with some other traveling buddies and stay for seven days (20:13). At this point Luke and some others sail to Assos, where they hook up with Paul again, who had made yet another long journey on foot—perhaps alone.

Paul knows his life is hard-core; it's what he signed up for. As a countercultural tentmaker and ragamuffin for God, he simply names it: "prison and hardships are facing me" (20:23). Yet with his tent and with God, he's learned to be radically content (more on this in chapter 10). He's gained the secrets of self-sufficiency, free and dependent upon no one: "I have not coveted anyone's silver or gold or clothing.... These hands of mine have supplied my own needs and the needs of my companions" (20:33-34).

Where did he learn these secrets of self-sufficiency, this wild readiness for the road? Therein lies a mystery.

INTO ARABIA?

Scholars agree that Paul undertook three major treks. His first missionary journey was about 1,400 miles long; the second

3,200; and the third 3,500. That makes a total of 8,100 miles traveled by Paul. Scholarly consensus says Paul took about ten years to accomplish the three journeys, each elaborated upon in the Scriptures.[2] However, scholars are clueless about Paul's *other* journey—his earliest, most mysterious, most suppressed, and perhaps most important travel: a lengthy trek into Arabia.

Into Arabia? In the entire New Testament, among all the words of Paul—and there are a lot—he only refers to this primary and formative trek into Arabia once. At the beginning of his letter to the Galatians, he starts with an unusually long autobiographical section—perhaps needing to explain himself to his audience. He sets the tone, then explains what he did immediately after being knocked off his horse by his encounter with the living Christ on the Damascus road: "My immediate response was not to consult any human being. I did not go up to Jerusalem to see those who were apostles before I was, but *I went into Arabia*. Later I returned to Damascus" (Galatians 1:15-17). In the next verse, Paul says that he eventually went to Jerusalem. The total time from the Damascus road experience until his arrival in Jerusalem, Paul says, was *three years* (1:18).

Modern scholars don't know why Paul went to Arabia, what he did there, exactly how long he stayed, or even to which part of "Arabia" he traveled. It seems some of Paul's peers in the New Testament were ignorant of his trek into Arabia as well, perhaps even more than we are. For example, did Luke, the writer of Acts, know about Paul's Arabian exodus? Apparently not. Luke tells the tale in Acts in a very different way: Paul didn't go to Arabia at all after his vision on the Damascus road. Rather, a blinded Paul was urgently led by the hand into the city, healed, baptized, and fed. As soon as he revived, he immediately started proclaiming Jesus as the risen Son of God in Damascus, and, after some time, goes to Jerusalem (Acts 9:8-20).

Despite the fact that the Acts tale is more famous, I'm guessing that Paul's own account is more authentic. Blown off his saddle, blown away by an encounter with a living and cosmic Christ, Paul—without asking for job leave, without talking to anyone, without consulting established leadership in the Jesus movement—goes away into "Arabia," only to show up in Jerusalem three years later, utterly confident in his call.

Why Arabia? How long was he there? What did he experience during that journey, and how did it change him? No one knows. No one knows even what Paul meant by saying he went into "Arabia." His experience there could have been starkly wild or highly civilized, since the region included uninhabited mountains and stark deserts, but also villages, cities, and kings. Some commentators think it was a time of necessary solitude and contemplation, while others assert it was Paul's first attempt at evangelizing non-Jews in distant lands. Me, I'm going with my gut: his world had just blown apart. I'm guessing that a confused and conflicted Paul—reeling from transformative shock—went on a vision quest into the wilds of Arabia. I don't think Paul's choice of words was an accident: he could've said he traveled *to* Arabia or spent some time *in* Arabia; instead, he reports that he went *into* Arabia. This connotes an immersion, a plunging, just as Jesus was not baptized *in* the Jordan but *into* the Jordan: it was a whole-being experience.

SEEKING MOUNT SINAI

Scholar and theologian N. T. Wright also thinks Paul went to the wilds of Arabia seeking discernment, but Wright has more rational reasons than I do. He lays out fascinating parallels between Paul and the Old Testament prophet Elijah: as young men, both were ultra-confident and zealously violent champions of Yahweh; and both experienced purpose-shattering identity crises that rocked them to their very foundations. Wright asserts that Paul, like Elijah hundreds of years before him, plunged into the wilderness of Arabia seeking new meaning and new identity through a vision quest. But not just any wilderness: Wright suggests that Paul, like his two heroes Elijah and Moses, sought out Mount Sinai, seeking the holy mountain to discern the will of God.[3]

On his wilderness sojourn, I'm guessing Paul crystallized a new call and a new identity. Although we can't be sure, his trek into Arabia may have lasted years. During that time, he must have done lot of tenting. I'm guessing he experienced the same raw, intimate, and wild relationship with the divine that the ancient Israelites experienced—the untamed relationship that Moses and Elijah experienced during their own vision quests at Sinai—and he came to know that his Lord tented with him, that God moved about in his camp. I'm guessing he was initiated into the mysteries of many of life's secrets. I'm guessing it was here that Paul learned, through living wild and on the loose, the secret of *autarkeia*—being content in any and every situation—which allowed him to be the fearless and untamed person God wanted him to be.

6

REWILDING EDUCATION

LOT OF CHRISTIANS today wonder why they should care for the environment. They're seeking to be educated by Scripture, and are looking for Bible passages telling them to honor the Earth. I get it; after all, that's what we're trained to do as Christians—look to the Bible to guide our behavior. But there are other primary texts we should be reading, too; like Jesus, we should always be reading nature and reading the signs of the times.

Would we look first to the Bible for guidance if our house was being bulldozed and our family was inside? No. We'd stop the bulldozer, or we'd bring our family to safety. Would we look to the Bible first if someone was pouring gasoline into our children's drinking water? No. We'd stop the perpetrator and make sure our family had clean water to drink. We need no book—even the Good Book—to urge us to these actions. They are natural.

Our current situation is this grave. Our house *is* being bull-dozed. Our water *is* being poisoned. By us. The Earth is the miraculous and abundant house that God gave us to enjoy, and we are destroying it. The Greek term *oiko*—as in *eco*nomics and *eco*logy—means home, and our *eco*system, our life systems, are being permanently degraded every day by our own actions personally and by industrial society globally. You might not sense it yet, because your water is still drinkable and your air still smells good and your grocery store still sparkles and your trash disappears and your neighborhood is not submerged under rising sea levels. But millions of other citizens of our Earth home—both human and not—are feeling it every day. And we keep wondering if the Bible exhorts us to do something.

READING NATURE: THE EARLIEST BIBLE

Authentic disciples have always read the Bible in one glance and read the big picture in another; they have always read the signs of the times, interpreted Scripture, and moved when the Spirit says move. Take slavery, for example. There are several Bible verses condoning slavery; if Christians took only those as a guide, without being guided by a larger sense of love and justice, we would be perpetuating a society that was truly anti-Christ, promoting the very cruelty, inhumanity, and oppression that Jesus came to liberate us from.

So please don't wait until Scripture convinces you to care for God's precious gift of creation. I'm doing exactly that in this book—providing Scripture-based encouragement for you to adapt your actions—but the time for transition is now. Don't wait for another Bible study or a worsening headline; God has been calling our culture to Earth-honoring repentance for a long time now. And we're the ones to do it. We just need to pay attention to what is sacred.

Many Christians feel God's presence in nature, sometimes more strongly than in church. How about you? Many of us feel unconditional love when touched by a sunrise, and we see resurrection hope when plants emerge in spring. In Romans, Paul speaks to this awareness: God's nature is plain to see in creation, in the things that have been made (1:20). Creation reveals God to us. Richard Rohr names the obvious: "the natural world is the first and primary Bible. . . . Creation is our first and final cathedral."[1] Sometimes Christians are so focused on being "Bible based" that they forget something vital: Jesus and his followers had no New Testament. Let me say this again: Jesus and his disciples did not rely on our Bible. They looked to nature, personal experience, and their tradition of Judaism to find God's good way. Think about how many times Jesus uses natural objects to illustrate his teachings: salt, light, mustard bushes, yeast, fish, figs, grapes, lilies, sheep, goats, cedars, palm trees, olives, mountains, rivers, sparrows, sand, stone, wheat, watering holes, ditches, donkeys, and many more. He was educating people about God and Spirit through nature. God's people have always paid attention to the wild world around them for holy education and divine direction.

We modern folks, in our race to improve our lives, have failed to pay attention to the world. Rohr observes that, with the invention of the printing press nearly six centuries ago, affluent people started reading books a lot more than nature itself. By doing so, we substitute ideas and words for direct observation and participation in the life that teems around us. This shields us from raw reality and prevents us from getting the vital dose of experiential education we need to stay wild.

WHERE LEARNING IS AN ADVENTURE

I love Outward Bound. I really do. I have been involved in wilderness leadership and public education for many years, and Outward Bound has transformed both fields for the better. Yet in the 1990s, when Outward Bound began marketing its mission to bring adventurous learning into American schools, they did something tragic: they gave up on self-denial.

Sensible self-denial was one of the five core pillars of vital modern education for Kurt Hahn, Outward Bound's visionary founder. For Hahn, education was not about memorizing Great Books or meeting state-mandated requirements. Education was soulcraft, pure and simple. "I regard it as the foremost task of education," Hahn wrote, "to ensure the survival of these qualities: an enterprising curiosity, an undefeatable spirit, tenacity in pursuit, readiness for sensible self denial, and above all, compassion."[2]

What if we trained American youth today not only in the domains of math, science, and English, but in the domains of curiosity, tenacity, self-denial, and compassion? What kind of citizens would we cultivate? Might we be closer to the people God has always wanted us to be?

As the founders of an Expeditionary Learning Outward Bound middle school in northern New Mexico, my wife and I tried to do just that. In 1999, we created Roots & Wings Community School, a crucible of learning that sought to instill wisdom, develop discernment, enhance courage, and deepen compassion. We created something very different, yet it still existed within the system and had to comply with most of the constraints of any public school. We were still required to meet state standards, perform well on standardized tests, and be free and open to all comers.

We had to fit into a conventional paradigm, yes, but from the outset we pledged that, here, learning would be an adventure. We knew what Walt Whitman knew: "Now I see the secret of making the best person," he wrote in *Leaves of Grass*; "it is to grow in the open air, and to eat and sleep with the earth."[3] Our mission statement reads: "Our mission is to inspire our students to academic and personal excellence. Our innovative learning community creates classroom, farm and wilderness adventure—engaging the head, hands and heart—enabling students to achieve more than they think possible and take active roles in our ever-changing world." At Roots & Wings, we address rigorous academic content, sure, but we also spend twenty or thirty nights in the wilderness each school year, combining weeks of traditional classroom settings with weeks spent boating, backpacking, snow trekking, and camping under the stars. Our middle school students have written hundred-page novels, put Kit Carson on trial, played monthlong high-seas swashbuckling games in math class, and experienced numerous overnight wilderness solos. In our own little way, I think we would have made Kurt Hahn proud; at our school's very core were semester-long learning expeditions of mind, body, and spirit.

More than anyone else, Hahn taught me the power of expeditions—the growth gained by setting forth, breaking free, climbing mountains, and facing unknown challenges in uncolonized space. *Expedition* was Hahn's word for going *cimarron*. "Expeditions can greatly contribute towards building strength of character," Hahn wrote. "Joseph Conrad in *Lord Jim* tells us that it is necessary for a youth to experience events which 'reveal the inner worth of the man; the edge of his temper; the fibre of his stuff; the quality of his resistance; the secret truth of his pretences, not only to himself but others.'"[4]

Kurt Hahn's educational philosophy runs starkly contrary to that of dominant culture. His strategy to develop better humans is about enhancing human *character*, not human *comfort*. "There is more in you than you know," was one of Hahn's deepest beliefs. His method of transformation: to propel people into experiences and see what comes out the other side. As we've seen, God's method has always been the same way. Hahn, like Yahweh himself, used wilderness and experiential testing as a crucible, a proving ground, to reveal our inner worth, the fiber of our stuff, our true natures, our secret hearts.

COURAGE AND CUNNING

When you die, what will you be known for? In these transitional times, this is a question worth meditating upon. Will your gravestone epitaph read: "In his mundane middle-class life, he perpetuated the American way"? In your eulogy, will a friend say, "She lived her self-serving life and only had enough time to love those who loved her"? Will the newspaper obituary report: "He often critiqued modern culture while sipping coffee and reading the news, but did nothing courageous to change it"?

Hahn was a man who changed things that were wrong. A former student said this about him: "He was the most helpful, most generous man I have ever known, rich in ideas and rich in the energy and cunning required to put them into effect."[5] To be rich both in ideas and in the cunning to implement them— this is the kind of fearless, imaginative living that God calls us to today. Kurt Hahn embodied the kind of good news that our world sorely needs.

Born a Jew in 1886 in Berlin, Hahn left Hitler's Germany to become one of the most influential educators the modern world has ever seen. He dedicated his life to educational initiatives aimed at profound human development. Hahn was a dynamo of influence, requiring neither position nor credentials to impact the world stage. Due to his magnetic and enthusiastic personality, he gained allies all over the globe—politicians, industrialists, officials, academics—who endorsed his programs, his philosophy, and his projects. He was a pragmatic idealist, engaging in the muck of reality even while believing in the world as it could be. As a personal counselor to royalty, he threw himself headfirst into the politics and immensity of the first-ever world war, and continued to strive for morality and dignity in the face of dehumanizing conditions. At several points Hahn tried to prevent Hitler from coming to power, but eventually was arrested and fled to England as Germany became ever more hostile to influential people of Jewish birth. Along the way somewhere, he became a Christian. In one being, he was both prophet and bridge builder, German and Englishman, educator and politician—in essence, a man who crossed boundaries and who, on multiple levels, tirelessly worked for and embodied a better world.[6]

EDUCATION AS ANTIDOTE

Hahn's chief educational aim was to prevent a sick society from infecting its citizens. Hahn didn't use the term *affluenza*, but he just as well could have. He held that modern Western consumer culture breeds diseased attitudes in adolescents—a set of unhealthy, immature traits that are carried into adulthood and passed across generations. Chief among these negative traits were irritability, apathy, and entitlement. Hahn insisted that this set of diseased attitudes was not natural but *cultural*, caused by a sick civilization.[7]

Sound familiar? Decades before most were thinking about it, Hahn was naming affluenza for the epidemic it is. Hahn had particular names for these dysfunctional attitudes of adolescence. His is a chilling and prescient list of all-too-familiar social conditions we find today in adults: "sedentary habits," "confused restlessness," "spectatoritis," "the weakened tradition of craftsmanship," "the ever-present availability of stimulants and tranquilizers," and an "unseemly haste." Hahn asserted that sick modern society prematurely snuffs out much of the best of healthy childhood—traits such as innate joy, uninhibited engagement with discovery, an enterprising curiosity, and a readiness to be involved in others' fates—creating a people both passionless and purposeless.[8]

Re-creating healthy young adults was the key to re-creating a healthy society, asserted Hahn. By doing so, he aimed to counteract civic apathy, lack of public spirit, and the decline of compassion, all of which he regarded as great threats to the survival of civil society. Hahn believed that authentic education could combat ill attitudes by arming the adolescent with a grand passion in which one could lose oneself. Hahn's educational plan was aggressive and activist, and fairly controversial—he did not wait for a child's inclinations to emerge but rather tossed kids into a wide range of activities and experiences. This kind of learning through immersion, or experiential education, could only be achieved by transferring children from diseased environments to "healthy pastures." In short, the school was to be the source and center of a counterculture.

HARDWIRED TO BE SELF-SERVING?

At the core of Hahn's philosophy was his unshakeable faith in the potential goodness of individuals. Some critics thought he was impossibly optimistic, while others accused him of being naïve. Kurt Hahn, naïve? Hardly; more than most of us, he knew the dark side of human behavior. After deeply engaging in German politics for years, after doggedly crafting international peace negotiations during the First World War, after seeing his home country follow Hitler's Nazism in lockstep, Hahn knew firsthand the moral decay permeating human society.

It wasn't that Hahn was naïve; it was just that, like God, Hahn refused to give up on people. And the problem of large governments and dominant culture, as he saw it, was not a lack of clever people, but the fact that in mass society clever people *too often lacked the courage of their convictions.* His observation is nothing new: faced with difficult circumstances, *far too many good people repeatedly fail to do what they know is right.*[9] Kurt Hahn saw his own good countrymen quail in the face of fascism and conform to Hitler's regime; Jesus saw his best disciples fall into *peirasmos,* falling asleep when he needed them most; and in the desert Moses saw his own liberated people grumble and grab rather than be transformed.

This eternal tension is at the heart of our crisis today: Are humans hardwired to be narrowly self-serving at the expense of others and the Earth? Or if we open ourselves to testing and transformation and grace, can we ever become the people that God yearns for us to be? I'm siding with Hahn, Moses, and Jesus. Despite the odds, despite our track record, I'm holding out hope for human potential. I'm holding out hope that enough humans can become God-filled people and lead the rest of us into the realization that the promised land is our own precious planet. I realize that my hope in human transformation is more desperate than data driven. It's just that a human-divine partnership of transformation is all that is left. Modern culture's promise of "better living through technology" only takes us so far; we also need to heed God's tough-love promise of better living through testing. Unless we can change into the people God has been waiting for, the human project is over.

7

ONE'S LIFE IS THE PROJECT

BILL MCKIBBEN compares modern culture to a child lost in the woods. Like a city kid out of his element, we're frantic, unsure, anxious, and disoriented. Tangled in confusing complexity, we see dimly. What new kind of reality lies just beyond our vision? Our best flashlights illuminate only a few steps into the unknown future.

Where to go next? What to do first? Well, like a lost camper, first we need to stop running, sit down, turn off our devices, and take a deep breath. We need to examine what we've brought with us in our pack, decide what baggage to abandon and what to keep, and then figure out our best next steps.[1]

Like the prophet Jeremiah at the crossroads, earnest God-followers today are asking two ancient questions. First, where is the good way? And then comes the question we don't like asking: In order to walk in it, how must we change our behaviors? How might we break from our all-too-cozy culture?

THE BLESSING OF A CORRUPT SOCIETY

Søren Kierkegaard is not an easy philosopher to digest. His judgments often appear too depressing, his expectations too demanding, and his concepts too difficult. Sometimes when wading into his writings I find them exhausting, unbelievably abstract, or just plain boring. Luckily I've had some interpreters to help me, most notably Donald D. Palmer, who wrote a slim volume refreshingly titled *Kierkegaard for Beginners.*

Kierkegaard, like the Jesus he tried to follow, was passionate about creating an authentic, new kind of person. How is an authentic, divinely led human being cultivated? Kierkegaard's answer is the same as mine: through unflinching self-examination leading to radical self-determination. In Kierkegaard's view, transformed reality began and ended with the individual who had accepted the power of choice and then completely surrendered to God. Corrupt society, despotic kings, unjust laws, and hypocritical churches were blessings, because confronting immoral institutions forced individual people of God to make their own moral choices.

To Kierkegaard, even the most amazing artists and innovative business people and clever style setters are still hopelessly dictated by society, constantly reacting against and comparing themselves to their peers and authorities. Having individuals choose a *particular* moral code was not Kierkegaard's goal; rather, it was a more elemental decision he felt must be made: whether to hold oneself to an ethical code *at all.* This is Kierkegaard's famous "existential leap": to acknowledge the self as responsible, to stand at the crossroads and choose the God-path in the face of everything. Once this leap happens— once this surrender happens—then one's life *is* the project. Choice making becomes a full-time job; any actions or expectations incompatible with one's moral commitment are eventually discarded.[2]

Everyone's a philosopher these days. Or should be, says Slavoj Žižek: ours is a unique time in history when everyone—in a very significant way—is forced to be some kind of philosopher, if we take our choices to heart like Kierkegaard encourages.[3] We live in a time when turning on a light may mean you are supporting a nuclear power plant. We live in a time when my dad has to decide whether he wants to put a piece of cow in his body to treat his heart condition. We live in a time when I can put my money in a bank that provides microloans to Ecuadorian farmers or supports Wall Street bailouts. In our age of techno-affluence, we are confronted with deep philosophical questions. Every day.

This, then, is the mixed blessing of an exhausting, exhilarating, complex, transnational, open-all-night digital society: today's age is a vibrant incubator for radical disciples seeking to live the Jesus Way, because everything—every single thing—becomes a moral choice. Modern life can be overwhelming, and it's easy to lose our sense of grounding and direction. Like that lost camper trying to reorient under a tree, we need to decide which tools we want to take with us, and which we don't.

Especially which watch we might choose to wear.

NEVER OFFLINE

"Never Offline." That headline, shouted from the cover of a recent issue of *Time* magazine, refers to an article within written by Lev Grossman and Matt Vella entitled "iNeed?"[4] Focusing on the Apple Watch, the article was powerfully ambivalent, naming several profound social impacts—both welcome and disturbing—that will likely arise with the advent of wearable, always-on technology. The article says up front, in bold letters, that this "may not be a good thing." Amid cheerful accolades about the dazzling powers of this new device, the authors also provide prophetic social critique: "This isn't just a new product; this is technology attempting to colonize our bodies."[5]

The arrival of this data-collecting watch is not just another incremental advance of technology as usual. Rather, the authors state that "this is a watershed, a frog-boiling moment" for mass culture, a society-wide commitment to an Internet that can never be turned off or put away. The authors speculate on the near future: once humans accept wearable tech such as this, "the only way forward is inward," and implants become the logical next step.[6]

THE TUG OF TECH

When modern people uncritically adopt technologies as fast as we do in the dominant culture, we take no time to reflect upon possible impacts that we never anticipated. We hardly ever see it coming; rather, we usually just get ambushed by massive change, and then reactively adapt without deep thought. Grossman and Vella note the recent, rapid rise of the iPhone, and our culture's uncritical, exuberant embrace of all related techs and apps.

Their view: nobody anticipated the extent to which smartphones now dominate our every moment and exert a "constant gravitational tug" on our eyes, thoughts, and attention. The reality of living with ever-connected, always-online gadgets like iPhones, they conclude, is that reality feels a bit less real. We become over-connected and disconnected at the same time; we tend to pay attention to the opinions of distant strangers over those of our loved ones standing next to us. We begin to lose the capacity to enjoy time without our devices or to be deeply focused or self-motivated. Not only does always-on social media captivate our attention, it now also validates our worth and our existence. As the authors note, experiences now don't feel fully real until we've used our devices to make them virtual and public, and until a significant number of distant individuals have validated us electronically for doing so.[7]

Even as we gain social reach and unimaginably powerful tools to impact the planet, we lose inner authority, self-knowledge, and self-reliance. Unable to be alone and undistracted, unable to find a location without a GPS, unable to deeply value an experience without the validation of others, we march on, gadgets in hand. The only problem, as we soldier onward guided by the devices of a techno-empire, is that we have trouble finding lasting purpose, contentment, and direction.

Our gadgets make us ever more free and powerful, and at the same time we become horrifyingly empty of authentic self, driven instead by the advice of our devices. Our devices tell us what is trending, who is doing something interesting, what events are transpiring, and who likes us. Our devices tell us what the weather is like, which investment to choose, and how we should feel about terrorists and resisters who are fighting against the status quo. I'm not sure if the article's authors meant their concluding words to be profoundly prophetic, but they were to me: "Every watch Apple sells will bind consumers more firmly to its closed technological ecosystem."[8] Bound and committed, we unwittingly become e-tethered to our devices, and maybe never bother to wonder whence our capacity for choice, morality, and self-reliance has gone. We become, in our own way, *reducidos*, tamed and utterly dependent upon the apparatus of empire, even if the systems are invisible and the shackles are crafted of the finest virtual networks and chased with silver.

SMACKDOWN: KIERKEGAARD VS. FACEBOOK

The Apple Watch brings our already tight, covenanted relationship to technology one step closer, to skin level. It now takes data from us at all hours of the day, addresses our wants before we know them, and becomes, far more than us, an expert and authority on our very selves, managing our personal choices and development so we don't have to.[9] We can now add interacting with our own bodies to the list of mediated, commodified, and alienated relationships we have chosen to contrive.

Plugged in to the corporate electronic teat, we have all we need. Things like community reliance, adaptability, local wisdom, and self-determination become irrelevant and old-fashioned. When you are speeding along the information super-highway, there are no crossroads, so why would you ever need to stand and look, or ask where the good way is? Why hone your own choice when tech can tell you what is right and wrong, what to trust and what is trending?

Long before the Apple Watch and the digital age—long before computers at all, actually, or television, or even electricity—Søren Kierkegaard was certain that "unplugging" was necessary for healthy spiritual and human development. He knew solitude brought a keen awareness of one's separateness, uniqueness, and an intimate awareness of the presence of God. From soli-tude emerges identity and connection to the divine, assets un-shaken by trends or shifting public opinion. Kierkegaard made a prescient prediction: if individuals lost solitude, they would find themselves irretrievably enmeshed in collective conscious-ness, "with only mass communications to shape their hopes, formulate their values, and arrange their thinking."[10] Long be-fore radio, Kierkegaard imagined this threat: "Suppose some-one invented an instrument, a convenient little talking tube which, say, could be heard over the whole land. . . . I wonder if the police would not forbid it, fearing that the whole country would become mentally deranged if it were used."[11]

In our era, new technologies seem to emerge almost daily, and we tend to embrace their promised benefits uncritically, without any real thought to how they will affect our lives and the planet. We rarely take the time to ask, how is this changing my soul?

In Kierkegaard's day, a troubling new technology arose: the daily newspaper. It was immediately and uncritically embraced by the society that surrounded him. Kierkegaard, however, dug in his heels. "There has never been a power so diametrically opposed to Christianity than the daily press," he wrote. The evil of daily newspapers, he declared, lay in their calculated intention to make the passing moment "a thousand or ten thousand times more inflated and important that it really is."[12] So often the trivial becomes essential, while the essential, in turn, becomes trivial. George Bernard Shaw said it this way: newspapers seem unable to discriminate between a bicycle accident and the collapse of civilization.

So what might Kierkegaard say about Facebook and other instantaneous social media? He believed that all moral growth "consists first and foremost in being weaned from the momentary." Constant referencing of peers—checking to see what others like or think or are paying attention to—might be fun, but it retards the authentic development of the true self. Ironically, seeking others' validation weakens even as it seems to strengthen.[13]

Attitudes of the majority, opinion polls, trending styles for the season—these are all immature associations that appear to strengthen individuals by forming them into a group, but actually weaken them ethically. It is doubtful that the age will be saved by networking and association, Kierkegaard observed. Not until each single individual has established an unshakeable ethical stance and connection to the divine—independent of the pull of peers and empire—can there be any hope of genuine communion.

If modern society is a confused camper lost in the woods, like Bill McKibben suggests, we need to stop running and take stock of our actions. Before we unthinkingly shackle ourselves to the latest device, are there attitudes or character qualities we need to cultivate? Jesus had some ideas on the subject, as he recruited for his God-movement.

REWILDING THE BEATITUDES

In Matthew and Luke, soon after returning from his forty days in the wilderness and calling his disciples away from their normal lives, Jesus goes up on a mountainside to pray and discern. After a time apart in this solitary, wild place, he then addresses his gathered disciples. He describes several types of people who are blessed. Here's one, familiar to most of us: "Blessed are those who mourn, for they will be comforted" (Matthew 5:4). Here's another: "Blessed are the merciful, for they will be shown mercy" (5:7).

This section of Scripture, called the Beatitudes, is so familiar that many of us forget to ask a basic question: What was Jesus' purpose in naming these blessed types of people?

Was he using this mountaintop moment with his raw recruits to deliver a series of heartwarming philosophical musings? Was he giving a needed cheer-up because his followers were feeling depressed? Or perhaps he was providing detached information about potential options: *if* one decides to be merciful, *then* one will be shown mercy. Was that what he had in mind?

I'm guessing he was doing something bolder and wilder up there on his mountainside. News was spreading about him. Crowds were coming. A movement was building. He'd been promising liberation and promoting a very different kind of upside-down society. He'd been urging people to repent, to drop business as usual, and to radically change their lives—and they were. He had just selected his inner circle of twelve apostles, and they were at his feet, expecting powerful teaching.

JOB QUALIFICATIONS

I wonder, with these proclamations, could he have been naming the *character* of his new community? Instead of making a series of passive future promises—as the text initially appears—was he instead laying out a manifesto for a movement?

For a moment, let's imagine he was. Let's imagine that his real intent has been buried a bit under a veneer of civilization. I don't know about you, but sentences beginning with "blessed are those" do not exactly spur me into action; rather, they invite me to muse over a tame cup of tea. Here is Jesus, on a mountainside with a ragged band of eager followers awaiting his word, and what does he do? Provide philosophical insights that require his listeners to do nothing but nod their heads approvingly? I doubt it.

If I had to guess, I'd say he was laying out job qualifications. As Ched Myers has said more than once, when you become baptized you're being drafted into a movement. Jesus was organizing a countercultural movement called the kingdom of God, and he had positions that needed to be filled. The phrase *blessed are those* can also mean "those pleasing to God" or "those aligned with God." *God's allies.* With this in mind, let's imagine a slightly creative translation of the Beatitudes found in Matthew 5:

> God's allies have no need for self-advancement;
>
> Living this way, they belong to God's ideal society.
>
> God's allies let themselves feel the pain of the world;
>
> Living this way, they will be sustained.
>
> God's allies do not grasp for more than their share;
>
> Living this way, they shall be entrusted with the wealth of the land.

God's allies hunger and thirst for justice and right living;

Their yearning will be satisfied.

God's allies are merciful;

Living this way, they will receive mercy.

God's allies are passionately singular in heart;

In their focus they will see God.

God's allies are makers and doers of peace;

Living this way, they will be called the children of God.

God's allies get persecuted for seeking justice and right living.

Living through this, they are partners in God's ideal society.

In uncolonized space, up on a mountainside, was Jesus plotting holy mischief, giving marching orders to his closest allies in the upside-down kingdom of God? It seems he was outlining attributes needed to live a brave new lifeway. He was encouraging his followers to make a wild departure from society's expectations, and take on some job qualifications that would cause a major disruption of business as usual.

Here, in the first part of the book—through the stories of Moses and Isaiah, Jesus and Paul, Tim DeChristopher and Kurt Hahn—I've described tamed Christianity, and how our wild God uses uncivilized space to craft divinely transformed human beings. But what characteristics emerge in the wilderness, allowing captives to become the prophetic people God needs us to be? What traits might God's allies need to embody in today's watershed moment, with the health of our very life systems at stake? We'll need some serious skills and serious grace if we are to resist the clutches of consumer culture, reduce the gap between rich and poor, and partner in the redemption and healing of God's beloved Earth. In part 2, I propose seven paths to wild our way so that we may become the people God yearns for us to be.

PART II

SEVEN PATHS TO WILD YOUR WAY

8

STEER BY INNER AUTHORITY

BEFORE WE STARTED a school together, my wife, Peg, and I ran wilderness camps for years. Recently our niece followed in our footsteps and became a camp counselor for the summer. She came to visit us, happy but exhausted, after a solid month at camp. "Now comes the deep relaxation," I said, remembering our own days as camp directors. "Every summer after camp ended, we would always sleep in late and then watch movies all day."

Her response caught me off guard: "Is that allowed?"

Is that allowed? It's a question most of us ask more than we'd like to admit, though perhaps without being aware of it. Most of us look to institutions, regulations, family, and peers for permission rather than look inward to our own value system to determine what is right. In order to cultivate inner authority in our students, at Roots & Wings Community School we encourage reflection more than regulation. When giving feedback to other members of the learning community, we encourage students to think before they speak, and to gauge the worth of their comment by asking three questions: Is it true? Is it kind? Is it necessary?

When individuals don't exercise inner authority, life can quickly get out of balance. Nature once gave us natural boundaries—choices largely dictated by daily rhythms, yearly seasons, regional geography. Technology has now liberated us from the limitations of almost all natural cycles, and in doing so, has given us a daunting array of decisions to make and options to consider. We have the ability to work at night, work on the weekends, work at home, work on vacation, work while commuting. And that's just work. What of our entertainment, our shopping, our eating, our socializing, our traveling? Basically, no one and no thing any longer tells us "this is how life should be lived." Common cultural norms have broken down. Instead, all we have are the examples of our peers, which are a sure recipe for anxiety. We see people working harder than us, and we wonder if we need to keep up. We see people earning more money than us, buying more things, going on better vacations, and we wonder if our lives are lacking. We see people celebrating themselves on social media, so we wonder what we're missing. We then spend more time posting on Facebook, making sure others know of the great things we're doing so they can feel jealous too and wish they were with us. Yet as we immerse ourselves ever deeper into the world of e-socializing, we see more and more exciting posts by smiling friends doing even cooler things, and we feel left behind. What is right for us? This question, if not answered by an inner authority, can lead to toxic levels of affluent exhaustion, insecurity, anxiety, and dis-ease, even as we pursue what we have been told is the good life.

Paul's business was cultivating inner authority among mature Christians. He stresses that inner authority does not mean just doing what you want; it means taking the time to discern deeply with God, to quiet the voices of peer pressure and parental expectation and conventional wisdom, and then to speak and act out of truth. Surrounded by the militaristic might and class-based economic system of the Roman Empire, Paul knew it was of utmost importance for Christians to develop their own, parallel society. But how is that achieved? "Do not conform to the pattern of this world," he says, "but be transformed by the renewing of your mind. Then you will be able to test and approve what God's will is—his good, pleasing and perfect will" (Romans 12:2). This is one of Paul's main desires for his developing Christian flock: to increase their capacity for inner authority, to test, approve, and apply God's will in their lives.

As a college student, I studied a bit about inner authority speaking truth to power. I gained a cursory understanding of Spirit-filled social change movements like the Diggers in England, the Tolstoyans in Russia, and Gandhi's Satyagrahis in India. But nothing taught me about inner authority more powerfully than when—right out of college—I encountered the transformative Christianity behind Tucson's Sanctuary Movement.

WELCOME TO SANCTUARY

Todd's weekly checklist in 1990:

- Work with Mexican immigrants Monday through Thursday.

- Wrestle with the war on Friday.

- Tiptoe over refugees sleeping in the sanctuary on Saturday.

- Examine everything on Sunday.

I was in my twenties, in Tucson as a VISTA (Volunteers in Service to America) volunteer, and this was the rhythm of my life. The first Persian Gulf War had just erupted a few months earlier. I was troubled, aware how this war was fueled by our nation's addiction to oil. I felt that I—we—needed to repent as a nation. Yet good Christian folks all over America were supporting the war wholeheartedly, with a clear conscience. Society felt insane. I was at an ethical crossroads, and I needed a guide.

"As a pastor, I'm supposed to follow the lectionary," Rev. John Fife would growl from the pulpit most every Sunday at Southside Presbyterian Church, nestled in the barrio of South Tucson, where I lived and worked. "Now, the lectionary's a fine thing; it helps us spread our attention throughout the Bible. But right now there's a war going on, my friends. People are dying because of us, and so American Christians need to focus on one thing. We follow a Lord who dared to tell us to love our enemies, so I'm going to preach about that."

Loving our enemies doesn't just mean resisting war, Fife taught me; a Christian's duty also includes sheltering the stranger and caring for the outcast. By the time I arrived in South Tucson as a naïve but well-meaning VISTA volunteer in 1989, the Sanctuary Movement had already borne its most prophetic countercultural witness, already provided safe haven and transport to thousands of refugees, and already endured its most controversial moments of persecution. In 1986, the U.S. Justice Department indicted Rev. Fife, some Southside church members, and several other religious folks on multiple counts of conspiracy and encouraging, aiding, harboring, and shielding illegal refugees. The trials were grueling, the public animosity painful, and the persecution ever present.

When I came to join the Southside Presbyterian Church congregation, I knew I was joining a communion of saints: a multicultural mix of Jesus-loving folks who, despite their differing politics and pocketbooks, were willing to provide sanctuary for vulnerable refugees fleeing intense violence, even when it meant breaking federal law. Even a few years after the trials, when I was there, the church continued to stand for what they knew to be right, and were still providing sanctuary to two to three dozen refugees sleeping on their property most nights.

COMPELLED TO ACT

The church people who spearheaded the Sanctuary Movement were not born agitators or revolutionaries. Theirs was a conversion of the heart, and it was contagious; by 1985, the movement included over five hundred congregations across North America. These were simply Christians willing to claim their inner authority, even at substantial risk, and put their values of love and compassion into practice. As an Ohio pastor stated in a *Time* magazine interview, "We're a very conservative group of folks politically. But once we encountered the refugees face-to-face, we couldn't justify not taking them in." These waves of refugee families, mostly from El Salvador and Guatemala, were fleeing intense violence and oppression caused by U.S.-trained paramilitary in their home countries. The vast majority of these fleeing villagers—especially children—had done nothing wrong, but were likely to face a quick death by abusive governments if they returned home. And so they streamed north to the U.S. border, seeking safe haven. The United States government—significantly responsible for funding much of the terror and paramilitary violence perpetrated in El Salvador and Guatemala—wasn't letting the refugees in. Deep injustice was being done, and followers of the Jesus Way felt compelled to act.

I'm told that the inspiration for the Sanctuary Movement began with personal encounters—American citizens encountering Latin American refugees telling horrific personal stories of unjust violence. For John Fife, those stories mixed with his

inner authority, his religious convictions, his passion for justice, and his creative imagination, and he decided he would do
something about it. In the spring of 1982, after discussing the
issue with other leaders of Southside Presbyterian, Fife posted
two big banners outside the church. One proclaimed: "This Is
a Sanctuary for the Oppressed of Central America." The other
addressed the Immigration Service, commanding "Do Not
Profane the Sanctuary of God."

John's courage and conviction—his inner authority—was
a light in the darkness to me when I first came to his church
in 1989. He helped me strengthen my own soul in a troubling
time. I was at sea. All week I was bombarded by popular media messages of victory through domination and exclusion of
the outcast; then on Sunday, Fife and my friends at Southside
told me a very different story about radical hospitality and the
nonviolent cross. I had to choose. I was at a crossroads, asking
for the ancient paths, seeking guidance toward the good way. I
took the advice of the prophet Jeremiah, who—three thousand
years ago—counseled his people to examine the ethical choices
they were making:

> This is what the Lord says:
> "Stand at the crossroads and look; ask for the ancient paths,
> ask where the good way is, and walk in it, and you will find rest for
>   your souls." (Jeremiah 6:16)

Jeremiah's directive comes in stages: first, station yourself
at the deciding point between different paths; next, ask elders
and dig into the tradition for wisdom; then, when you have dis-
cerned a right way to live, get busy walking it.

This process is the *foundational life-practice* Christians must
cultivate today—to steer by inner authority, following the path
of Jesus and the prophets. In the face of the dominant culture's

all-consuming cult of voracious, unconscious, and ecocidal living, like Jeremiah we must stand at the crossroads and look. Sometimes we might need to stand at the crossroads and Google; we need to search for the good way, ask for alternatives, learn from both ancient tradition and modern technology. My time with the Sanctuary Movement showed me that choosing a path of right action in the face of state-sponsored injustice may be difficult, unpopular, or lonely, but it will give your soul clarity, peace, and purpose in a confusing and conforming world.

Jeremiah called for prophetic discernment-on-the-move in a changing moral climate, encouraging us to exercise inner authority as often as we exercise our muscles. For most of us in this tame generation, our inner authority is flabby, unused, out of shape. We tend to let the dominant culture make our ethical decisions for us rather than cultivating the inner authority that Jesus embodied, John Fife practiced, and Jeremiah preached.

John Fife was a moral powerhouse for me, a wild force of nature in a tame world. However, it was another modern-day prophet in Tucson's Sanctuary Movement who truly catapulted me upon Jeremiah's path of radical self-determination: the legendary goat-man of southern Arizona, Jim Corbett.

CROSSING PATHS WITH CORBETT

Jim Corbett was a key architect of much of the religiously rooted cultural defiance that energized the Sanctuary Movement in the 1980s. His words and his visage were shocking, and burned into my memory. Up to that point in my young and fairly sheltered life, I'd never heard or seen anyone who so defied cultural norms. Squinty eyes, pinched face, ragged goatee, mottled skin—by this phase of his hardscrabble life, Jim Corbett sometimes seemed more goat than man. He didn't wear a cloak of camel's hair, but he might as well have. He'd been a rancher and wanderer for decades, and now spent weeks at a time roaming the Sonoran Desert with a few goats as partners. Arthritic, curled fingers displayed broad, yellowed nails, and a walking cane served as an additional hoof.

Corbett was a genius—deeply spiritual, incredibly cerebral, and highly creative. His inner authority led him to think and move along pathways I'd never thought allowable, or even possible. His book, *Goatwalking*, rewilded my brain; somehow Corbett coherently wove together animal husbandry, Zen Buddhism, nomadic rambling, civil disobedience, radical compassion, legal counsel, and wild-land recipes into a book that was part Exodus, part Underground Railroad, part anarchist manifesto, and devastatingly Christian. He was a desert prophet come to life.

He was the first to show me that according to the domesticated institutional Christianity of our day, Jesus' teachings are not only foolish, but subversive, even dangerous. To give our wealth to those without, to refuse to protect our property from plunderers, to stop concerning ourselves with plans for the morrow, to love enemies and outsiders—these are the kinds of teachings that destabilize hierarchies, break down barriers, and disrupt business as usual. To be truly free to follow an untamed God, we need grab on to our inner authority and hold everything—every little choice—up to the light.

Let's look at our own situation today. How do we steer by inner authority in this watershed moment in history? Environmentally, we are at a crossroads like no other time in history. How do we discover and walk in the good way, learning to live lighter on God's Earth even as the systems we are part of scream for more petroleum? At some point, if you are an authentic follower of the Jesus Way, you exercise your inner authority in the face of a dysfunctional and destructive dominant culture. At some point, you upturn the tables of the money changers and the power brokers. At some point, like Tim DeCristopher, you say, "Enough."

THE PROPHET KNOWN AS BIDDER 70

What is it about Tim DeChristopher that caused him to become a prophet for millions of modern Americans? Was it the audacity of his actions? The courage of his convictions? His inspiring example, illustrating how one individual could make a world of difference?

For me, it was all three. Surrounded by a sea of tame environmentalists, he dared to walk a wilder Way in the footsteps of Ezekiel, Isaiah, Elijah, and John the Baptist. He exercised his inner authority like the rest of us would exercise a muscle.

The tale of Tim's outrageous and prophetic civil disobedience in 2008—and how he later landed in prison—is already steeped in legend. It is a myth for our times, slightly more fantastic with every retelling. Why? He exploded our paralysis, embodied our hopes, and expanded what we think is possible.

The facts are these: On December 19, 2008, Tim entered a building in Salt Lake City, where the Bureau of Land Management (BLM) was auctioning off leases to drill for oil and gas on Utah's public lands.[1] It was just a month before George W. Bush's final day as president, and the BLM had cobbled together a last-minute bargain auction, offering leases for drilling rights on seventy-seven public land parcels in southern Utah. Attending the auction were "energy companies eager to mine the rich landscape for oil and gas," and "a handful of heartsick environmentalists watching yet another climate disaster unfold."[2]

Somehow, when Tim entered the room in a suit, he was taken for a valid corporate bidder participating in the auction, and was presented with a paddle emblazoned with "Bidder 70." After the auction was well underway, he began raising his paddle to bid. Tim acquired the rights to fourteen parcels— a total of 22,500 acres for $1.8 million—before he was escorted out of the auction and held and questioned by federal officials.[3]

A CRIMINAL FOR OUR TIMES

Tim DeChristopher has become something of a folk legend. He has captivated our imagination, and now we don't want to let him go. Not only did *Rolling Stone* dub him America's most creative climate criminal; dozens of other publications were also powerfully taken by his actions.[4] Media reports have described his story as a "folk hero tale of a man who went to jail for his principles," and "'a Rosa Parks moment' for the climate justice movement."[5] In a word, he inspires us.

How premeditated was his act of counter-corporate courage, dramatically disrupting the usual mundane business end of climate destruction? This, too, seems already to have become a matter of legend. Several commentators agree that his was a "spontaneous act of civil disobedience," a "spontaneous decision to take up the number 70 paddle and bid money he did not have."[6]

That fateful morning, Tim felt he would be led to protest the auction of oil-and-gas leases on Utah's federal red rock lands. He wasn't sure how. When an official at the auction asked him if he was there to bid on land parcels, he agreed. As Tim recalls, "that seemed like a good place to start."[7] He remembers it this way. As he walked into the room that morning, someone said, "Hi. Are you here for the auction?" He said, "Yes, I am." The man then asked, "Are you here to be a bidder?" And he responded, "Well, yes, I am."[8]

Tim began bidding at first just to increase the prices. "That was one of the things that pushed me to the edge," he recalls. "I was feeling outraged that most of the parcels were going for $10 or $12 an acre. Some were going for as little as $2 an acre."[9] But after seeing that more than half the leases were being purchased by oil-and-gas companies, something changed inside him. He started bidding to win. In the midst of his despair and rage, Tim saw something that energized him and gave him the impetus to channel his righteous anger. "I saw toward the back of the room someone I knew from my church, and she started crying. I think what drove her to tears was watching the inhumanity of it and the coldness of it—that there was absolutely no respect for what was being lost. The depth of her emotion justified the depth of my emotion; it made me feel like I wasn't crazy for feeling outraged."[10]

By the end, he'd amassed a total of 22,500 acres at a price of $1.8 million.[11] Taking a bidder's paddle and winning leases that he had no intention or means to buy became, for Tim, an act of spiritual devotion.[12] It was a liberating act of defiance that brought the nation's attention upon an auction that was illegitimate, unwise, and ecocidal.

The auction of those lands, initiated under the Bush administration, was later ruled illegal and rescinded. Despite the impropriety of the auction, the Obama administration continued to press the case against the man who dared to play with corporations, and Tim was found guilty. On April 1, 2009, he was indicted on two felony counts: interfering with a federal oil-and-gas leasing auction and making false statements. He pled not guilty on both counts and rejected the offer of a plea bargain, so he faced ten years in prison and a fine of $750,000.[13] His supporters raised cash to cover the first payment on the leases he'd won, but the BLM refused to accept it, for reasons unclear to me.

Perhaps because popular sentiment was on Tim's side and the largest oil spill in history was inconveniently happening at the same historical moment in the Gulf of Mexico (the British Petroleum disaster of 2009–10), the government postponed his trial nine times, dragging out the legal process over two years. Eventually Tim served twenty-one months in a federal prison, part of that time in isolation. What did he decide to do during his three years of mandated probation following his release in April 2013? Something that probably made secular eco-activists scratch their heads, but likely made sense to a young man refining his inner authority and passionately partnering with God: he enrolled at Harvard Divinity School.

9

RELY UPON RADICAL GRACE

B OTH CHRISTIANS AND environmentalists tend to slip into smugness. Christians do so when they feel securely saved; environmentalists do so when they realize just how cool and conscious they are. Since I aspire to be both—Christian and environmentalist—I'm twice as likely to fall into the smugness trap.

Except I don't—at least not as often as I might. When I take my inner authority seriously and look at the state of our world soberly, my smugness falls away. We moderns have to face one stark conclusion: our deep complicity. Right now, in our daily routines, through our participation in a rabid consumer culture, we are destroying God's greatest gift: the Earth that we love, our one and only home. The Greek verb "to sin" comes from an archery term meaning "to miss the mark." In terms of honoring God's creation, we in North American industrial society have been missing the mark for generations.

REWILDING SIN
How deeply are you enmeshed in affluenza? If you're like most of us, your engagement with consumption amounts to an

addiction. Occupied, enthralled, and enamored, our sober-ing reality is this: we can't stop ourselves from engaging in a rapacious way of life that is utterly out of control. Unable to quit—this is the very definition of addiction, is it not? "I do not understand what I do," Paul admits in his letter to the Romans (7:15a). I don't want to smog the air, pollute the water, and waste resources, but like Paul I keep doing the things I know are wrong, every week of the year. "I have the desire to do what is good, but I cannot carry it out. For I do not do the good I want to do, but the evil I do not want to do—this I keep on do-ing" (7:18b-19).

We protest weakly as we march along, exhausting ourselves and our planet. Wendell Berry nails our condition perfectly when he says, "The great obstacle is simply this: the conviction that we cannot change because we are dependent upon what is wrong. But that is the addict's excuse, and we know that it will not do."[1]

Our awe-inspiring modern society rightfully prides itself on being the pinnacle of human civilization. Never before in human history has there been such cutting-edge technology, such global distribution for worldwide markets, such manipu-lation of natural resources, such opportunities for affluence, such death-defying advances in healthcare, such enlightened explanations of scientific and natural phenomena. We are as powerful as gods. Yet we keep doing the evil that we know we should not do.

Our modern problem, says Berry, is that we are repulsed by the idea of raping nature, but our voracious standard of living demands that the raping continue. We live opulently but schizo-phrenically, pursuing life and liberty and opportunity, while at the same time we are bound and shackled to a voracious death machine we did not create and cannot stop. Do we really think that freeways are free of environmental consequences, or that the cost of Costco is just what we pay out of pocket, or that the damage of fast food happens only to our bodies? Ched Myers explains it this way: the socioeconomic system we rely upon to exist every day—importing endless food, energy, and gadgets while exporting endless waste—is built on structures that destroy the land and dehumanize workers.[2] We are so enthralled—meaning in thrall, held captive—by our habits, appetites, and systems that we are unable to invent a different kind of society.

In the United States, where we have let profit-making corporations rule, the dominant culture only tends to change when someone can make money doing so. In an article detailing California's recent drought conditions entitled "We're Running Out of Water," Jon Gertner attempts to explain why no substantial improvements are being made. America doesn't improve water systems, Gertner says, for the same reason America is slow to improve its transportation systems: the current technologies are so established that it is difficult to imagine anything new.[3] So we lurch through yet another day, dependent upon flawed systems for our survival and riding a death train we can't imagine getting off.

If our modern civilization is so enlightened, so powerful, why can't we stop our rapacious ways? Could it be . . . *sin*?

I hesitate to use the word. Just to bring up *sin* in modern secular culture makes one seem outdated, irrelevant, a laughable prude who's trying to control divergent behavior. And in mainstream churches the meaning of sin is so distorted—limited to personal acts of wrongdoing—that it cannot begin to name the generational and systemic problem we face. We have missed the mark on a massive global scale.

Douglas John Hall says that no single term in the English language is as poorly understood—in both church and wider society—as the little word *sin*. Did you know the Spanish term for a sin is *un peccadillo*? It's the same term used to describe the minor-league annoying barb that a bullfighter pokes into the back of a bull to goad, distract, and infuriate. In Western cultures—speaking English, Spanish, and a host of other European languages—sin has not merely been misunderstood, but also domesticated, privatized, belittled, and ignored. Ched Myers suggests that Christianity makes a tragic error when it switches its focus from *sin*—an eternal "missing of the mark" and an inherent part of being an imperfect human—to *sins*, meaning personal failings that are to be "catalogued, condemned, and controlled."[4]

AFFLUENZA ANONYMOUS

It's not your fault you're addicted to affluenza. Like Ethan Couch, the Texas teen who blamed his consequence-free upraising for his actions, you were born into it. So was I. We were raised in a soup of shortsighted capitalism, steeped in a culture that holds consumption as its highest ideal. It's not your responsibility that you're addicted to affluenza; but now that you've diagnosed your addiction, it *is* your responsibility to face the consequences.

How can we kick the affluenza habit? We might need to get wild. Fifty years ago, Thomas Merton suggested that the modern world, captive to values of empire, needed a counter-cultural movement inspired by the radical example of the early desert fathers and mothers. These men and women were feral followers of the Jesus Way during the fourth and fifth centuries who fled to the desert rather than be complicit with Constantine's version of state-sponsored Christendom.

Copying their prayerful, austere, and creative way is not the point, Merton emphasized. Rather, we should learn from their bold example how to "ignore prejudice, defy compulsion, and strike out fearlessly into the unknown":

> We must liberate ourselves, in our own way, from involvement in a world that is plunging into disaster. But our world is different from theirs. Our involvement in it is more complete. Our danger is far more desperate. . . . We cannot do exactly as they did. But we must be as thorough and as ruthless in our determination to break all spiritual chains, and cast off the domination of alien compulsions, and find our true selves, to discover and develop our inalienable spiritual liberty and use it to build, on earth, the Kingdom of God.[5]

Repenting of affluenza is the sacred duty of our time. And yes, it is daunting. Our complicity is complete, our danger desperate, but repent we must. In an age when almost all of Christianity is captive to corporations, God calls us to break free of our addiction to ecocidal behaviors. But how to break free? To get a really good look at how we affect our planet every day, we need to take a page from the twelve-step tradition of Alcoholics Anonymous. We need to conduct a fearless moral inventory.

FEARLESS MORAL INVENTORY

My friends who are recovering addicts tell me that the fourth step of the Alcoholics Anonymous twelve-step program is by far the most daunting. The first three steps speak a language of surrender with which most Christians identify: first, we admit we are powerless and our lives are unmanageable on our own; second, we acknowledge that a relationship with God could restore us to sanity; and third, we turn our will and our lives over to the Divine. Many Christians may say that these first three steps sound just like their own powerful conversion experience—that these words name the experience of all who consciously turn their lives over to a living Lord.

It's the fourth step that stops us in our tracks: conduct a searching and fearless moral inventory of yourself. Let me spell it out: *Conduct. A. Searching. Unflinching. Fearless. Moral. Inventory. Of. Yourself.* No excuses, exemptions, or shortcuts. From what I gather, step four requires me to list all the things I've done wrong, name all those I've hurt, and examine all the ways I continue to fall short every day. Just thinking about conducting this kind of fearless moral inventory makes me nervous and exhausted. How about you? Like me, are emotions being dredged up for you—maybe feelings like anger, guilt, shame, defensiveness, helplessness, and grief?

Before you panic, meditate with me a little deeper on step four. It does not say, "List all the bad things you have ever done and beat yourself up about it." It says to inspect your path unflinchingly. Without denial or excuse, take a deep look at the impact of your behaviors, both constructive and destructive. Step four is not about shame or judgment; it's about sober self-awareness. The fourth step requires us to step out from behind our excuses, disguises, and unconscious habits and stand naked to be counted. Poet William Stafford describes this encounter in his poem "Easter Morning." In Stafford's scene, Jesus stands at your front door, and at that moment, "all you ever did, or said, / or even thought, suddenly wakes up again," not in judgment, but in recognition. You know it's all true. "You just shiver alive and are left standing / there suddenly brought to account: saved."

For Christians, this is our good news. Like the prostitute who—according to the Jewish law—deserved to be executed by stoning, we stand before Christ, helplessly addicted to affluenza, shivering without disguise, guilty, suddenly brought to account. Instead of executing us for unrepentantly destroying God's precious Earth—as would be just—our Lord says something utterly wild: "Who is there to judge you? No one but I, and I have forgiven you. Go now and leave your life of sin."[6]

REWILDING FORGIVENESS

Institutional Christianity has a long-standing schizophrenic relationship with sin and judgment. Jesus clearly teaches abounding mercy; at its very core, his message teaches us to love our enemies and treat our neighbors as ourselves, which topples all of our best-laid plans for excluding and punishing others. But more pointedly, he teaches us to forgive outrageously and forever; in the language of the times, he says to forgive not just seven times (already a big stretch for me) but "seventy-seven times" (Matthew 18:22). To forgive *that* much would utterly break me open in love—which, I have a feeling, has been God's idea all along. So how does this encouragement for us to forgive eternally fit with a very different concept at the core of institutional Christianity: our eternal judgment in hell?

Is God telling humans, "Forgive more than I do"? A loving God who commits the vast majority of his children to eternal hell has always been hard for me to understand. How could a loving God do this? The God I know and love and follow would never do such a thing, but—because I was raised in Christendom, which preaches the threat of an eternal hell for most of humanity—I rarely spoke out loud about this glaring disconnect.

Richard Rohr helped me find the words.[7] He observes that institutional Christianity's understanding of hell as a place of eternal judgment and torment is not scriptural. Rohr tells us that, in his book *Inventing Hell*, Jon Sweeney asserts that our "fire and brimstone" concept of eternal torment and damnation was envisioned by the poet Dante eight centuries ago, but it is not the imagery of the Bible. He notes that the word *hell* is not mentioned in the books of Moses, the Pentateuch. Neither Paul nor John uses the word. The bottom line: eternal damnation for all non-Christians is not the worldview of the Bible.

Rohr observes that institutional Christianity has for far too long presented a religion that is both conflicting and schizophrenic: on one hand, Jesus tells us to love our enemies, but then the church tells us that God himself doesn't do so. "Jesus teaches us to forgive seventy times seven," Rohr notes, "but apparently God has a cut-off point." This kind of unloving and judgmental God is theologically untenable if we are followers of the teachings of Jesus. Why? "Humans can't be more loving and forgiving than God—it's just not possible!" In the end, we are all saved by God's mercy, Rohr concludes—a mercy expansive enough that it neither demands payment nor keeps score.

In a world like ours, this kind of radical grace and expansive mercy can be hard to find. I had to be desperate and alone on a snowy mountaintop in Greece before it found me.

COMING TO MOUNT ATHOS

After two hours of an early-morning sea voyage, I knew we were close. The feeling of apprehension that had been bubbling up my stomach reached a peak when the morning mist parted to reveal a stone quay. Everything seemed etched in grey— our boat's metal hull cutting through the choppy winter sea; the seagulls keening mere feet above the rudder, attentive for fish and food scraps; the granite cliffs and harsh shoreline now looming close. Forty-five minutes ago, back when the boat still moved on the open waters, the peninsula of Athos itself had risen out of the sea fog like one of several long, giant fingers in the distance. Now we were here.

I'd been traveling for more than forty-eight hours: from Oakland to New York; from New York to Athens; after a noisy and sleepless night in Athens, on a rickety little plane to Thessaloniki; then by car over rutted stone roads to the "gateway to the Holy Mountain," the isolated little coastal village of Ouranopolis. From there, this two-hour voyage across choppy water was finally bringing me to Mount Athos.

Black and white and grey continued to dominate my vision as I took in the quay through the morning mist. Several dark lumps that I had assumed were rocks, part of the stone pier, now materialized into unmoving human figures. *Monks*, I realized. *Waiting*. The Athonites sat apart from one another, dressed entirely in black wool with hoods drawn against the weather, white and grey beards flowing down to their midsections. Unmoving. Had they been sitting there forever? It made for a striking photo, with the backdrop of the stone quay and the severe cliffs. I took a few pictures as I approached.

The operator cut the motor as the boat sidled up to its moorings, the sea still choppy, and threw a rope to a man in a cap and wool coat who waited at the dock. My fellow passengers surged forward, giving rapid orders to one another and handing bags and parcels onto shore, but I stood at the rear of the boat, transfixed. I couldn't keep my eyes off of the waiting monks, who were now moving slowly toward the vessel. There were five in total, and each wore a simple black wool cassock and carried a traveling bag. Ancient, inscrutable, they were exotic in their simplicity. One monk in particular, his eyes more striking and beard greyer than the others, drew my attention. His visage looked as if it had been carved from the granite of Athos itself. As he approached the boat, I respectfully approached to get his attention. Making motions with my camera to show my intent,

I asked in English, "Excuse me, sir, may I take your picture?" I began to focus the lens.

His dark eyes pierced me with a direct gaze as he grabbed my forearm. In perfect English, he said: "Do you need to?" With that, he loosened his grip, turned away, and stepped down into the departing boat.

That was my introduction to Mount Athos, when I was a twenty-year-old seeker. For more than a thousand years, Orthodox men had come to live on Athos as monks. I'd come to the Holy Mountain on a research scholarship, seeking to discern how monks could *love* the world by *leaving* the world. Little did I know my sojourn there would be one of the most miserable—and transformational—experiences of my life. I was about to encounter radical grace.

FREE AND UNEASY

Twenty-eight main monasteries and hundreds of isolated hermits uphold a long tradition of hospitality for those who need Mount Athos—those who seek solace, spiritual counsel and training, academic study, relief from the troubles of the outside world. Or those who are on a pilgrimage for religious truth, like I was. Food and a bed for the night are free, although the conditions are basic. Visitors are expected to conduct themselves with modesty, quietude, and decorum. Almost all travel is either by boat or on foot, for the roads are narrow, steep, and often in ill repair.

Do you need to? The monk's question, and his blazing eyes, stayed with me those next days as I traveled the Holy Mountain in silence. I tried to strike up conversation at the monasteries I visited. Funny, the monks of Athos weren't that interested. By day seven or eight, I had read all the books I had brought with me. I felt an itch to write a letter, but, oddly, there weren't a

lot of neighborhood post offices. Really, I wanted to *get* a letter—two decades before Facebook, I was itching for someone
to validate me, to ask me a question, to pat me on the back, to
friend me, to let me know I was alive.

My ego unease reached a climax one night as I traveled to
yet another nearly abandoned, ancient, crumbling monastery.
It was Xenophondos—"the voice of the stranger"—a vast complex built of stone to house several hundred monks. These days
it housed eighteen, the youngest in his eighties. As the evening
service began, the incense braziers filled the small chapel with
thick smoke, and the muttering of unintelligible prayers began. I and eight skeletal monks half-stood, half-sat along the
walls of the stone chapel, leaning on thin wooden armrests with
no seats. Suddenly the ancient black-robed monk to my right
began to cough violently. No one moved. His rattling coughs
seemed endless, and I was afraid he would hack up his lungs.
The coughing, the heat, the incense, the swirling smoke, the
skeletal men, the closed-in claustrophobia was just too much
for me, and I burst out of the chapel, gagging. I ran up a short
set of stone stairs to take ragged breaths of the piercing winter
starlight. I had never felt so out of place, so utterly alone.

The next day I left before breakfast and found passage on a
boat heading around the coast. I determined to cut my trip short
and head back to the Greek mainland. At this point I didn't care
in the least how monks could love the world by leaving it. If I
could get to Athens and then book a flight back to the States in
the next few days, I could surprise my family for Christmas. In
fact, I was convinced by now that this was the message God was
trying to tell me: forget all this exotic seeking, love your family.

But an encounter on the boat changed my course once again.
I met Costa, a scruffy Greek man with a roguish smile, probably
in his early thirties. To find someone on Mount Athos under

fifty seemed a minor miracle; the other supernatural thing was that he actually talked to me. I'd studied modern Greek two years prior, so we stumbled through a conversation. He was an architect from Kos, headed to see a friend of his, a hermit at the very top of the Holy Mountain. After gauging my distressed state, he offered a proposition. Join me, he said. Climb up the Holy Mountain. I politely declined. You came all this way, he said. What do you have to lose?

I started to respond, then stopped. What *did* I have to lose? I'd come all this way, spent all this money, committed all this time, devoted all this study, and I was going to refuse this opportunity because I felt lonely and depressed and uncomfortable? Here I was in a wild and remote part of Greece forgotten by time, being handed a chance to be personally guided on a hike up the Holy Mountain to meet a friendly hermit, but I was going to pass because I missed my mom? Within the hour I was hiking behind Costa, packs on our backs, on our way to see Father Theologos.

ENCOUNTER AT THE TOP OF THE MOUNTAIN

Theologos the hermit was younger than I expected, and more cosmopolitan; he had studied in France and continually smoked a pipe, usually with a slightly amused look on his face. Life was simple here. Boredom and loneliness set in again, but at least I wasn't gagging and running out of incense-filled chapels like a man possessed. After two days Costa left, but I made a deal with Father Theologos to stay a bit longer. In exchange for soup and bread, I split wood and kept the two fireplaces going in his little stone cottage. Theologos was going to a feast day in a few days where he would meet other hermits, and he invited me to come. As the days passed, I started getting excited about meeting this strange group of men.

Then Father Theologos fell mysteriously ill, for reasons I still don't know. All I knew was that he was suddenly bedridden, uncommunicative, feverish. And I was the only one to help. The next day I was peeling the last potato I could find, wondering how I could find some more food for us, when the snow came—fierce, biting, relentless. Day after day it came. I ran through the blizzard to the outhouse in the middle of the day, and I couldn't see my hand in front of my face. By the end of day two, a wall of snow completely blocked the front door of his stone hut. I had brought firewood inside, so that wasn't a problem, but food was. I found some celery, a half-box of crackers, and two cans of tuna, but that wouldn't last us long. It was also hard getting the stuff into Theologos's mouth—potato soup had been easier.

I think it was about this time—late on day two of the snowstorm—that I started going crazy. Cut off from anything familiar, I no longer knew who I was. Already close to despair, now this driving snow forcing me to stay shut inside a stone room pushed me over the edge. I was tired of reading Greek books, tired of journaling, tired of making up mental games, tired of no letters and no phone calls and no friends and no family, tired of caretaking a mute monk, tired of living with only my own face looking back at me. I did push-ups and paced like a tiger in a cage. Little could I name it at the time, but I had become a socioholic—needing a steady stream of recognition by others to feel good—and there I was, an addict without drugs. That stone cottage at the top of the Holy Mountain became my personal hell. I began having waking daydreams of throwing up excrement, over and over again. Without the affirmation of others, I was nothing, I was a piece of crap. My friends had abandoned me, my family had abandoned me, my God had abandoned me. No one heard my cry. Over and over, these thoughts and images came over me until I fell asleep in the darkened stone hut, exhausted beyond tears, snow relentlessly piling up over the eaves, lonelier than I'd ever been in my life.

I awoke sometime after midnight to a full moon pouring in a high window. The snow had stopped completely, and the clear sky was almost painful. It wasn't quite a voice, but as the huge full moon filled my entire vision, a message filled my entire being, with a word earthy enough that my publisher won't print it: *Todd, you are a piece of s——.*

And a second later: *And I love you anyway.*

RELEASED

Was this God talking? It sure felt that way to me, and the scandalous grace made me laugh out loud. Divine mountaintop encounter or not, this experience changed my life. It was a process of unflinching self-examination, an acknowledgment of my colossal imperfection, which led to completely unexpected redemption, forgiveness, and release. That night on the top of Mount Athos, it felt like the moon was speaking, like God was speaking, like Jesus was speaking, like my deepest self was speaking. The message sunk into my bones: *I love you anyway.* It wasn't nearly the majesty of a dove descending or the heavens opening, but I gained a hint of what Jesus must have experienced coming up out of the river Jordan when he heard God say, "This is my Son, whom I love; with him I am well pleased" (Matthew 3:17). Despite my unworthiness, it felt like God ripped open my reality to let me know I was fundamentally okay just as I was—radically accepted, embraced, and approved. Even now—decades later—that experience of radical release remains a touchstone, and helps guide me as I navigate our ego-ridden world, reminding me like a prodigal son that I am already embraced, and that I don't have to do anything, prove anything, earn anything, or defend anything to be loved by God. I felt free, utterly released.

Have you felt this liberation, in your own way? I hope so, with all my heart. The prophet Isaiah has a Hebrew word for people like us: *geulim*, the released ones of God. In Isaiah 35, the prophet has a vision in which humanity and creation are redeemed *together*. One does not transform without the other. Isaiah foresees an abundant wilderness in a restored future, and proclaims that the *geulim*—a transformed group of humans liberated by God—will walk into God's ideal society.

Jesus grew up steeped in the transformative words of Isaiah and other prophets. Reading straight from the scroll of Isaiah, Jesus proclaimed he was anointed by God to share good news with the poor, set the oppressed free, and proclaim the year of the Lord's favor (Luke 4:16-19). Isaiah staked out the role of releaser; hundreds of years later, Jesus ran with it, embodied it, fulfilled it, and transformed it into the ultimate divine liberator. After his sojourn in the desert, Jesus told the world he was here to make *geulim*—released ones—who, released from bondage, could become the people God ached for them to be.

Biblical forgiveness means a lot more than just telling someone they're still okay after doing a bad action. It means to release and redeem—from social guilt, from economic debt, from personal wrongdoing, from political and systemic oppression. It is an act of economic, political, and spiritual liberation, and God is the grand Redeemer. This is why our English translations of the Lord's Prayer are diverse—the words Jesus used could mean forgive us our sins, release us from our debt, pardon our trespasses, free us from bondage. In fact, I think Jesus meant all of those things. I think Jesus was teaching his disciples to pray like this: again today, liberate us from all that binds us, so in turn we may liberate and release others. Jesus was generating a gang of *geulim*—released ones of God—who were then liberated and empowered to heal and release others from all that darkened their God-given potential.

Ever since that moment on a mountaintop on Athos, I have felt radically accepted, embraced, and released. I hope that you feel radical acceptance, too, and know in your being how much God loves you, just as you are. As *geulim*, we have a gift for the world. We are free to be fools for God. We are free not to worry about the dominant cultural obsessions of earning, coveting, competing, protecting, winning, judging, and maintaining. We are liberated to lift our focus from constantly upgrading our current status. As released ones who have experienced radical grace, it is both our privilege and our task to transform our economics and our roles so that we might help create God's new society within the shell of the old.

10

EMBODY ENOUGHNESS

LEGEND HAS IT that John Muir was once asked the main difference between himself and John D. Rockefeller. Muir replied: Rockefeller doesn't have enough money.

That's a funny statement, but only if you understand this piece of U.S. history: Muir was a wandering conservationist, while oil tycoon Rockefeller was the richest man in America in the late 1800s. Muir was content with what he had; Rockefeller, never.

The search for contentment—it's a theme that echoes through Scripture, that haunts our culture today. Consumer culture says contentment is just a click away, and you deserve anything you want, whenever you want, from wherever you want. Want new furniture? Get it. Want a bigger house and a nicer car? Grab them. Want to go out to eat? Go out. Want the newest iPad? Buy it. Want the latest smartphone? You need it. Want gourmet food? You deserve it.

You deserve it?

Really?

Scripture has a very different take on the search for contentment. It says that chasing after your own self-satisfaction

is a prison. "People who want to get rich fall into a temptation and a trap," Paul writes bluntly to his trusted apprentice
Timothy; people like that get caught in "many foolish and
harmful desires that plunge people into ruin and destruction"
(1 Timothy 6:9). It's not getting rich that is dangerous, Paul
says; it's *wanting* to be wealthy that leads us to ruin. Interesting.
Last I checked, wanting wealth was the backbone of the modern American dream.

What's the key to contentment, then? In contrast to consumer culture, the Bible presents a very different message:
minimize your focus on your own desires so you can focus on
satisfying God's desires. They say the secret of contentment is
learning the mysteries of adaptive self-sufficiency in God.

WHAT'S ON MY PLATE

I was at a potluck recently, and after serving myself a blend of
dishes, I found a seat next to several young kids I didn't know
well. One boy, maybe six years old, looked up from his meal
when I sat down. His smile encouraged me to start a conversation, so I asked him a question kids love to answer: "What's
your favorite food?"

"What's on my plate," he answered, looking down.

I was a little confused at the jumble he was eating, but pasta
seemed predominant. "You mean spaghetti?"

He just looked at me and shrugged. With a smile, he re-
sumed talking with his friends.

Upon reflection, I am certain that this little kid's answer is
one of the greatest spiritual teachings I have received: *My favorite food is what's on my plate.* Whatever I have on my plate is
here, now, my daily sustenance, present and available for me as
a real and necessary gift, rather than an idealized fantasy that
is located somewhere else, a wishing that leads to unsatisfied

desire. It's the same sentiment as expressed in the title of Sinead O'Connor's album *I Don't Want What I Haven't Got*. It's the same sentiment in Wendell Berry's poem "What We Need Is Here." Check out these last few lines: "And we pray, / Not for new earth or heaven, / but to be quiet in heart, / and in eye, clear. / What we need is here."

Deep experience in practicing the Jesus Way allowed Paul to learn the secret of adaptive *autarkeia*—the Greek word for being content. Like that little boy, Paul learned to be happy with whatever arrived on his plate. Check out how, in Philippians, he describes his life philosophy: "I know what it is to be in need, and I know what it is to have plenty. I have learned the secret of being content in any and every situation, whether well fed or hungry, whether living in plenty or in want" (Philippians 4:12).

In times of abundance or in times of scarcity, Paul is chill. He's learned the art of *autarkeia*—adaptive self-sufficiency—so he knows how to be content in *any and every* situation. His secret: he requires very little from the world. To be happy, he's not chasing the next product, he's not adjusting the temperature, he's not angling for a higher salary, he's not trying to solve something that might happen tomorrow, he's not wishing he had something different on his plate. In his writings to his partner Timothy, he advises: "But if we have food and covering, we will be content with that" (1 Timothy 6:8). Keep to the basics, Timmy my boy, he seems to be saying. Chow and a tent. That's all we need.

THE MYSTERY OF ENOUGHNESS

How did Paul learn to be so content? Probably the way we all do: through experience and testing. *I have learned the secret*, he writes. In Greek, the term he uses here literally means "I have been initiated into the mystery." It's the same term used by the Eleusinian mystery traditions and Gnostic groups of the time, referring to secret knowledge, unknown except to the initiated.[1]

Paul has learned—through experience, through his time of wandering and testing in Arabia, through putting himself in all kinds of situations—that food, shelter, and God are enough. This seems to be a rare level of Christian autonomy—perhaps even a kind of enlightenment—which allows him to be satisfied and content *even in conditions others would consider too tough*. Can you see how free from dominant culture this makes him? What would it be like if Christians today embodied this kind of fearless *autarkeia*—an inner "enoughness" that allowed us to unshackle from our culture's affluenza-driven anxieties of insecurity and scarcity?

GOD-POWERED, NOT SELF-POWERED

In the text above, Paul says something else very interesting: he's learned how to be content whether well fed or hungry. The term he uses for "well fed" here, is *chortazesthai*: "to be full." It's an ancient Greek word originally reserved for animals, as in "to be foddered." In the New Testament, though, we find it's used for humans as well as animals, and for satisfying hungers deeper than for food. In Matthew 5:6, the same root verb, *chortos*, is used when Jesus says in the Beatitudes, "Blessed are those who hunger and thirst for righteousness, for they *will be filled*." So when Paul says he has learned to be content whether well fed or hungry, he's speaking of far more than a happy stomach. He's speaking of a profound interior sufficiency he has attained, an unshakeable state of daily enoughness.

Paul's self-sufficiency is impressive, but so far he sounds just like dozens of secular Greek philosophers of his era who valued inner calm and self-sufficiency. Paul also sounds extremely

Buddhist, advocating for the practices of being present, simple living, and self-control. But then he does something wild: he adds in the God factor.

In Philippians, just after saying he's learned to be content in any situation, he adds this key line: "I can do all this through him who gives me strength" (4:13). Paul experiences his profound sufficiency and satisfaction by grounding his contentment not in self-control, not in material adjustments, but in his Lord. His call and purpose stem from his Lord, his source of abundance comes from his Lord, and his sense of radical well-being is grounded in his Lord. With this grounding in God, Paul says he experiences deep *autarkeia* even when surrounded by violent threats, unjust systems, political persecution, insecure finances, religious judgment, fearful famine, or harsh conditions.

PAUL'S PREDECESSORS

The concept of *autarkeia* did not begin with Paul; rather, he ran with it, deepened it, transformed it. Greek philosophers prior to Paul preached a self-controlling *autarkeia* as a disciplined tool for self-liberation; Paul steeped himself in *autarkeia*, owned it, and expanded its meaning, considering it not merely a self-liberating tool but a God-powered gift to promote the liberation of all creation. This divinely empowered self-sufficiency freed him *from* the world, *for* the world.

The virtue of adaptive self-sufficiency goes back at least as far as Plato. Frederick E. Brenk, in his essay "Old Wineskins Recycled," traces how the concept of *autarkeia* traveled and transformed within the philosophical traditions of later Cynics, Stoics, and Epicureans. A Cynic philosopher who lived three centuries before Paul, Krates of Thebes, saw self-sufficiency as a pathway to the divine: "Practice being in need of little, for such is nearest to God and the opposite farthest away."[2]

Many strands of ancient Greek wisdom contain messages of *autarkeia*. Check out this example of a classic Socratic dialogue:

> A seeker of wisdom asked: Who is the wealthiest man?
> Sokrates replied: The one who is self-sufficient with least; for self-sufficiency is the wealth nature gave us.[3]

Paul, raised in cosmopolitan Tarsus, grew up in a city filled with philosophical wisdom such as this. He was formally trained as a young man among practicing philosophers, and probably saw many excellent lives where the truth of *autarkeia* was lived before his eyes: needing little brings true wealth and leads one to God, while chasing after riches drives one away. Paul uses these same philosophical teachings in his own writings. Look again at the words of Paul, and how closely his own teaching mirrors that of Krates: "But if we have food and clothing, we will be content with that. Those who want to get rich fall into a temptation and a trap and into many foolish and harmful desires that plunge people into ruin and destruction. For love of money is a root of all kinds of evil" (1 Timothy 6:8-10a).

TAKING *AUTARKEIA* TO THE NEXT LEVEL

Did the Greek philosophers strive for *autarkeia* solely for self-liberation? Or did they also do it to practice ever-deeper levels of compassion? It's not clear. Krates, for example, distributed the majority of his inherited wealth to his fellow citizens; yet letters from the time record his money-giving as primarily a "liberation of the interior self" that resulted in personal peace.[4]

Paul took this idea and expanded it, making *autarkeia* the foundation that gave him closeness to God, inviolable joy, independence from the wiles of empire, and the freedom to give himself away to others. His statement in Philippians reveals he has learned the secret of needing little, content in whatever circumstances he finds himself. This sentiment is right in line with the vital yet self-focused liberation of the ancient Greek philosophers. Yet Paul goes a step further in two key ways: his liberation from need is utterly rooted in God; and this liberation frees him not *from* others but *for* others.

Paul's concept of Christ-rooted *autarkeia* allows him to liberate the rest of his resources—material, intellectual, spiritual—in charity and compassion to others. This God-filled altruistic aspect of Paul's *autarkeia* raises his practical philosophy to a whole new level from those who came before. The practice of *autarkeia* liberates Paul to live large, and frees him to become bread for the world.[5]

PORTMANTEAUS AND OTHER MASHUPS

Ever heard of a *portmanteau*? No, it's not a piece of furniture, it's a special category of made-up word: a word created from combining two others. *Affluenza* is such a word, created from *affluence*, an overabundance of wealth, and *influenza*, a contagious sickness. Here's a portmanteau I love from the ancient Greek: *epiousion*. In English it is customarily translated as *daily*, as in the line from the Lord's Prayer that implores, "Give us today our *daily* bread."

What's wild about *epiousion* is that the Lord's Prayer is the *only* place scholars know of where the word appears—it is found nowhere else in extant Greek literature. *Strong's Concordance* suggests the word was likely created by the early Gospel writers to express, in Greek, a wild concept spoken of by Jesus—a concept foreign to the citified, Hellenized world but with deep roots and nuances in both in Aramaic and Hebrew, languages born of nomadic cultures steeped in migratory wilderness wandering. *Epiousion* is a combination of the Greek *epi* (fitting or suitable) and *ousion* (essence, substance). Taken together, it means "aptly substantive"—in other words, a daily amount, enough for the day's needs. Origen, in the mid-third century AD, translated the sentence into Latin in this way: "Give us to-day our needful bread."[6]

In the last century, the world of ancient Christian scholarship got very excited when the word *epiousion* was discovered somewhere else: on a fifth-century shopping list. On a scrap of parchment, the word seemed to have been written next to several household grocery items. Its placement gave rise to speculation: Perhaps, in this context, the word meant a list of what is needed now? Of what must be purchased for tomorrow? Of what daily rations or regular ingredients should be obtained to-day? Unfortunately, the original transcriber, A. H. Sayce, was apparently a poor scholar, and reexamination of the original papyrus found no authentic use of the word.[7] Still, it captures the imagination, does it not?

TIME FOR ANOTHER EXODUS?

It's tempting to think that Jesus' petition asking for "daily bread" was original. Not so. He knew his Jewish audience would be familiar with it as a concept deeply embedded in Israel's collective history. Check out Proverbs 30: The author, writing at least six hundred years before Jesus lived, is sharing wisdom and asking rhetorical questions, when suddenly the nature of the passage changes. He makes a direct request of God: "Give me neither poverty nor riches, but give me only my daily bread." If you give me too much, the author continues, I'll be tempted to think I earned it myself and I won't need you, God; and if you give me so little I can't survive, I'll be forced to steal and be unable to do the right thing, dishonoring my God (Proverbs 30:7-9). *Give me only my daily bread.* Where have we heard this phrase before? The Hebrew word *lechem* can be translated equally as "bread" or "food," as it was one and the same—the ordinary, daily meal of the Israelites, one's proscribed portion, the necessary food to sustain them.[8] Enough for the day.

The necessary food to sustain them each day. Now where does this image take us? Jesus' prayer for daily bread echoes not only the daily *enoughness* requested in Proverbs, but even further back, to the daily manna provided in the deep wilderness of exodus. Manna wasn't glamorous, but it was enough. From my church upbringing, I've always pictured manna as some sort of miraculous, puffy white snack—I remember using cotton balls on construction paper to create a diorama in Sunday school—but the reality was much more down to earth. It wasn't glamorous, but it was enough for the day: "The manna was like coriander seed and looked like resin. The people went around gathering it, and then ground it in a hand mill or crushed it in a mortar. They cooked it in a pot or made it into loaves. And it tasted like something made with olive oil" (Numbers 11:7-8). After their long journey in the desert and finally settling in the fields of Canaan, the book of Joshua says that the Israelites ate produce from the land for the first time (5:11-12).

When they did, the manna stopped. The manna ceased once they started eating the crops of the land of Canaan. The time for manna had ended; it was traveling food, sufficient for people on a migratory journey, enough to sustain them as they passed from the land of bondage to the land of promise. N. T. Wright calls manna the road food of the inbreaking kingdom, a food for a culture in transition, a food that "signals that the Exodus has begun, but also that we are not yet living in the land."[9]

Jesus, with the Jewish people captive and oppressed, declared the time for manna had returned. Numerous times in the gospel of John he compares himself to the manna of the exodus: "I am the bread of life" (John 6:35, 41, 48). *I am enoughness for you as you travel,* he's saying. His invitation: total communion while embodying a parallel society walking on a wilderness journey.

N. T. Wright proposes that Jesus saw his kingdom work as a new exodus, and that the Lord's Prayer is Jesus' daily marching orders for a new breed of wilderness-wandering people.[10] Perhaps a thousand years after the first exodus, Jesus knew that God's people needed to break again from business as usual, to go on a journey of transformation, to be liberated from bondage to empire so they could live large once more, as God intended.

Two thousand years after Jesus, is it once again time for a new exodus? Instead of always wanting more, can we learn the secrets of *autarkeia* in God? Facing an uncertain future, can we help manifest God's kingdom by learning to be content with our daily bread?

11

LEAD THROUGH MEEKNESS

THE WORD *MEEK* has been tamed for too long. It's time to
redeem its reputation.

In his Sermon on the Mount, Jesus famously says,
"Blessed are the meek, for they will inherit the earth" (Matthew
5:5). His words are a direct reference to a psalm composed by
David centuries earlier: "the meek will inherit the land and enjoy peace and prosperity" (37:11). In New Testament Greek,
praus is the word Jesus uses for meek; in Old Testament Hebrew,
David uses a complementary word, *anav*.

Did David and Jesus mean that the *wimpy* will inherit the
Earth? Somehow I doubt it. In English we translate *anav* as poor,
needy, weak, lowly, vulnerable, afflicted, oppressed, humble, depressed in mind or circumstances. The book of Job is one of
many Old Testament texts that use *anav* like this, to describe
the dispossessed fleeing in the face of oppressors: self-advancing
men steal poor people's sheep, move boundary stones to their
advantage for illegal land-grabs, and "force all the *anav* of the
land into hiding" (Job 24:2-4).

Anav. Praus. Meek. Someone weak and needy, someone
pitiable. Not something you really want to call yourself, right?

So why did Jesus?

Jesus called himself meek. "Take my yoke upon you and learn from me," he invites those who would be his disciples, "for I am *praus* and humble in heart" (Matthew 11:29). Is Jesus really saying follow me because I'm weak? Join my wagon 'cause I'm wimpy? To me, a man who stands in front of a synagogue and boldly proclaims he's the embodiment of an ancient vision is not meek. To me, a resister who disrupts the status quo by overturning tables in the temple is not wimpy.

I'm pretty sure that when Jesus described himself as *praus*, he was calling himself something far more than weak, and he was inviting—even mandating—his followers to be that something, as well. As scholars note, it's difficult to translate *praus* and *anav* into English because we do not have a word for the trait. It seems the Roman Empire did not either. Remember, Jesus spoke in the peasant language of Aramaic, and empires founded upon the precept of "might makes right" sometimes can't understand the trait he was describing: humility with power, gentleness with strength, surrendering the self to be empowered by God.[1]

A WAY THAT DELIGHTS THE LORD

In Job, being *anav* is vulnerable and powerless—a trait inherent to those who are poor, oppressed, and afflicted. In the Psalms, however, being *anav* is a choice; like Jesus uses *praus*, *anav* is both a trait to deepen and a lifeway to follow. In Psalm 25, notice how the psalmist shapes his prayer for guidance: "Show me your ways, Lord, teach me your paths; guide me in your truth. . . . He guides the *anav* in what is right and teaches them his way" (Psalm 25:4-5a, 9).

A little later, in Psalm 37, whole pages are devoted to the contrast between two paths: the way of "evil men"—a path of greedy, violent land grabbing and self-advancement—and the way of *anav*, a lifeway that delights the Lord. In this psalm, when the writer describes the qualities of "evil men," I wonder, how much does this describe our modern economic way of life? According to Psalm 37, evil men and unjust societies grasp for wealth and power; they plot and succeed in unjust schemes; they borrow and do not repay; they damage the Earth; they draw the sword and bend the bow to bring down the poor and the needy. Ouch—this sounds a little too much like some of us.

Those who follow the way of *anav* stand in stark contrast to those following the way of "evil men." The *anav* commit themselves to a God-delighting lifeway and are referred to in different places in Psalm 37 as the humble, those who hope in the Lord, those whose ways are upright, the righteous, the blameless, those the Lord blesses. Looking again at Psalm 37, but through a different lens, here are some traits of those who follow the way of meekness, of *anav*: They do not fret, they show restraint, they are not envious, they refrain from anger. Instead they trust, they do good, they share, they live in wisdom. They are always generous and lend freely. They wait patiently before the Lord, they delight themselves in God's presence, they are people of peace, and their tongues speak what is just.

HUMILITY = SUSTAINABILITY + RESILIENCE

Digging deeper into the nuances of *anav*, I think again about what Jesus meant—and what the psalmist meant—when both assert that the meek shall inherit the Earth. Is Jesus saying it's only the *anav*—only those who do not grasp and hoard, only those who do not think too highly of their own importance and needs—who *are able to coexist* and live within the blessing of creation, while the haughty and hoarding are unable? Is Jesus saying that overconsumers who live like the evil men—the grasping ones—are unable to inherit the land because they grasp and exploit too much and cannot accept the gift of creation on its terms? This is starting to sound a lot like bioregional sustainability and learning to live within one's ecological niche. Psalm 37 is clear in its prescription for social ills: by living with restraint and in communion with all others, the people will be able to live with the land as an eternal inheritance; they will receive the desires of their hearts and are able to dwell in the land forever, enjoying safe pasture and great peace. They receive the gift of what the modern Transition movement calls "community resilience": in times of disaster they will not wither; they will not be forsaken; they may stumble, but their feet will not slip. When times are hard, they will not fall. Thinking like a tree, the psalmist concludes, it is far better to have the enough of the *anav* than the too much of the wicked.

BUDEO-CHRISTIANITY

I've often wondered why dissolving the ego isn't an overt part of the core curriculum for Christian praxis like it is in Buddhism. Though I was raised within Christianity, I first learned about letting go of the small self when I was twenty, from the amazing Buddhist teacher Thich Nhat Hanh. In one of his poems, he describes his brother, back from a long adventure, who yearns for stability, a harbor in which to anchor. The brother builds a shelter and seems content to stay secure there for the rest of his days. The next lines are a surprise: "One night I will come / and set fire to his shelter, the small cottage on the hill," the narrator says. "My fire will destroy everything / and remove his only life raft after a shipwreck." Amid the ashes, the narrator says, the brother's shell will break, and with that breaking will come glorious deliverance and liberation. Commenting on the meaning of the verse, Thich Nhat Hanh explains that in the poem he is the brother, and he is also the narrator who burned down the cottage.[2]

It took the poetry of a Buddhist for me to understand it, but when I did, I began to see this kind of ego-surrender and *anav* thoughout the Bible. Our tradition overwhelmingly reminds us that the authentic path of faith is not so much about God *protecting* our lives *for ourselves*, but transforming them for others; not about God *saving* our souls, but *inhabiting* them. Richard Rohr said something extremely powerful once when I asked him about the Lord's Prayer: when you dare to say *thy kingdom come*, you better be prepared to say *my kingdom go*. Reciting the Lord's Prayer gets your agenda out of the way to make room for God's. This is the transformative meekness that Jesus embodied and taught—a kind of enlarging and emptying that diminishes the small ego and tosses dreams of self-advancement onto the trash heap.

MISTER MEEK

I don't normally think of Moses as "Mister Meek," do you? *Meek* is not usually the word one uses to describe someone who went face-to-face with Pharaoh, dragged his people on a forty-year exodus through wild lands, and brought the commandments outlining God's ideal society down from the mountain. This kind of bold leadership is usually accompanied by arrogance and egotism; yet the Torah describes Moses as a "very humble man," more *anav* than anyone else on the face of the Earth (Numbers 12:3). I'm guessing Moses's desire for self-promotion and special status might have been burned out of him during his ego-destroying God-encounter in the flaming bush. Here's a great example: During a particularly trying part of the exodus, stumbling through the desert on basic rations, the Israelites done had enough—not just a few, but the whole assembly wants to quit.

They grumble against Moses's leadership, saying it would have been better for the whole tribe to die in Egypt. They grumble some more, question Moses's competency and authority, and plan to choose another leader and go back to Egypt. They even jab him personally, saying he has made his people a stench to Pharaoh and an offense to empire (Exodus 5:21).

In the face of this crisis of confidence, what does Moses do—show them who's boss in a display of power? Threaten military action? Pout and tout his credentials? No. Moses throws himself *down on the dusty ground*—in battle, a sign of surrender, vulnerability, and submission—and *lets them decide* if he should die by stoning (Numbers 14:2-10). At his core, I think Moses knew he was just a tool, clay in the potter's hands, a servant leader who had nothing to prove, no position to win, and no ego to defend. Time and time again, in speech and in action, he foreshadows Jesus' own word and deed: not my will, but thy will.

And while Moses captures the Old Testament headlines as "the most humble man who ever lived"—an ironic twist on humility if there ever was one—there's another character weaving her way quietly through the Old Testament who may embody *anav* even better: Ruth.

YOUR WAY IS MY WAY

Ruth did not have an easy life. In fact, she's downright desperate from the moment we meet her in the Old Testament: a vulnerable and penniless widow with no family support, descended from an outcast tribe despised by Israel, living in a time of severe and widespread famine. Soon, Ruth gets to add refugee, wanderer, migrant farmworker, and unwelcome alien to her resume. When I call her "unwelcome alien," it's a bit of an understatement: Ruth was a Moabite, and the Moabites and Israelites shared a generations-old relationship of feuding, fighting, insulting, accusing, and competing. The Moabites were a hardscrabble people, living on a plateau to the east of the Dead Sea bordered by the rugged Dead Sea escarpment and the Arabian Desert. The Israelites had a long history of squatting on Moabite land, and—even if they were largely the bully—they felt so wronged by the Moabites that "no Ammonite or Moabite may ever come into the assembly of the Lord, nor may any of their descendants even to the tenth generation. . . . Never seek their welfare or prosperity as long as you live" (Deuteronomy 23:3, 7 NABRE).

Never promote their peace and prosperity so long as you live? Yikes! How's that for being neighborly? Ruth, a young Moabite widow married into a clan of refugee Israelites and heading back to the lands of Israel, didn't have a lot going for her. In fact, Ruth would be the epitome of *anav* as defined in the book of Job: desperate, powerless, and on the run. So how does Ruth come to be the Old Testament's best embodier of Jesus' kind of *anav*—powerful servant leadership through meekness?

She does so through a great Hebrew term I mentioned earlier in chapter 4: *hesed*, or "covenanted loving-kindness." Just as God practices covenanted loving-kindness with his people, so Ruth practices covenanted loving-kindness with Naomi, her helpless mother-in-law. Boaz, the kind-hearted Israelite who eventually marries her and increases her blessings abundantly, in turn practices *hesed* toward Ruth far beyond the norms of the culture around him. In fact, the whole book of Ruth is about unexpected *hesed*—from humans, but especially from God.

Back to the story: Ruth's father-in-law dies right away, leaving her mother-in-law, Naomi, a widow (Ruth 1:3). When we first meet Ruth, we hear that her husband also just died, along with her sister's husband (1:5). She seems to have no family of her own prior to marriage, so very quickly the story shows us a harsh picture: three women alone in a male-dominated world, all widowed, all without resources during a time of famine.

Without other recourse, the three set off together on the long journey back to the land of the Israelites. Suddenly, though, at some point along the journey, Naomi turns to the young women and says, go back, my daughters. Go back home, seek security, and if you're lucky God might give you the best you could hope for in times like these: a new husband. "May the Lord show you *hesed*," Naomi says, "as you have shown *hesed* to your dead husband and to me" (1:7-9). Orpah and Ruth protest, saying they will remain faithful and continue with Naomi. Naomi, at this point, becomes bitingly blunt. Forcing her daughters-in-law to face reality, she asks: Why would you come with me? What hope could you possibly have? Get real, she says: I have no husband, no children, no money, no land, and no options. I'm used up. You two, though—you might still have a chance, if you return where people know you (1:11-13).

REWILDING RUTH

Facing bleakness, the three women are devastated and weep together, wailing without hope. Eventually, Orpah does the sensible thing and heads back to her homeland. Ruth, however, does something completely unexpected. As the Scripture states, "Orpah kissed her mother-in-law goodbye, but Ruth *clung* to her" (1:14).

Naomi tries one more time to get Ruth to go back, but Ruth is done with listening to voices of self-preservation. You might expect a penniless young widow to cling to her mother-in-law out of fear, or insecurity, or a desire for familiarity in a terrifying time. But Ruth transforms all that and clings to Naomi not out of fear but out of solidarity—out of a deep, abiding *hesed* that turns her into a figure far stronger than her surroundings.

I'm not goin' nowhere, she essentially says, and then channels the very persona of God, voicing one of the most profound covenants ever made: "Where you go I will go, and where you stay I will stay. Your people will be my people and your God my God. Where you die I will die, and there I will be buried. May the Lord deal with me, be it ever so severely, if even death separates you and me" (Ruth 1:16-17).

I wonder: In the uncertain era we live in today, how can God's *hesed*—covenanted loving-kindness—bring good news to an anxious world? It's amazing how many Christians are as nervous as the rest of the world about financial upheaval, declining energy resources, and a changing climate. Just as Ruth clings to a hopeless Naomi and walks with her in solidarity, dare we trust that God continues to be with us, clings to us powerfully, pledges to be with us in all of our trials? Remember, God didn't immediately remove Ruth's difficulties but rather walked with her through the uncertainty and despair.

In times of uncertainty, it's tempting to lock up our stuff and close our gates. Yet Ruth's example of solidarity makes me ask a second question: What kind of covenanted loving-kindness might God's allies be called to practice in today's shifting world? What vulnerable aspects of creation, both human and other-than-human, might we commit to protect and serve? Will we pledge to a local farmer and covenant together so that the fate of her land and business becomes *our* business? Will we conjoin our well-being to that of our local river and think of its health as our own? If we did, we might localize Jesus' famous dictum as Wendell Berry did, and follow this rewilded wisdom: do unto others downstream as you would have them do unto you.

12

CULTiVATE A DiVINE INSECURiTY

IN **1985**, a deep summer drought significantly lowered the level of the Sea of Galilee. The lower waterline revealed large swaths of sandy mud around its shoreline, exposing a shallow sea bottom rarely seen by humans. In early 1986, two brothers discovered a large, fragile boat sunk in the mud opposite Migdal, or Magdala, very near their family home.

Three things about the boat made it deeply intriguing to archaeologists:

1. It was two thousand years old, dating from the time of Jesus.

2. It provided valuable clues to the life conditions of peasant fishermen during that time.

3. Its wood was the consistency of a soft cheese like you might spread on a cracker.

Archaeologists spent a decade restoring and improving the boat's structural integrity before they decided it could safely be put on public display. What makes this two-thousand-year-old boat stand out from other relics of the period? Certainly not its make and model: this eight by twenty-six foot boat was typical of reliable, workaday transport on the lake. Not its configuration: like many of its kind, it had a stout mast, a sail, four oars, a rudder, and could hold around fifteen people. No, what made this boat stand out was the absurd degree to which it had been repaired and reused.

Like an old jalopy nursed along with spare parts, duct tape, and a prayer, this boat had been nursed along by skilled shipwrights using poor-to-bad materials. The craft contained at least seven—and possibly as many as twelve—different types of timber. Whoever built and maintained it were master artisans, and may have literally scraped the bottom of the barrel for any wood they could get their hands on. John Dominic Crossan describes the vessel: "The boat was constructed by cannibalizing other boats. Half of its keel was quite adequate—but reused— cedar wood, and the other half was rather inadequate jujube wood. Furthermore, its planking had been replaced not with new boards but with bits and pieces patched together."[1]

Then one sad day it was no longer seaworthy. At that point, Crossan tells us, the boat was completely stripped of anything salvageable—stem post and stern post, sail and mast, oars and rudder, *every single* iron nail—and pushed into the lake for its final rest, sinking in a graveyard of discarded boats near a Magdala shipyard. Two thousand years later in 1986, a drought and two brothers brought it again to human attention.

REWILDING THE DISCIPLES

Why is this derelict vessel important to this book? Because this boat shows us a wilder, rougher, grittier reality for Jesus' disciples than most of us imagine. Perhaps, like me, you always pictured Jesus' gang as a bunch of fairly happy fishermen. This boat shows,

however, in excruciating clarity, what life was really like for peasant fishermen under the conquering, commercializing, industri-
alizing Roman Empire. I find it haunting that every single iron
nail had been removed before the boat went to its nautical tomb.

Remember, things had gotten tougher by Jesus' time. For
generations, ordinary peasant families had lived close to the
coast and been able to fish freely while the lake was called
Galilee. But at the time of Jesus, its name was changed; it was to
be called the Sea of Tiberias, as in Tiberias Caesar. It was property of the empire now. Everything about it was under Roman
control. Crossan asserts that nothing about the lake was free
any more—not tossing a net, launching a boat, or landing a
catch. All activities were likely taxed. Herod Antipas's factories
for salting, pickling, and drying fish took the lion's share of any
catches, and the empire controlled all coastal businesses.

The scrap lumber used in the boat's construction is perhaps
an ideal physical metaphor for the overall economic situation
of the period. This excavated boat, Crossan suggests, represents
and reveals the violence normal to civilization in Roman times
in Galilee.[2] So what did Jesus and his peasant disciples do in the
face of such oppressive conditions? History is not certain, so
we'll have to do some guesswork. If we turn to the Gospels for
an answer, do we hear tales of James and John wearing Roman
aprons and clocking in at Herod's fish factories? Do we read
reports of Peter turning in his catch to the authorities for coin?
Or do we read stories about the disciples fishing *anyway*?

It leads me to wonder, was freelance fishing a feral act of
resistance to empire? Instead of joining Rome's ranks of serf-
workers for the sake of security, did Jesus' disciples choose a
divine *insecurity* and trust in providence? Did they assert that
the sea was God's, and did they glean their daily meal from the
bounty of the waters, as promised in the Lord's Prayer?

NIGHT FISHING

Through this lens of fishing-as-resistance, the final place where the resurrected Jesus appears in the Gospels becomes all the more intriguing. Do you remember? At the end of John 21, the author tells the story—in an intimate, folksy manner—of Jesus having a last hangout with his disciples on the shore of the Sea of Tiberias. "It happened this way," the narrative begins, and I picture them sitting around a campfire, listening to a familiar tale. Peter and Thomas and several others close to Jesus were together at the lakeshore. I imagine they were trying to go through the motions of normal life, but reeling from a barrage of mind-boggling events: in recent days their master had been tortured and crucified, and then after death impossibly appeared to them in a locked room. John's story puts them gathered at the lakeshore, probably stunned.

"I'm going out to fish," Peter declares out loud, perhaps convincing himself to get back to business as usual. "We'll go with you," his mates respond. So they get into the boat, and go out into the night (John 21:3).

Into the night. Sure, it could be that the Roman Empire expected all fishermen in their employ to go fishing at night. Perhaps this was a normal, imperially compliant activity. But since Peter declares it out loud like a choice, might it be that fishing at night was a subversive act of economic self-sufficiency? Was fishing under cover of darkness a way to avoid unjust authorities? Peter's actions call to mind the tales of Robin Hood and other more real medieval English bowmen who felt it their right to hunt for deer as they always had, despite attempts by land-grabbing monarchs to claim and control swaths of forest as the King's Wood.

Whether they were obeying empire or resisting it, Peter and the boys eventually head back to shore in the early morning—only to find the risen Jesus waiting for them at a campfire, roasting fish and bread on the coals like any other morning. He takes the bread and the fish and gives it to them, just as he had with the bread and wine only days earlier, before he had been crucified. What profound words does he utter when they come ashore? A phrase both heartwarming and familiar: "Come and have breakfast."

This is one of my very favorite passages in the entire Bible, probably because it is one of the most down to earth. The risen Lord, cooking breakfast over the campfire at the seashore, hanging out with his closest friends, liberated from the clutches of empire, liberated from the power of death. Wild life practically sings out of this passage. *I'm still here*, Jesus seems to be saying. *I'm still with you, when you're eating, when you're cooking, when you're fishing. Trust that your daily needs will be met. You can count on me.*

FISH AS FREEDOM

If this reading is right, the fish becomes the symbol of divine insecurity and feral freedom. It is food caught at night by untamed disciples in uncolonized space, right under the nose of the empire. "Give us today our daily sustenance" becomes an exercise in trusting God's great economy, plying God's waters, and resisting the state-controlled marketplace. How empowering it must have felt for a group of peasant followers of Jesus—an intentional community that Jesus called the kingdom of God— to experience themselves as self-reliant and God-dependent, acquiring enough fish and bread not to be shackled to Herod's industrial economy.

No wonder the symbol of the fish became such a powerful image for the earliest church. It was a swiftly drawn sign for a body-on-the-move who thrived on divine insecurity—a body of people who met in secret under government oppression, freely took care of one another without hoarding, and had no regular gathering places, yet somehow thrived as a parallel society even under intense persecution by Roman authorities.

Ever since I was a young Christian, I've understood that the fish symbol was a code sign—like a secret handshake—for these earliest followers of Jesus. Organizers in Jerusalem or Rome would draw it in charcoal over the doorway of a hastily arranged meeting place. An underground Christian, wondering if a stranger might be a spiritual ally, would draw a single arc in the dirt, and the other, if also a Christian, would complete the secret sign by drawing the second arc, completing the outline of a fish. It was a doubly inspired symbol because the Greek word for fish—*ichthus*—works as an acrostic for the Greek phrase, "Iesous Christos Theou Uios Soter," or "Jesus Christ the Son of God, Savior."

Among affluent Christians today, worship and economics are too often utterly separate domains. Not so for the early followers of the Jesus Way, gathering in caves and catacombs under the sign of the fish. The fish symbolized an utterly different society, the interdependent and self-sufficient kingdom of God, in which worship and wealth were shared. When joined, the covenanted body became a *socioeconomic alternative*, a body that disciples counted on to provide daily bread. It was a parallel economy that stood in stark contrast to the kingdom of Caesar, which for daily bread demanded sweat, labor, dependence, and allegiance. You could be a member of one or the other, but not both.

Hmm . . . I wonder, how are we moderns doing on that last account?

THE FIRST STEP: STAY LOOSE

Jesus' vision of the kingdom of God—wild, free, fearless, and immediate—operates from very different values than those of security-focused dominant society. Look at this intriguing collection of cross-cultural encounters, which are presented back-to-back without interruption in the gospel of Luke:

> As they were walking along the road, a man said to him, "I will follow you wherever you go." Jesus replied, "Foxes have dens and birds have nests, but the Son of Man has no place to lay his head."

> He said to another man, "Follow me." But [the man] replied, "Lord, first let me go and bury my father." Jesus said to him, "Let the dead bury their own dead, but you go and proclaim the kingdom of God."

> Still another said, "I will follow you, Lord; but first let me go back and say goodbye to my family." Jesus replied, "No one who puts a hand to the plow and looks back is fit for service in the kingdom of God." (Luke 9:57-62)

A few decades ago, some well-meaning Bible editors working on a New International Version (NIV) translation titled this section of Scripture "The Cost of Following Jesus." I'm guessing these scholars were living comfortably in our industrialized society, perhaps employed in modest, air-conditioned offices. No wonder, then, that they came up with that title. But should this section really be called "The *Cost* of Following Jesus"? Instead, it might be better named "The *Practice* of Following Jesus." For Bible editors raised in a civilization filled with personal comforts and social obligations, Jesus' words in the above encounters seem shocking and raw, even impossible. But for a people on the move, living lightly on the land and seeking a massive shift in conventional culture, these words are not horrifying; they are simply the way of doing business.

Jesus' wish for his followers to cultivate holy insecurity is brought to a very real level when—right at the beginning of his ministry—he sends his disciples out in pairs, telling them to take nothing for the journey. In Mark, Jesus gives these brief traveling instructions: "Take nothing for the journey except a staff—no bread, no bag, no money in your belts. Wear sandals but not an extra shirt" (Mark 6:8-9). Luke and Matthew report the same mandate: Go, and *take nothing* for the journey.

When modern, affluent Christians analyze this passage, they tend to focus on the great missional work that the disciples were doing: increasing Jesus' reach, spreading the good news of the kingdom, healing the sick, and casting out demons. This part is of course important—but I'd like to focus on Jesus' directive. Could taking nothing for the journey be a *necessary rite of passage* for any Jesus follower who wants to move into authentic discipleship? Could separation from the securities of civilization be a *necessary* rewilding for those who seek to rely upon an untamed Lord?

I do believe it is. Like the exodus to the ancient Israelites, so this sojourn was to the disciples: a test of trust, a step on the Way, a break from bondage to the things that keep us small and secure. Take nothing, and do not be afraid, Jesus tells them as he sends them out to unknown towns. Remember, this challenge was the first thing he asked of his disciples after he gathered them: rely upon the mercy of the road, and trust that you'll be okay. Later, in Luke, Jesus asks them about how they experienced this walkabout, and they confirm that they lacked nothing during their journeys (Luke 22:35). This gave them a basis of trust upon which all other actions were built. It was a rite of passage, a catechesis: a vital, primary training for feral followers of God.

OH, ONE MORE THING: HATE YOUR FAMILY

Jesus laid down many daunting teachings about cultivating holy insecurity, but none troubles me more than when he says *hate your family*. I mean, living with few possessions is difficult enough, but within the realm of possibility for a half-done disciple like me; as I mention in chapter 14, I gave half my clothes away a few years ago, and I found it wasn't too hard. Taking nothing for the road isn't an experience I've undertaken, but because I backpack and hitchhike with just a few things, at least I can consider it as a challenge I might undertake as a disciple.

But *hate my family*? Not gonna do it. It just feels wrong. Yet Jesus' message seems painfully clear: "If anyone comes to me and does not hate father and mother, wife and children, brothers and sisters—yes, even their own life—such a person cannot be my disciple" (Luke 14:26). Yowch! Jesus the lover, telling us to be a hater? Is he saying, just kidding, what I said earlier about *honoring* your parents—what I really meant to say was *despise* them and wish them ill?

I have to believe otherwise. As I wrote in the first chapter, I'm a family man. I believe in my bones that God wants us to raise loving children and care for our families, even as we live in a world-changing manner. So my question remains: How can we nurture great families *and* practice radical discipleship?

With this as my foundational belief, I then ask, what could Jesus have meant when he said *hate your family*? Too many nice Christians, including me, confused by such an uncharacteristically harsh statement by their Lord, simply ignore it and keep living deeply entrenched in dominant culture, enmeshed with their parents, and in love with their families.

We might want to ignore it, but this sentiment doesn't occur just the once. It rears its disturbing head again later in Luke. During an emotional interchange, Peter says to Jesus,

"We have left all we had to follow you!" (Luke 18:28). In the next verse, a painful awareness emerges: To meet Jesus' conditions of membership, it's clear the disciples underwent a drastic dislocation from their families. Peter and at least some others "left home or wife or brothers or sisters or parents or children" in order to commit fully to the society-changing intentional community that Jesus called the kingdom of God (Luke 18:29).

Why would Jesus expect his followers to forfeit family as usual in such a drastic way—wasn't he all about love? Far more than family-centered love, Jesus was about a *larger* love. *Miseó*, the Greek word translated as "to hate" also means "to love less." It can mean to love one thing far less than something else, or to renounce one choice for another. Did Jesus really want his followers to *hate* family—meaning harbor a permanent ill will toward them? As a family man, I sure hope not. Rather, I'm guessing Jesus wanted his disciples to focus on the common good instead of the personal good. He demanded that they defect from the typical familial expectations that keep our lives small, safe, self-serving, and secure.

NOTHING TO LOSE IS A GOOD THING

A few years before his audacious moment winning oil drilling rights as Bidder 70, Tim DeChristopher realized something profound: he and his generation had nothing to lose. He had a personal experience of stark, spiritual depression—a sobering reality check in which his hopes for the future came "crashing really hard." This dark night of the soul—facing the fact that humanity's future was never going to be "normal" again and that our current human civilization, busily damaging the Earth, is simply not able to mend its ways—became a strange source of courage and liberation, allowing him to act as daringly as he did at the Utah auction. He was ready to embrace a larger love because he had nothing to lose: "What empowered me to take that leap and have that insecurity," he said later, "was that I already felt that insecurity. . . . My future was already lost."[3]

Tim's transformational moment came when he met Terry Root, a Nobel Prize winner and one of the lead authors of a major report by the Intergovernmental Panel on Climate Change (IPCC) during a presentation at the University of Utah. She presented all the IPCC data from the report, and Tim couldn't believe what he was hearing. He recalls the event:

> I went up to her afterwards and said, "That graph that you showed, with the possible emission scenarios in the twenty-first century? It looked like the best case was that carbon peaked around 2030 and started coming back down." She said, "Yeah, that's right." And I said, "But didn't the report that you guys just put out say that if we didn't peak by 2015 and then start coming back down that we were pretty much all screwed, and we wouldn't even recognize the planet?" And she said, "Yeah, that's right."[4]

If our situation is so dire, thought Tim, why are these scientists so calm? He asked Root if he was missing something.

"You're not missing anything," Root responded. "There are things we could have done in the '80s, there are some things we could have done in the '90s—but it's probably too late to avoid any of the worst-case scenarios that we're talking about." She put her hand on Tim's shoulder and said, "I'm sorry my generation failed yours."

"You just gave a speech to four hundred people and you didn't say anything like that," exclaimed Tim, aghast. "Why aren't you telling people this?"

"I don't want to scare people into paralysis," Root responded honestly. "I feel like if I told people the truth, people would just give up."

For Tim, the truth did the exact opposite—it set him free for action. "Once I realized that there was . . . no hope for me to have anything my parents or grandparents would have considered a normal future—of a career and a retirement and all that stuff—I realized that I have absolutely nothing to lose by fighting back. Because it was all going to be lost anyway."

Robbed of a hopeful future, Tim plunged into a period of deep despair. "I was rather paralyzed," he remembers. "It really felt like a period of mourning. I really felt like I was grieving my own future, and grieving the futures of everyone I care about." He looked around for support and found some. "I had friends who were coming to similar conclusions. And I was able to kind of work through it, and get to a point of action."

Tim believes strongly that it's this type of authentic grieving that's missing from the environmental movement and preventing us from being the people we need to be. He struggles, though, because he knows how painful this kind of honest grieving really is. "I struggle with pushing people into that period of grieving. I mean, I find myself pulling back. I see people who still have that kind of buoyancy and hopefulness. And I don't want to shatter that."[5]

GOOD NEWS IN THE ASHES

For Tim, it was strangely comforting and liberating to realize that things are going to fall apart. It allowed him to let go of worry, let go of expectations, freed him of illusion, and gave him an opportunity to change things drastically. Prior to his dramatic act of civil disobedience, Tim felt the weight of the world on his broad shoulders. He felt burdened by heavy thoughts and an intense sense of anxiety, urgency, and duty. Disrupting the auction had intense consequences, but it was something that had to be done, something worth sacrificing his freedom for.

Jumping into action turned everything on its head. Like Jesus' upside-down kingdom, what seemed like death turned into abundant life. Rather than being the one who had to inspire, he was being inspired. Rather than being the one who carried this cause, he felt carried by it. Tim describes his experience of liberation: "I thought I was sacrificing my freedom, but instead I was grabbing onto my freedom and refusing to let go of it for the first time, you know? Finally accepting that I wasn't this helpless victim of society, and couldn't do anything to shape my own future, you know, that I didn't have that freedom to steer the course of my life. Finally I said, 'I have the freedom to change this situation. I'm that powerful.' And that's been a wonderful feeling that I've held onto since then."[6]

PRISON AS LIBERATION

Author and activist Terry Tempest Williams loves the Utah wilderness fiercely, just as Tim DeChristopher does. The two have become friends, and during Tim's trial, Terry was one of many who rallied and fought to keep him out of jail.

Tim laughs good-naturedly at the irony of these efforts, because he never attempted to escape legal consequences. His goal was never to keep himself *out* of prison; rather, his aim is to get more people to join him *in* prison. The experience liberated him. When I checked up on what Tim was up to (more than a year after being released from jail), I discovered that he was speaking in Boston about "Civil Disobedience as a Spiritual Path."

Just hearing the title of Tim's talk made me nervous. It challenged me to my core and reminded me about Jesus' daunting demands. *Join him in jail?* Yeah, right. *What of my wife and kid?* I immediately thought. *What about the school we started?*

Digging a little more, I discovered that Terry Tempest Williams had talked with Tim DeChristopher about the very topic of civil disobedience, and the conversation had been printed in *Orion* magazine. More than a little uneasy, I plunged into it. My attention was riveted when Terry asked Tim about other valid alternatives for those who don't have the option of going to prison, such as parents with children.

Tim's response was blunt: "Everybody has a reason why they can't."

Ouch. I can only imagine the pause that must have transpired in the conversation. I imagine Tim as John the Baptist, implacable, dragging his people toward repentance. Terry then tried a different tactic, using a personal story. "I was arrested in front of the White House, protesting during the buildup to the Iraq war. . . . I looked around [and noticed] it was a lot easier for me to be arrested than others, you know? I didn't have a traditional job, I didn't have children. I mean, some people have more at stake than others."

Reading this transcript a year after the conversation happened, I found I was rooting for Terry, aching for her to voice the questions that are in my heart as well, aching for the two of them to help me find a third way.

"Civil disobedience is one path," Terry continued. "It's a path I've personally chosen at times—certainly not with the stakes as high as they are for you. . . . But what about other alternatives?"

Tim softened—a bit. "If people aren't willing to go to jail, there are alternatives in which they can be powerful and effective. But if people feel they've got too much to lose—they've got all this other stuff in their life, and they might be risking their job, or their reputation, and things like that—I don't think they can be powerful in other ways."

Terry voiced my own burning question: "So you can't be powerful as an organizer or as a support person behind the scene? Or as a teacher or educator?"

"You can," Tim responded, "but I don't think people are going to realize their power as revolutionaries if they feel like they've got all this stuff to lose." Reading between the lines, I can feel Tim struggling here—wanting to agree with Terry but refusing to let go of the hard truth that burns like a coal in his belly. At the core is the *willingness* to go to jail, the willingness to let go of everything, the willingness to walk through life comfortable with divine insecurity. This is the same hard truth that Jesus shared with his disciples two thousand years ago.

A true cultural revolutionary must have the willingness not to hold back, not to be safe, Tim gently insists. "People can do it without getting arrested," he allows. "But people can't be powerful if their first concern is staying safe. . . . Our current power structures only have power over us because of what they can take away from us. That's where their power comes from—their ability to take things away."[7]

LET'S SLIP INTO SOMETHING MORE UNCOMFORTABLE

"Sometimes you jump off the cliff first, and build your wings on the way down." These words of Annie Dillard from more than fifty years ago mean a lot to Tim. Ever since he woke up that fateful day, Tim has been making his wings as he flies, making his road as he walks it. "First I didn't know what I was going to do at the auction, but I knew I was going to disrupt it," he remembers. "And then, after disrupting it, I had no idea who was going to support me and how that was going to play out. And no idea whether or not I could handle that role."[8]

Step by risky step, we become the people God yearns for us to be. For Tim, getting arrested and defying the government was the liberating step that freed him to become a powerful agent of change.

The challenge I hear from Tim, the challenge that I hear through history from our prophets, the challenge that God's endangered creation is asking of us today, is this: it's time to get radically insecure. As Tim says to Terry toward the end of their interview: "What's the most uncomfortable thing you can do—the greatest risk, with the most at stake?"[9]

13

EMBRACE THE UNRAVELING

WHAT'S WITH THE LONG LINE? I asked silently as I pulled into a crowded gas station queue in the winter of 2013. I was coming into civilization from our little mountain home for my weekly town errands, and I was puzzled. Dozens of cars waited their turn. *Taos is never like this*, I thought, and craned my neck out the window to see better. My breath turned white in the bitter cold. Up at the pumps, two men suddenly broke into a fight, each grabbing hold of the same nozzle. One slipped on the ice, and the other jerked the gas line away in victory.

Weird, I said to myself, reversing my car to get out of a crazy situation. I decided to do my food shopping first. I pulled into the grocery store lot and circled, amazed. Every single space was full, including a variety of illegal parking jobs and curbside hoverers. *Is there a party I don't know about?* I ended up parking half a block away, wedged between others on a normally empty street.

As I entered the store, it finally dawned on me that something was very wrong. Each of the six grocery store registers had lines *forty to sixty* carts long. Shoppers' carts were stacked with produce and frozen meats and piled high with cans.

"What's going on?" I blurted out loud. "Zombie apocalypse?"

"Almost," the nearest checker responded, smiling grimly as he continued his never-ending job of swiping and bagging mountains of food. "We got no heat, and our refrigeration seems to be on the fritz. We're closing early, and we don't know when we're opening back up. Taos is out of natural gas."

The shortage lasted four days. Truck fleets from Texas, which northern New Mexicans rely upon for natural gas, failed to arrive, right during the coldest streak of winter in recent memory. Thousands of homes were suddenly without their primary heat source as temperatures plunged. So what did people do? Naturally, they reached for the next available heat source. They all plugged in electric space heaters and kept them running, causing a massive and unexpected spike in demand that suddenly put the entire overloaded electrical grid at risk. Stores and services dependent on natural gas closed without warning. People panicked, leading to the kind of crowding, confusion, hoarding, and high tensions I'd witnessed earlier. Fights broke out, and rumors circulated of elderly people freezing in their homes. Like a row of falling dominoes, the building blocks of business as usual fell in Taos over those four days. I saw just how easily the veil of civilized normality can unravel.

Unexpected aid and neighborliness showed up, as well. In the midst of the crisis, neighborhood groups went door to door, checking in on the most vulnerable and elderly. The local radio station became a clearinghouse of information and support; scores of people called in to offer firewood, heaters, blankets, and carpooling options. Extra food lines were set up, offering hot meals for those dependent on natural gas for their cooking. Hospitality reigned in the midst of hardship.

This four-day jolt provided me with a small window into the chaos—and the community—that can happen when things rapidly fall apart. Since that time, I've learned that what we experienced in Taos is typical. Rebecca Solnit, in a book aptly titled *A Paradise Built in Hell*, examines the extraordinary communities that arise during times of disaster. Living the Bay Area, Solnit experienced the earthquake that shook the central California coast in 1989. She remembers loving the earthquake; well, not loving the earthquake itself but rather the way communities responded to it with aid and collaboration. "We don't even have a language for this emotion, in which the wonderful comes wrapped in the terrible," she writes. "We cannot welcome disaster, but we can value the responses, both practical and psychological."[1]

BLESSED ARE THOSE WHO FEEL THE PAIN OF THE WORLD

As our very world falls apart, activist Joanna Macy teaches us to do something wild: embrace the unraveling. *Feeling* the depth of what human industrial society has done to the Earth helps us grasp the true nature of our situation. For decades Macy has led workshops helping people come to terms with both the crisis and the opportunity of our historical moment. Instead of immediately trying to fix or deny, in her workshops Macy encourages people first to embrace what is happening. She notes that—as participants express their grief, dread, and outrage at the unraveling of our world—a connected awareness grows that we are, all of us, *living in a disaster zone*. Hearing one another name the unraveling gives us a strange reassurance, defies our culture's tendency toward numbness, and reminds us we're not crazy for noticing.[2] Like Tim DeChristopher and many others, we come to realize that things will never be the same. This sobering truth is incredibly painful, yet catalyzing.

I wonder, is this what Jesus meant when he said, "Blessed are those who mourn, for they will be comforted"? Earlier in this book I suggested a creative translation of this text: *God's allies let themselves feel the pain of the world; living this way, they will be sustained.* To mourn means to feel the pain. In Jesus' day, he was encouraging his followers not to hide from the pain of their world but to feel and embrace the suffering and injustice surrounding them. What would it mean for us today to feel the pain as a way of life, to feel the pain as a spiritual path? I think it means to do what seems impossible: to embrace the unraveling of the Earth.

Recently Joanna Macy cowrote a book called *Active Hope: How to Face the Mess We're in without Going Crazy.* It's good medicine, and sorely needed. In it, she highlights the need for our culture of affluenza to drop the "veil of normality" that screens out the very real perils we face. In this current moment, she notes, the impact of the global unraveling is unevenly distributed. While climate-related disasters have deeply affected the lives of millions, there are many millions more who, from the comfort of their privileged homes, don't believe there is much of a problem.[3] Far too many cozy Christians in North America fall into this group. *Geez* magazine, one of the most creative and prophetic voices in emerging Christianity today, captures our entitled naïveté in a poignant quote from a Sudanese man: "Ah yes, when it finally comes to America, then it will be real."[4]

DARING TO LOOK DOWN

As a private in the U.S. Army, Roy Scranton drove into a living hell. "Driving into Iraq just after the 2003 invasion felt like driving into the future," he remembers. His team drove all day and all night, past burned-out tanks and devastation, until Baghdad appeared in the desert morning light like a vision from a nightmare. It was the end of the world for a city of six million, about the same size as Houston or Washington:

> Flames licked the bruised sky from the tops of refinery towers, cyclopean monuments bulged and leaned against the horizon, and broken overpasses swooped and fell over ruined suburbs, bombed factories, and narrow, ancient streets. The infrastructure was totaled: water, power, traffic, markets and security fell to anarchy and local rule. The city's secular middle class was disappearing, squeezed out between gangsters, profiteers, fundamentalists, and soldiers. The government was going down, walls were going up, tribal lines were being drawn, and brutal hierarchies were being savagely established.[5]

Back home safe in America more than two years later, Scranton thought he would never see such a thing again. Then Hurricane Katrina hit New Orleans, and the same "chaos and urban collapse" he'd witnessed in Iraq played out on home soil. Civilization unraveled, food systems fell apart, and the Eighty-Second Airborne hit the ground with automatic weapons, patrolling the city under implicit martial law. Scranton's unit was placed on alert to prepare for riot control operations. The grim future that Scranton had witnessed in Iraq had come home—not through enemy attack but through social collapse in the face of an extreme and unpredictable climate. For Roy Scranton, this was a wake-up call to a new normal: modern civilization unable to recuperate from shocks to its system.

PRACTICING DEATH

Learning how to die isn't easy. At first, Army private Roy Scranton was terrified by the idea. In combat in Iraq, his chances of survival were strong—in his own words, "I had good armor, we had a great medic, and we were part of the most powerful military the world has ever seen"—but still, he was in the midst of enemy territory, getting shot at and mortared, with IEDs potentially hiding along every stretch of roadway. His life was on the line every day, and death was ever-present. Scranton kept waking up each day to see death in the mirror, and it nearly paralyzed him. He found a way through his paralysis and fear in an unexpected place: an eighteenth-century samurai manual. For the practicing samurai, the manual gave the following advice: "Meditation on inevitable death should be performed daily."[6]

Scranton was stunned into a new reality. "Instead of fearing my end, I owned it," he recalls. Every day he would envision a litany of the macabre: "I'd imagine getting blown up being run over by an IED, shot by a sniper, burned to death, run over by a tank, torn apart by dogs, captured and beheaded, and succumbing to dysentery." After such visualizations, it was easier not to worry because he had already accepted death. A particular line from the samurai manual spoke to his condition: "If by setting one's heart right every morning and evening, one is able to live as though his body were already dead, he gains freedom in the Way."

Although this text is referring to the Way of the Samurai, I think the same could be said for the Way of Jesus. By accepting death, by looking into the chasm of nonexistence, a strange liberation emerged for Scranton. Fear was replaced by resolve. No longer needing to protect anything, no longer attempting to ensure a cherished vision of the future for himself, he was able to act and imagine boldly. Instead of obsessing about self-preservation, a new goal emerged: "The only thing that mattered was that I did my best to make sure everyone else came back alive."[7]

EMBRACING A HARD TRUTH

Roy Scranton says he got through his tour in Iraq one day at a time, following ancient wisdom from a medieval samurai text, meditating each morning on his certain demise. After immersing himself in the chaos that followed in the wake of Katrina and confronting the "new normal" of our era, he came to another devastating yet liberating awareness: we moderns have to learn how to die, not as individuals but as a civilization.

We humans as a species aren't used to imagining radical future change. We obey existing laws; we follow current trends; we devise conventional solutions to anticipated problems. Our expectations for tomorrow are based upon the rules of business as usual today. Roy Scranton describes our current condition this way:

> Across the world today, our actions testify to our belief that we can go on like this forever, burning oil, poisoning the seas, killing off other species, pumping carbon into the air, ignoring the ominous silence of our coal mine canaries in favor of the unending robotic tweets of our new digital imaginarium. Yet the reality of global climate change is going to keep intruding on our fantasies of perpetual growth, permanent innovation and endless energy. . . . We face the imminent collapse of the agricultural, shipping and energy networks upon which the global economy depends, a large-scale die-off in the biosphere that's already well on its way, and our own possible extinction. If homo sapiens (or some genetically modified variant) survives the next millenniums, it will be survival in a world unrecognizably different from the one we have inhabited.[8]

The biggest problem climate change poses, Scranton declares, is not how our government should plan for resource wars or what type of flood barriers we should erect to protect coastal cities. Our biggest challenge is not about protecting what *is*, or defending what we currently define as the "American way of life." The biggest problem we face is grasping a philosophical and spiritual truth: our current mode of civilization is already dead. Like the samurai, we need to envision daily the death of life as we know it, the end of business as usual. The sooner we embrace this hard truth, the sooner we can—with creativity, faith, and humility—get down to the work of adapting and attending to God's dream, being active players in God's wild new story of creation.

REWILDING OUR STORY

As I encountered Roy Scranton's frontline stories of social upheaval from Baghdad and Katrina, up bubbled these words from a group called the Dark Mountain Project: what witnesses of war observe, time and time again, is not only the fragility of modern civilization's fabric, but the speed with which it can unravel.

The Dark Mountain Project fascinates me. Founded by Dougald Hine and Paul Kingsnorth, it is a group of artists and writers devoted to an uncommon genre: uncivilized thinking. The project emerged out of a "feeling that contemporary literature and art were failing to respond honestly or adequately to the scale of our entwined ecological, economic and social crises." Uncivilized thinking, they say in their darkly captivating manifesto, emerges not from the "self-absorbed and self-congratulatory metropolitan centres of civilisation" but rather from out on the wilder edges of human society—from the unruly places, "woody and weedy and largely avoided." From these places, "insistent truths about ourselves can drift in"— truths that displace humans as the center of all things and that we're not always eager to hear.[9]

I find the writing of the Dark Mountain Project to be so beautiful and haunting that I am tempted to quote them for pages on end. From their perspective, human civilization is like a shawl, an intensely fragile construction, woven of thin material. Out beyond the view of self-important cities, "unchecked industrial exploitation of the environment frays the material basis of life in many parts of the world and pulls at the ecological systems that sustain it."[10] Our era is a time of great unraveling, these writers say:

> Human civilization . . . is built on little more than belief: belief in the rightness of its values; belief in the strength of its system of law and order; belief in its currency; above all, perhaps, belief in its future. We live in an age in which familiar restraints are being kicked away, and foundations snatched from under us. . . . A familiar human story is being played out. It is the story of an empire corroding from within. It is the story of a people who believed, for a long time, that their actions did not have consequences. It is the story of how that people will cope with the crumbling of their own myth. It is our story.[11]

THE EMPIRE HAS NO CLOTHES

The authors at the Dark Mountain Project name a zeitgeist—a spirit of our times—that feels spot-on to me. They strike at the core of our current cultural condition. People today no longer are true believers in the stories the agents of empire have been spinning. We do not want to fit happily into the military-industrial complex. We are not content with business as usual, because the promises are not being delivered. Compared to previous generations, we are less trusting of "progress." Work blurs into all hours of the day, but we experience less security. We experience a nagging fear of crime, social breakdown, police power, and environmental ruin. We seek authenticity but fear being offline. We have far more choices and far more anxiety. Our physical health is better, but our mental health and spiritual well-being are far more threatened. Our suspicion of governments and corporations is on the increase. Deep down, we moderns know the empire has no clothes.

We have listened to the promises of empire and found them lacking. Fundamentally, we do not believe that the future we are inheriting will be better than the past, but none of us want to look too deeply into what might be coming. The agents of empire tell us we are on an unending escalator of technological progress. Just don't look down, and we'll be fine, they assure us:

> Things may be changing, runs the narrative, but there is nothing we cannot deal with here, folks. We perhaps need to move faster, more urgently. Certainly we need to accelerate the pace of research and development. We accept that we must become more "sustainable." But everything will be fine. There will still be growth, there will still be progress: these things will continue, because they have to continue, so they cannot do anything but continue. There is nothing to see here. Everything will be fine.[12]

"We do not believe that everything will be fine," say the writers of the Dark Mountain Project. "We are not even sure, based on current definitions of progress and improvement, that we want it to be." They believe that "this is a moment to ask deep questions and to ask them urgently. All around us, shifts are underway that suggest that our whole way of living is already passing into history."

May the task of the Dark Mountain Project also be ours: to fan the flames of imagination, embrace the unraveling of what once was, and dare to look for new paths and new stories, ones that can lead us through the end of civilization as we know it and out the other side.

14

TRUST IN THE SPIRIT

ONCE CALLED Father Richard Rohr, OFM, at three in the morning, crying my guts out into the phone. It's probably not something one should do to internationally renowned spiritual guides—Lord knows he had enough on his shoulders already. But I was in the throes of divorce. I was hurting, ripped wide open, and didn't know where else to turn.

It seemed natural at the time. I was in my early twenties and had recently moved to Albuquerque to get involved with Richard's new initiative, the Center for Action and Contemplation. Like no one else, Richard gave counsel that helped me mend brokenness, abide opposites, and make sense of a confusing world. So at three o'clock in the morning, from a solitary phone booth on a deserted high school campus, I phoned him, like a man lost at sea grabbing for a lifeboat.

REWILDING FAITH

Richard picked up. I started in. Everything I'd counted on had fallen apart. What would the future hold? How do you live each day, ripped wide open? Somewhere in the midst of my blubbering, I heard him say something like, "Todd, even more than loss, even more than anger, I hear a lot of worry. Stop worrying. Stop worrying about what you can't control. Stop worrying about tomorrow. Trust, even when it's hard. Have faith in God. Remember, the opposite of faith is not doubt. The opposite of faith is anxiety."

The opposite of faith is not doubt; it's anxiety. So keep living, Todd, Richard said. Live into tomorrow, and see what the day brings. Trust life. Trust God. Divorce is a death, yes, but it's only a part of your small self that is dying. Your bigger self needs to live into what is next for you.

That phone call—and that divorce—happened twenty-five years ago. Looking back, I simply smile and give thanks for what seemed monumentally tragic at the time. From that experience I learned that faith is not intellectual belief; it is trust, lived out. Faith is a continued experiential stance, risked and tested true every day.

Does my confusion about faith resonate with you? I think it might, if you grew up around institutional Christianity. Somehow Christendom has tamed the term *faith*, co-opted it, twisted it to mean a dogmatic set of beliefs *about* God-reality instead of *living in* God-reality. It's time to get back to a wilder, more vigorous faith, an ever-deepening trust in the Spirit gained from ever-expanding practice.

THE PRACTICE IS THE THING

Mark Scandrette and some friends in the Bay Area entered into an audacious experiment a few years ago: each participant would sell or give away half of their possessions and donate the profits to poverty relief. For people with too many possessions, what kind of deeper security comes from selling those possessions and giving to the poor, like Jesus told his disciples to do

(Luke 12:33)? Mark and his friends thought they'd find out by taking a step in that direction. So they took John the Baptist's advice about extra shirts and surplus food and gave half of their belongings away. This experiment turned into a multi-week adventure for Mark's group: one week it was books and music; another week clothes, furniture, and housewares. Fascinating questions arose: How many bicycles are enough, if they serve different functions? Why do I have things I don't actually need? What about things that are beautiful or meaningful but non-functional? All in all, the experiment caused this group to make profound realizations about their attitudes toward money, possessions, hoarding, and consumption.[1]

A group of us in Taos decided to emulate Mark Scandrette's "Have2Give1" experiment, but with an uncomfortable twist: we pledged to give as many of our things as we could directly to people who truly needed them. We added this catch because almost everybody we knew needed nothing. Giving to friends who had surplus already or giving anonymously to charity organizations was easy. Giving face-to-face to someone in true need would get us out of our comfort zones and into the world. I ended up finding owners for my men's clothes by working a food distribution line as I sometimes do, but as I handed out food, I also assessed the passing men with an eye toward what piece of clothing I had that might fit each man's size and style. It was a small gesture on my part, but still powerful. Too often I treat "the poor" as an anonymous group of people to be pitied; this practice helped me see individual guys with individual needs, just like me.

Getting rid of half my stuff taught me something else: how little I needed it. We tend to confuse having a surplus with security. But true security—and true faith—means leaping out in trust, trusting something far bigger than your own self and the visible things surrounding you.

EVIDENCE OF THINGS NOT SEEN

William Hutchison Murray was a Scottish mountain climber who was regularly getting into uncomfortable situations that taught him to trust the Spirit. His words have inspired my own attempts to walk in trust. It is fitting that Murray's autobiography is entitled *The Evidence of Things Not Seen*. The phrase refers to a passage from the King James Bible: "Now faith is the substance of things hoped for, the evidence of things not seen" (Hebrews 11:1). Murray was an experienced traveler in the pathways of trusting the Spirit and pursuing things not seen. He routinely initiated projects far larger than were reasonable.

One of his most fascinating projects was writing a book—while a prisoner of war. Guess what he wrote it on? Toilet paper. Held by the Nazis for three years during World War II, ailing due to a near-starvation diet, forced to scribble on scraps, Murray the writer did not have bright prospects of publishing a book. Yet publish he did. He felt the call, committed to the project, gave it his all, and trusted in the Spirit to do the rest. The story is even more amazing when we discover that Murray's first manuscript—written on toilet paper, mind you—was discovered and destroyed by the Gestapo. What did he do in the face of such despair? He began again from the start, just like reattempting a mountain ascent, which he did regularly when not imprisoned in foreign countries. Murray's was a tested faith in the unseen; time and time again he saw results materialize that he could not achieve on his own. In a book he wrote after the war, it becomes clear that Murray the mountaineer is also Murray the mystic. Here he is, writing about the mundane and sometimes frustrating preparations for a mountain expedition to the Himalayas, when he suddenly pens a profound truth. His team had endured numerous setbacks and difficulties, but they eventually book passage on

a ship to Bombay, despite the fact that they didn't feel completely ready. Murray realizes something powerful, a law of
the universe:

> Until one is committed, there is hesitancy, the chance to draw
> back, always ineffectiveness. Concerning all acts of initiative
> (and creation), there is one elementary truth, the ignorance of
> which kills countless ideas and splendid plans: that the moment
> one definitely commits oneself, then Providence moves too. All
> sorts of things occur to help one that would never otherwise have
> occurred. A whole stream of events issues from the decision,
> raising in one's favour all manner of unforeseen incidents and
> meetings and material assistance, which no man could have
> dreamt would have come his way.[2]

I stumbled upon this quotation at just the right time in my
life. My wife and I had just committed to start our wilderness-
based public charter school from scratch, a project to which
we felt deeply called but for which we had no professional experience or training. We had also just committed to adopt a
baby from Ecuador, and the idea of becoming a dad scared me
almost as much as it delighted me. Finally, we'd also committed
to leave our jobs and friends in Albuquerque to move to a tiny
mountain community near Taos, living along dirt roads and
heating with a wood-burning stove.

As we jumped into these new commitments all at once, we
found Murray's wisdom to be true: Providence moved with us.
All sorts of unexpected blessings and incidents occurred as
we stumbled our way into new callings. As we worked, Spirit
worked; opportunities were revealed and ways opened. Starting
the school was a project that to me felt distinctly Spirit-initiated
and Spirit-led. Like Moses thousands of years ago, God was
not requiring that I be professionally trained or previously

skilled; my task was to be obedient to the vision. Time after time our dream of a new kind of public school was halted in its tracks—stopped because of a permit that was rejected, because of an exemption that was refused, because of funding that was retracted—only to be given new life through unexpected ways and means. Through multiple steps and many months, I watched—sometimes in satisfaction, sometimes in awe—as a force far greater than our sweat and labors worked with us and through us to create a new possibility in this world.

ARE YOU EXPERIENCED?

Feeling led by the Spirit is a difficult thing to write about without sounding cheesy or grandiose. I certainly was no Moses, but I *was* daily experiencing a Spirit-infused reality I had only read about—something Jesus called the Helper, something that Gandhi called Satyagraha, or truth-force. I could feel it: I was a channel and a tool. Through my actions (and through far more than my actions) the Spirit was manifesting something that God wanted to see. Gandhi knew this kind of power in his bones—and knew that by surrendering to it, he became part of it. Gandhi subtitled his autobiography *Experiments with Truth*, because that's what his life became: a series of tests, probing the truth of a Spirit-filled universe.

I wonder, are today's Christians, by staying too cozy, selling ourselves short? How many of us prevent our best spiritual development by cementing ourselves into commitments that, although good, prevent us from being available and open to something wilder? To follow an untamed God into an unknown future, we'll need to have a robust trust in the Spirit. Like Gandhi, we'll have to conduct our own experiments in truth. We'll need to have deep confidence, tested through experience. In order to exercise our faith like a muscle and get ourselves in shape, we'll need to consistently put ourselves into positions of discomfort. We'll need to channel Kurt Hahn, the founder of Outward Bound, who would routinely throw people into all kinds of challenging situations, shouting after them, "There is more in you than you know!"

A LARGER FORCE WORKS THROUGH US

Discerning a call defines us. Responding to that call empowers us. Once we embark upon that path, situations emerge that increase our capacity to respond further. A whole constellation of support often shows up. Unexpected allies appear. Unforeseen assistance arises and divine providence surprises.

If we think of ourselves as disconnected individuals, then we will understand our sense of call in individualistic terms. I sometimes fall into this trap: *me*, doing something that *I* was meant to do to fulfill *my* destiny and *my* potential. Or *me*, making a living in *my* profession so *my* family can have a good life. But when we recognize a holy pull to a new kind of work or a new way of living, it's vital to remember it isn't just us who are involved—in addition to the Spirit, another part of the web of life is calling to us.

For example, when John Fife shared with me why he felt called to do the work of Sanctuary, he described three strong pulls. One came from the Spirit, calling him in this place and this time to this particular action. One came from the voices of the immigrants themselves, pulling him out of his complacency and comfort. And one came from what he called the "communion of saints"—those who had come before, thousands of God's people in previous generations who had offered shelter to the outcast and the orphan and the widow, who were now holding us in the light, supporting us, calling to us, encouraging us to continue in the work. These days, many of us also hear God's very creation crying out, the web of life re-minding us we are part of it. Rainforest activist John Seed says, "I try to remember that it's not me, John Seed, trying to protect the rainforest. Rather, I am part of the rainforest protecting itself."[3]

PART III

OUR WORK AHEAD

15

LiVE MORE WiTH LESS

MENNONITES DON'T MAKE the headlines all that often. Most try to avoid the corridors of power, stay out of the limelight, stay close to their communities, deflect attention, and live by example. Because of this, sometimes their most inspiring models of authentic discipleship do not receive national exposure.

But every now and then a Mennonite meme gets our society's attention. Such was the case with the *More-with-Less Cookbook*, which emerged in the 1970s. Countless people—not only in North America but all over the world—were captivated by its simple premise: eat better while consuming less of the world's resources. The theme of "more with less" was brought to an entirely new level with its companion volume, *Living More with Less*, which came out a few years later. This book somehow managed to be both homespun and prophetic. "This is a book for people who know something is wrong with the way North Americans live and are ready to talk about change," author Doris Janzen Longacre writes in the foreword. "This is a book about rediscovering what is good and true. This is a book about

beauty, healing and hope, a book about getting more, not less."[1]
The book project, sharing hundreds of practical and inspirational ways to live more with less, was a shared effort: contributions from about 350 practitioners from across the globe were
included. The work is a delightful mixture of pragmatism and
philosophy, part how-to guide and part manifesto, wrapped
into an elegant pattern for a coherent and countercultural lifeway. Nestled near advice on home sewing, energy-saving tips,
and instructions for making rubber-tire sandals are statements
like this: "North Americans seem to have almost unlimited political, economic, and personal freedom. . . . Yet we submit daily
to brainwashing by commercial interests that must be equal to,
if not more powerful than, the political posters and slogans of
totalitarian governments."[2]

Living in the world today cannot be separated from making
economic-political choices, Longacre writes, just as one cannot
take the yolk out of an egg that has already been scrambled. By
living, you are political. Eating is a political act. When you go
to the grocery store or get gas, you are making economic and
political choices just as strongly as someone who is growing
their own food and refusing to own a car.

Longacre grew up Mennonite, and her community taught
her how to live more lightly than most of us in the modern
world do. With her book, she wanted to take that a step further
and help people move toward right living in a deeper way. She
chose to provide guiding patterns to pursue—lifeways to live
by, rather than rules to obey. She came up with five themes: do
justice, learn from the world community, nurture people, cher-
ish the natural order, and nonconform freely.

Decades after its initial publication, *Living More With Less* is
enjoying a bit of a renaissance, and in 2010 it was rereleased in
a thirtieth anniversary edition. "This book was decades ahead

of its time, and is just as relevant today as it was thirty years ago," Shane Claiborne states on the book's cover. "It is like a cookbook for life."[3]

HOW MUCH DOES YOUR CHANGED LIFE CHANGE THE WORLD?

In the spirit of *more with less*, my family and I have changed our lifeways a lot in the last six years, living a simpler life of greater sustainability and watershed citizenship. As I mentioned in the introduction, we've been living in a yurt in the mountains, using a composting toilet, heating with forest wood, eating locally, growing some of our food, milking goats, living in community, taking fewer showers, and skimping on non-necessities.

But Derrick Jensen gives me pause. *Why do you think your little lifestyle changes make any real difference?* That's the provocative question Derrick Jensen asked in his 2009 article "Forget Shorter Showers."[4] I read this article when it was first published, and years later it's a question that still stews in my soul.

How globally effective is personal lifestyle change? Is it enough to follow the words of Gandhi and *be* the change I want to see in the world, believing that change will somehow spread beyond me? Derrick Jensen says no. In his article, he powerfully argues that personal lifestyle changes—dramatic as they may be for individuals—do almost nothing to forward the massive, systemic change needed today:

> *An Inconvenient Truth* helped raise consciousness about global warming. But did you notice that all of the solutions presented had to do with personal consumption—changing light bulbs, inflating tires, driving half as much—and had nothing to do with shifting power away from corporations, or stopping the growth economy that is destroying the planet? Even if every person in the United States did everything the movie suggested, U.S. carbon

emissions would fall by only 22 percent. Scientific consensus is that emissions must be reduced by at least 75 percent worldwide.[5]

To drive his point home, Jensen quotes Kirkpatrick Sale's sobering conclusion that personal changes have little impact upon planetary crises: "For the past 15 years the story has been the same every year: individual consumption—residential, by private car, and so on—is never more than about a quarter of all consumption; the vast majority is commercial, industrial, corporate, by agribusiness and government [he forgot military]. So, even if we all took up cycling and wood stoves it would have a negligible impact on energy use, global warming and atmospheric pollution."[6]

DON'T PRETEND IT'S POLITICAL

Jensen's message is painfully clear: taking shorter showers may be a good choice to make, but don't pretend it's a powerful political act, or that it's deeply revolutionary. Remember, he says repeatedly, *personal change doesn't cause social change.*

Or does it? After wrestling with Jensen's argument, I'm still convinced that personal change *can* cause social change. It's often the necessary catalyst that leads us to it; because I fill my cistern from a mountain stream and not a city tap, I care more about stream health in other parts of the world.

Jensen states that organized political resistance is necessary to confront and dismantle corporate and industrial power. No doubt. But Jensen doesn't ask the real question: What *kind* of organized political resistance? He seems to think there's only one kind of organized political action, the kind that is essentially an externalized *re*-action—citizens opposing injustice by demanding that our governments or corporations do something, putting legally binding limits on faceless institutions already damaging our planet. This kind of external activism is designed to *get our government or a corporation to improve*, even as our own lifestyles may stay unchanged. Examples of this might include demands that our government force extractive petroleum corporations to stop fracking or require industrial food producers to follow healthier practices.

I'm certain, with Jensen, this kind of organized political resistance is vital for social change. But unlike Jensen, I'm certain that an *equally necessary* form of organized political resistance arises from a groundswell of collective lifestyle change. We must remember that the root of politics is *polis*—people, not politicians or laws—and that organizing culturally defiant, lifestyle-changing parallel societies has been the modus operandi of such transformative movement leaders as Dorothy Day, Mahatma Gandhi, Vaclav Havel, Rigoberta Menchu, Thich Nhat Hanh, and Saint Francis of Assisi—not to mention the one who called upon a small group of disciples to follow him and change the world.

THERE'S A TURNING GOING ON

Joanna Macy says there's a powerful movement bubbling just below the surface, something much more profound than the surface that Derrick Jensen observes. She calls it the Great Turning, and this is the wild hope she shares: this Great Turning is not only crucially needed, it's already underway. Huge transitional shifts are already being made every day by countless individuals in all realms of society. Millions of people are freeing themselves from egocentric and ecocidal lifeways to lifeways that honor the Earth and the common good.[7]

Macy articulates three dimensions of the Great Turning, each mutually reinforcing and equally necessary:

Dimension 1: "Holding actions" that reduce damage to Earth and its beings. Holding actions encompass a great variety of pragmatic actions to defend healthy life on Earth: legal measures like "progressive legislation and regulations, political actions and lawsuits" and "direct actions such as boycotts, blockades, whistle-blowing, protesting, and civil disobedience."[8] These holding actions seem to be the "organized political resistance" that Derrick Jensen urges—immediate efforts to curtail the most damaging aspects of our industrial society. But while Jensen sees holding actions as the sole focus of what we should be doing, Macy sees them as a crucial stopgap, providing time to do the vital work of the other two domains of the Great Turning: envisioning and implementing a life-sustaining society.

Dimension 2: Analysis of structural causes of destruction and creation of alternative institutions. We must investigate the inner workings of our industrial growth society, comprehend how its seductive and destructive mechanisms work, and then create alternative social institutions. Bill Plotkin, in *Nature and the Human Soul*, notes that countless individuals involved in the Great Turning are already crafting new life-sustaining structures and practices in all our major cultural establishments: economies, food and energy systems, government, religion, parenting, and education.[9]

Dimension 3: Fundamental shifts in personal worldview, values, and practice. This dimension is the most basic, Macy asserts, as the courageous resistance and creative new alternatives needed for the Great Turning cannot take root and flourish without deeply ingrained values and spirituality to sustain them.[10]

The Great Turning needed today is not just about urgent political protest; it is equally about organizing a groundswell of *collective lifestyle change* through new worldviews, transformative practices, and alternative structures. And so, Derrick Jensen, I am here to tell you that I won't forget shorter showers.

I won't forget composting toilets and buying less plastic. These actions are not just personal. When organized and disciplined, they become deeply political, and can be revolutionary.

How? Jensen tells us that wasteful corporations and industry are the chief culprits of climate devastation, and that personal changes in consumption won't matter. In doing so he overlooks an essential truth: an industry's degree of success—and its degree of destructiveness—is utterly dependent upon millions of us buying its stuff. When organized people and businesses make independent choices and stop buying, then industries stop producing, and when they stop producing, they stop polluting.

The bottom line is what Gandhi taught us all along: even in the face of empire, you still control your choices. He showed just how politically potent our personal lifestyle changes can be when shared, spread, and organized.

TIME FOR A MOREWITHLESS FEST

Longacre's *Living More with Less* is one small part of the Great Turning. Although the book's influence may have gone underground in the last three decades, the "living more with less" ethic is by no means gone. Many Mennonites I hang out with in Albuquerque have continued quietly to practice this ethic in their lives through cohousing, reinvesting in neglected neighborhoods, economic redistribution, community gardens, bicycle lifestyles, and tiny home construction. Like leaven in the loaf, expectant and percolating, *more with less* waits to infuse the whole of society when the conditions are right.

Are the conditions right today? Sure seems like it. A few years ago, my Menno friends and I started asking, does *more with less* have something to say to our society today? Might it encourage a new kind of connection in the larger community? Is it time to go big? From these questions emerged the MoreWithLess Fest

2013. Mennos worked with other community groups interested in healthy localized living, such as the Albuquerque Alternative Energy Enthusiasts, to spread and celebrate the more-with-less ethic. Passionate neighborhood folks shared solar power demonstrations and water conservation techniques; others offered compost bin construction and bike maintenance workshops. Urban homesteaders displayed rooftop veggie gardens and a two-story chicken coop on wheels. I brought some flint corn we'd grown, a hand-grinder, boiling water, and a portable griddle, and on the spot we made corn cakes slathered with butter and honey.

This was nothing revolutionary, nothing remarkable. Yet it was profound. More than anything, Mennonites—joining with scores of other folks representing their own traditions and disciplines—were simply declaring *this is the new normal*. It was quiet and joyful community cultural resistance.

After the success of our MoreWithLess Fest, I began to pay more attention to community initiatives happening elsewhere. I began hearing about a similar but much larger phenomenon bubbling up in hundreds of places all over the globe: the Transition movement. As I learned more, I became convinced this movement was something churches needed to know about. Excited, I began writing an article to introduce Christians to the Transition movement—but then I discovered it had already been done.

CHRISTIAN, MEET TRANSITION

Living within a dominant culture bent upon overextraction, overproduction, and overconsumption, North American Christians need to reclaim the ancient practice of Sabbath. But pastor and writer Ric Hudgens urges us not to settle for a legalistic and compartmentalized kind of Sabbath; Sabbath must be broader and more systemic than just taking a day off.

Christians need to live out Sabbath as a "revolutionary practice contrary to everything that the global economy demands."
Hudgens suggests that instead of being our temporary respite,
a transformative practice of Sabbath could become the primary
form of communal resistance in the near future for Christians
living in the midst of a mad world.

Where might Christians find this kind of Sabbath being
lived out during these uncertain times we live in? One bright
spot is the Transition movement, an international grassroots
network of communities working toward a post-carbon society, equipping local communities to deal with the challenges of
climate change and diminishing oil reserves.

Transition is not an individualized philosophy but rather
a community movement. Similar to discipleship, you cannot
just *believe* in Transition, you must *do* Transition. Its key practice is not a vague sense of sustainability but rather *measurable*
community resilience. As Hudgens observes, the movement
centers not upon "creation care" but rather upon a retooling
of the economy called "energy descent." Hudgens spells it out:
"Human energy use, which began a rapid ascension with the
Industrial Revolution and has been climbing madly ever since,
must now start descending—and learn how to keep descending.
Resilience—the ability of a system to negotiate disturbance and
thrive while restructuring, experiencing hardship, and undergo-
ing significant change—becomes the primary attribute of value,
and the key to survival." In Transition terms, resilience is the
capacity of a local community to adjust well as the environment
around it rapidly shifts.[11]

What might human life look like, what might modern society look like, what might Christian community life look like
without depending upon cheap oil and rabid consumerism? The
Transition movement is one place to find hope, for its paradigm

envisions a post-carbon world beyond globalization that is not a barren, apocalyptic nightmare. As Ric Hudgens says, today's Christians can begin right now to live into this coming Sabbath "with the deep conviction that this will not be a lesser life than we have lived, but in fact a better life, a more beautiful life, a more abundant life."[12]

Once I found an article introducing Christians to Transition, I figured a book would not be long in coming. Soon it arrived— a thin volume, concise and compelling. *Transition Movement for Churches*, written by Tim Gorringe and Rosie Beckham, fittingly emerges from the United Kingdom, and begins by explaining how Transition was first ignited.

THE IGNITION OF TRANSITION

The Transition movement began with a teacher, a class, and a movie, when Rob Hopkins showed *The End of Suburbia* to his permaculture students in Kinsale, Ireland. The movie points out that in the 1950s, when North America was self-sufficient and producing enough oil for its needs, an oil geologist named M. King Hubbard predicted to a disbelieving world that American oil would run out by the early 1970s. By the early part of this century, his prophecy had come devastatingly true: the United States produced only 2 percent of the oil it consumed.[13] What were America and other overdeveloped, oil-dependent nations to do in order to fuel their ravenous oil-based economies? Countries like Canada and the United States faced a daunting dilemma: we have no more oil, yet we are completely dependent upon oil, especially for food. As expanding economies like China and India continue to grow, the demand for oil worldwide continues to increase. Big problem. What to do?

Rather than asking citizens to *reduce* their consumption in any way—for reduced consumption would be considered un-American—the United States aggressively sought alternative oil sources. So did Canada. For example, in a rather progressive move, the administration of George W. Bush mandated that 40 percent of the domestic maize crop should be processed for fuel. Canada, in a different strategy, searched for alternative methods to extract oil; somehow, the nation decided it would be ethically acceptable and economically viable to extract oil from tar sands, even though the process is fiscally expensive and environmentally destructive.[14] As of 2015, it seems the United States has settled on fracking as its response to supply our oil needs, suddenly making oil cheap again in the short term, while polluting precious groundwater.

These responses, though providing short-term gluts of extractive fuels, are perpetuating our planetary energy crisis. These responses do not call on us to reduce in any way, but rather to seek alternate sources, sometimes in very desperate and destructive ways. How can we free ourselves from this trap? Is it even possible? Most of us depend upon oil for transport, food, work, clothing—everything. Our governments, schools, and corporations seem to encourage us to stick with business as usual. In the face of such immense social pressure to continue with business as usual, how can we reinvent our very lives?

Back in Ireland, after viewing the film, Rob Hopkins and his students conceived of an "Energy Descent Plan" for their town of Kinsale, proposing in detail how the town could reinvent itself in terms of food, work, and transportation—essentially, how the town could transition from an oil-soaked reality to a new kind of society in which other forms of energy took the lead. When the town council accepted the plan, Kinsale became the first Transition Town, inaugurating a contagious movement that is spreading across the world.[15]

PUT AWAY THE HAIR SHIRT

Caring for our planet doesn't have to be miserable? Life can actually be *better* with less stuff and less frenzy? This core philosophy from the Transition movement is a promising new message in environmentalist thought. For far too long environmentalists, like angry prophets, have proclaimed depressing messages about stopping the bad rather than choosing something good. In the words of Rob Hopkins, Earth-honoring lifeways all too often come across in a way that is about as appealing as "cold tea and soggy toast."[16]

The Transition movement changes all that. As I wrote in the preface, millions of us moderns are realizing that "the good life" isn't so good; so often, daily life feels frantic, exhausting, out of control. What once was good—personal advancement, increased consumer choices, technological progress—has gone haywire. The Transition movement instead offers a positive vision of enoughness for all: a near future that's "energy-lean, time-rich, less stressful, healthier and happier."[17] It is not about suffering and protesting; it is about finding the good way and walking in it.

Of course we need to stop ecocidal activities. Of course we need to fight against systems. Yet too often we campaign against things and lose sight of where we want to go. I feel so much stronger and positive when I can be *for* something instead of just against, don't you? A great example of this kind of activism comes from the Transition group in Lewes, East Sussex, England. Confronted by a company that wanted to "develop" a key part of the town with high-rises, car parking, and chain stores, the group responded not with protests and petitions but with their own vision of what could be done with the riverside property.[18]

Hundreds and hundreds of Transition communities across the globe are coming together in ways like this to vision the futures of their communities—pragmatic yet inspiring plans for food and farming, housing, industry, medicine and health, education, economy, and energy—and then building the capacity to act on it. These are neither disempowering, apocalyptic scenarios nor pie-in-the-sky fantasies. Rather, these visions of transition address the questions all communities need to ask: What kind of future do we want? How do we build the capacity and the resilience we'll need to get there?

RESILIENCE AND THE WAY

Resilience, the primary goal of the Transition movement, is about embodying Paul's *autarkeia* as a community—knowing we can be content, we can thrive, we can work together to have enough, whether in a time of abundance or scarcity. Ultimately, resilience is a spiritual matter, which is why many Transition communities have members who focus upon *inner Transition*.

How do we bounce back from daunting challenges? How do we maintain a sharing spirit in times of scarcity? How do we deal with despair? These are vital questions for our time. A minister who is a member of Transition Liverpool says, "It seems to me that religion and spirituality have always been about transition."[19]

This comment makes me think about concepts that are at the heart of Christianity: conversion, repentance, awakening, revival, enlightenment, rebirth, renewal, resurrection. All of these have to do with transition and transformation. Transition always affects both inner and outer aspects of reality; it is about changing minds and hearts, as well as changing behaviors, practices, and policies.

Tim Gorringe and Rosie Beckham believe the emphases of the Transition movement are aligned with many of the core emphases of the Christian life.[20] Their book is a compelling invitation calling for Christian communities to get involved in Transition worldwide. Why should Christians engage with the Transition movement, they ask? Because Christians walk a Way that cares about creation, and about our neighbors, and about the generations coming after us into this blessed and broken world. Christianity has much to learn from the grounded hope and transformational energy that Transition embodies; so, too, the Transition movement could learn from the Christian tradition's passion for justice and praxis of forgiveness. A Christian discipleship community aligned with the Transition movement and following the Way of Jesus could become a beacon of resilience, spreading good news and social and environmental justice in its community.[21]

16

GET IN RELATION WITH CREATION

AS A TEENAGER, I lived in my mom's house. I loved her magic refrigerator: no matter how much I took out, she'd have it restocked the next day. She had a great garden just outside, but I was a lazy kid, so instead of getting what I needed for that day from the land, I'd just go pillage her fridge. I'd leave the refrigerator door wide open all day to make it easier for me. Whenever I had the urge, I'd just rifle through it and have a feast. I'd leave scraps all over the table, push trash onto all the chairs, and throw meat to rot on the kitchen floor. Finally, when I was done, I'd take a pitcher of her drinking water and crap in it. Then I'd do the same thing the next day.

Did this actually happen in my parents' house? No. But not so long ago, the obvious hit me: this is what I'm doing. Every day of our lives we dwell in our Mother's house and ravage it. Most of the damage becomes invisible quickly, so each day we whistle a happy tune while we blissfully choke her nostrils, dump plastic into her body, and pay others to rip her flesh for more oil and gas and minerals to fuel our latest desires. The next day everything despoiled has been hidden just out of sight, like a bunch of overflowing trash cans in the side yard after an all-night keg party.

Yesterday in New Mexico I bought bananas originating from Ecuador for nineteen cents each. I almost shouted out loud about such a bargain, but I stopped my tongue—and surely prevented a mad rush to the banana aisle—when I saw this wasn't a sale. *Nineteen cents was simply the customary price* for a piece of fruit that was planted, grown, harvested, packaged, and shipped from thousands of miles away. It was the price for business as usual.

In empire, we imagine our planet as a limitless supermarket that operates for our benefit. Without reflecting upon the repercussions, we think it absolutely normal to have incredibly low prices, ever-restocked shelves, never-ending variety despite the season, and waste that simply disappears. Even if we're frugal, even if we buy organic, even if we conserve, we still see the environment as a commodity for us to use however we wish.

What if we saw the Earth as a living being that has feelings, wants, and needs? If we consider our Earth a living *entity* rather than merely a *commodity*, a whole new set of actions arises. In order for our Earth-destroying practices to change, our *laws* and *attitudes* have to change. Right now we're in the habit of protecting our personal rights and freedoms—but what if we got in the habit of protecting the Earth's rights and freedoms? Like other relational habits we cultivate—going out on a date with your loved one or bringing a pie to a neighbor or going to Grandma's once a week—we need to maintain right relation with creation.

NATURE GETS DOWN

Clearly it was a good year: lush fields, good grain, great harvest. About 2,500 years ago, the author of Psalm 65 was loving his watershed, and he decided to write about it. "You have crowned the year with your bounty," he proclaims. The grasslands are providing rich pasture; the fields are so amazing that they "drip with fatness" (65:11 NASB). The author extols the bounty around him, and in response gives bounteous thanks to God.

If someone from our current culture was the author, the psalm might continue: "The Lord is good. Let the cash roll in! This is going to feed my family and make us a ton of profit. We can store and hoard this bounteous harvest for years, and be more secure than all of our neighbors. Hallelujah!"

The real psalm, however, is very different. Instead of choosing to *commodify* nature, the author *personifies* it. Responding to the bounty laid out before him, the author proclaims, "the hills wrap themselves with joy" (65:12 ISV) and the valleys "shout for joy, yes, they sing" (65:13 NASB).

He's saying the Earth *itself* is happy.

This is not the only time a Scripture writer portrays the Earth having feelings. Rather, personifying nature is a deep part of the cultural consciousness. In one chapter of Isaiah, the mountains and forests burst into happy song (Isaiah 44:23); later the mountains are joyfully singing again, but the author also envisions the trees all clapping their hands (Isaiah 55:12). Elsewhere, in the Psalms, we find it's the rivers that are clapping their hands and the mountains singing together for joy because God is coming to make things right for the Earth (Psalm 98:8-9).

In short, creation is psyched, and showing it. It's undeniable: our sacred Scripture says nature has feelings, and the Earth is happy under certain conditions.

Let the gravity of this sink in: *the Earth is happy under certain conditions.* If this is true, then, as partners in a covenanted bond wouldn't we as God's people want to do our part and be in right relationship with the Earth, just like we would with anyone we love? The ancient Israelites sure did.

TO SERVE AND PROTECT

How much should humans manipulate their environment? This question rears its head in dramatic ways today, since—under our noses—our very life systems of water, soil, and air are eroding due to human manipulation. Rabbi Saul Berman tells us that this question has ancient roots, going right back to the dynamic tension found between two verses in early Genesis.[1]

In the first chapter of Genesis, God blesses the newly created humans, saying: "Be fruitful and increase in number; fill the earth and subdue it. Rule over . . . every living creature" (1:28). Hmm: *Rule over . . . every living creature.* On the surface, this seems to be a divine grant of unexamined, unfettered power, and countless critics throughout history have cited this text to prove the Bible is at fault for—not just in league with, but rather *responsible* for—humanity's long-term habit of exploiting and destroying nature.

But blaming the Bible because of this one line would be a very skewed reading of Scripture. Just one chapter later, God takes the newly created human "and put him into the garden of Eden to cultivate it and keep it." Other translations deepen the meaning of this phrase: God tells the first human in the garden to "work it and guard it," to "care for it and maintain it," to "serve it and to keep it."[2]

Berman emphasizes that, from the earliest pages of Genesis, God imposes upon humans a *sacred servanthood relationship* to the world in which they live. The Earth is yours, says God, but there's a condition; you can only rule the Earth if you first become *anav*—a servant who leads through meekness. Enjoy the blessings *of* my creation, Yahweh seems to be saying, as long as you are a blessing *to* my creation.

THE EARTH SHALL HAVE ITS REST,
AND SOME OTHER RIGHTS, TOO

As the Israelites ended their forty years of wilderness traveling and entered Canaan, Moses reminded them how to relate
to this new land: "For six years you are to sow your fields and
harvest the crops, but during the seventh year let the land lie
unplowed and unused. . . . Do the same with your vineyard and
your olive grove" (Exodus 23:10-11).

After being worked pretty hard, the land deserves a time of
refreshment, Moses reminds his people. This wisdom is scattered throughout the Bible's first five books. To our modern
mindset of continued development and progress, however, this
counsel seems primitive, unrealistic, unbelievable. Don't harvest and consume and extract for a year—come on, who are
you kidding?

Let the land lie unplowed and unused, Moses said. It's
tempting to think this is optional advice, some folksy plant-
ing wisdom in Exodus that could be followed or not. But later,
in Leviticus, any hope that this law is optional is extinguished.
Instead, it's amplified as a mandate from God: "The Lord said
to Moses. . . . The land is to have a year of rest" (Leviticus 25:1,
5). Other translations are even stronger: "The land must have
a year of *complete* rest" and "It must be a year of *complete* rest
for the land."[3]

In short: Developers, desist. Stop the madness, humans.
Curb your constant exploitation. Nature's got inalienable rights.

REDEMPTION AND RESTORATION

"The land must not be sold permanently, because the land is
mine and you reside in my land as foreigners and strangers.
Throughout the land that you hold as a possession, you must
provide for the redemption of the land" (Leviticus 25:23-24).

Drawing meaning from ancient texts in foreign tongues is a fascinating exercise, and this text is one of the most fascinating. This ancient property law from the time of Moses states: for anything you own, "you must provide for the redemption of the land." What does that mean in ancient Hebrew—to provide for the *redemption* of the land? Most likely, this phrase in Leviticus connotes economic redemption. *Redemption* in Hebrew means restoration, once again bringing to wholeness. In the New Living Translation, the phrase "you must provide for the redemption of the land" is translated as "you must grant the seller the right to buy it back." The logic of the next verse then follows: "If a fellow countryman of yours becomes so poor he has to sell part of his property, then his nearest kinsman is to come and buy back what his relative has sold."

Following this economic logic, most translations interpret this passage to mean that a new purchaser of land must grant rights to the kinship community of the people who had previously been living on the land. This is fascinating to me: in this passage, God is *giving rights to place-based communities of poor people* who want to get their land back.

Another possibility is even more fascinating: What if "you must provide for the redemption of the land" meant not *economic* restoration to a former owner but rather *environmental* restoration of the land itself? Modern English translations of this text hold key differences: several versions say the landowner must provide redemption *of* the land, while others say *for* the land, and yet others say the landowner must provide redemption *to* the land.[4]

Wait a minute. Could it be that God, through Torah law, was saying: "Remember that the land is mine, and you are my renters. For all land in your care, you must provide restoration *to* the land"?

I know that I am bucking hundreds of years of historical opinion here. But perhaps prophetic imagination requires doing just that. When you read the Bible deeply, you see evidence that the Bible treats nature not merely as a commodity to be guarded, but as an entity with feelings and rights. My hunch is that in God's ideal society it has always been God's expectation—and a legal mandate—for landowners to provide restoration *to* the land for any abuse they cause. Since ancient times, land-based cultures like the early Israelites understood that land has the right to rest when cultivated, and the right to restoration when violated, because *they knew* their land. They were related to it, intimately connected to it. Our current technocratic and transnational culture—in its unrooted, arrogant, and frantic race to develop, exploit, and extract—knows a region of land only as a commodity to exploit. We must recover a view of the land as a diverse patchwork of ecosystems that we must get to know and then trust.

REWILDING PLACES

Kim Stafford is a gatherer of stories, a craftsman of words, a noted author, and a keen observer of place. He also is a friend and guide who came into my life when I was a student in college. As I prepared for my pilgrimage to the monasteries of Mount Athos as a young man, he wrote me a thoughtful letter addressed "to Todd, afoot, somewhere in Greece," and made me vow to open it sometime during my monthlong journey when I was in wide-open space. What kind of professor would take the time and care to do a kind deed like that for someone he barely knew? One like Kim Stafford, that's who.

Kim is also is a miner of names, sifting through our continent's spotted history and remnants of culture. He tells us how the Kwakiutl people of America's northwest coast gave their places names of character. For them, a place name was a story unto itself, a rich clue, a telling of something that had happened, or happens. Kim gives some examples: "They called one patch of ocean 'Where Salmon Gather.' They called one bend in the river 'Insufficient Canoe.' When the tidal waters receded, two islands were sometimes joined: 'Two Round Things Meeting Now and Then.'"[5]

In the late 1800s, German-American anthropologist Franz Boas recorded these place names in his book *Geographical Names of the Kwakiutl Indians*.[6] Boas was observing Kwakiutl culture even as the first European settlers were just moving into the Kwakiutl territories at the north end of Vancouver Island.[7] Upon reading Boas's century-old book, Kim Stafford reflects that "it is a shock to follow the active [Kwakiutl] names along the beach near Alert Bay—'Tree Standing on Flat Beach,' 'Having Coho Salmon,' 'Sound of Dripping Water,' 'Having Brant Geese'—and then to come to the names of the new white tribe: 'Cannery,' 'Court House,' 'Cemetery,' 'House of White People.'"[8]

"I want to fight my way back in time," Kim writes, "where the new names have not yet pruned away stories with a chain-saw." I do, too. Today's tamed Christians need to know that our tradition was not always uprooted and abstract and heavenly focused, alienated from both Earth and place. Our spiritual an-cestors, the ancient Israelites, were a people close to the land. In Genesis, the writer identifies a man named Anah *not* by his pro-fession, like Baker or Smith, *not* by his father, like Henderson or Johnson, not even by direction, like West or North, but rather by saying, "This is the Anah who discovered the hot springs in the desert while he was grazing the donkeys" (36:24). What does that tell you about people, place, and story? Whether wander-ing or rooted, the names the Israelites gave places were stories unto themselves, rich clues for their children, telling of things that happened to the people. All the ancient Israelites would have known that Massah was "the place of testing," Meribah was "the place of argument," and Bethlehem was "the house of bread."

Kim reminds us that there are still places on our modern sailing maps—usually crossing dangerous shoals to safe water—where it states in bold print: "local knowledge is advised." Even in this displaced era of GPS and smartphone, local knowledge remains essential, perhaps more than ever. As Kim states in his droll manner, "The alternative to local knowledge is shipwreck."[9]

One Kwakiutl place name that entrances both Kim and me, calling across hundreds of years, is "Having Everything Right." It is the name of a meadow, near water, where people gather abundant berries and make good life. It is that kind of place where everyone yearns to dwell, at least for a while. What's interesting to me is that it is a name for *more than one* place. Kim mentions at least two locations, two meadows identified by Boas bearing the same Kwakiutl name. "Having Everything Right," Kim concludes, "is a portable name, an expandable place. It could be what we call earth."[10]

WELCOME TO THE DOCTRINE OF DISCOVERY

What happens when a voracious, expansionist culture encounters a place-based culture like the Kwakiutl, people who have adapted themselves to their particular land over thousands of years? Usually something not good. Somehow Christians have been conquering indigenous people and justifying their actions as godly for hundreds of years.

This is something that a lot of us cozy Christians have a hard time dealing with—but deal with it we must. For those of us today who seek to walk the Way of Jesus, yet also benefit from

European colonization, this history is our legacy, our shadow. What to do? We can't make this shameful inheritance disappear from our past. We can't change it, yet neither can we ignore it. What to do, then? I'm not sure. Maybe, if we understand our colonizing legacy better, we'll be less likely to do damage in our future. One of the first steps we can take is to dig into our history and truly grasp the damage our Christian ancestors have done across the world.

I was introduced to the concept of *terra nullius*—"empty land" in Latin—by Sarah Augustine in 2014 at a gathering of about two dozen Mennonites and friends from across North America. We gathered because we were seeking to understand our own colonizing history better so that we might dismantle some of the worst destructive habits of our modern culture—hardwired habits that even now encourage good people to destroy indigenous cultures and healthy watersheds in the name of progress and growth.

Sarah opened my eyes to a lot of history I did not know well. In the early stages of the Crusades, almost a thousand years ago—1095 to be exact—Pope Urban II set forth a papal bull he entitled *Terra Nullius*. This bold decree gave kings and princes throughout Europe the right to "discover" or claim land as long as it was "empty"—empty of Christians, that is. Building on this foundation over three centuries, the first set of international laws was established in the fourteenth century by expansionist Christian states. Rules had to be created, of course, once European countries began to bump elbows in their zeal to colonize; they didn't want to go to war with each other, after all. Nor did they wish to lose their eternal souls for their unjust deeds. So, the church created very complex, well-researched doctrinal arguments grounded in Scripture to justify the seizure of lands discovered by these Christian "princes." This body of legal and theological justification, termed the Doctrine of Discovery, made seizure and subjugation legal and approved in the eyes of both church and state.

The Doctrine of Discovery grew and mutated over the decades, as colonization became an ever-expanding business. In 1452, Pope Nicholas V issued the bull *Romanus Pontifex*, which declared war on all non-Christians throughout the world and authorized the conquest of their governments and territories. One common thread ran through all of the papal edicts that became part of the Doctrine of Discovery: each law continued to classify non-Christians as uncivilized and subhuman, and therefore *without either rights to land or free will*. Bolstered by these laws, Christian explorers claimed a God-given right to seize control of all lands and used these concepts to justify war, colonization, and even slavery.

By the time Christopher Columbus set sail in 1492, this Doctrine of Discovery was fully embedded, a long-established code of conduct for agents of colonizing Christendom.[11]

NOT ANIMALS, EXACTLY

The Doctrine of Discovery created a legal process that allowed rulers from Christian nations to colonize and claim a place—with the blessing and cooperation of Holy Mother Church—if another European invader had not already done so. Native inhabitants of a "discovered" land were not animals, exactly, but neither were they considered fully human. Rather, they were a different kind of creature. *Terra Nullius* gave European colonizers the legal right to define a new land as "devoid of human life" if not ruled by a Christian prince.

Stop a second. Did you get that? The new land had to be ruled by someone who was *both* a Christian *and* a prince for it to be seen as off-limits for colonization.

So what about the rights of the original inhabitants of a "discovered" land? They were not quite human, clarified the Vatican, but they could be baptized. Once Christianized, they gained the right to occupancy, but not sovereignty. This means native peoples who had lived in a place *perhaps thousands of years* had the right to continue to exist there without being massacred, but the colonizers reserved the right to control them.

Such nakedly unjust decrees couldn't stand out in the open forever in cultures that claimed to follow a nonviolent Lord; at some point, I'm guessing that some Christians started feeling a little guilty. So in 1573—long after colonization had taken place successfully worldwide—Pope Paul II issued the papal bull *Sublimis Deus*, which denounced the idea that Native Americans "should be treated like irrational animals and used exclusively for our profit and our service." More than fifty years after that, Pope Urban VIII (1623–44) went a step further and formally excommunicated anyone still holding Indian slaves.

Such corrective measures, however, were too little too late; the Doctrine of Discovery had already rooted itself into the European consciousness and was justifying the continued colonization and conquest of non-Christian lands and people throughout the world.[12]

WATCH OUT: THE NUNS ARE COMING

This horrific legacy is difficult for us moderns to deal with. Lucky for us, it's completely in the past. The Doctrine of Discovery— what a medieval and unenlightened set of rules, huh? What an outdated Christian justification for blatant, self-serving exploitation and oppressive greed, right? How primitive. Sure is nice to know the enlightened, diverse civilization we have today is so much more evolved than in that era.

Except we're not. Guess when the Doctrine of Discovery was last cited to justify action in a legal case? 2005.[13] Its continued influence—both overt and surreptitious—continues to influence how indigenous, land-based peoples are treated by those who are driven by the diseases of affluenza and colonization. It's enough to get a lot of people mad.

In November 2014, an American nun hand-delivered a letter to Pope Francis's ambassador in Washington, D.C. Sister Maureen Fiedler was her name, and in the letter she and many others urged the new pope to renounce the medieval papal documents comprising the Doctrine of Discovery. As of this writing, she isn't sure if the letter made it to the Vatican. And she knows the Vatican has written later bulls and papal apologies attempting to show the church no longer supports the doctrine. But she's hopeful that her letter—a resolution by the Leadership Conference of Women Religious—will spur this pope to repudiate these five-hundred-year-old church documents that justify the colonization and oppression of indigenous peoples.

"When I learned about it, I was horrified," said Fiedler. She's a member of the Loretto Community, a congregation of religious women and laypeople who seem to be serious about authentic discipleship and naming their own tradition's dark side. Just recently, they marked their two hundredth anniversary by challenging the religious sanctioning of Christian enslavement and power over non-Christians. Hence the letter.

The ancient Doctrine of Discovery continues to exert significant influence upon modern North American culture even now, Fiedler asserts. Its colonizing attitude shows up in seemingly small ways, like the use of Native Americans as sports mascots. The *Huffington Post* states the Doctrine of Discovery "has justified efforts to eliminate indigenous languages, practices and worldviews, and it affects Native American sovereignty and treaty obligations."[14]

These nuns—and our small group of Mennonites, who met up to learn from Sarah Augustine—are by no means the first groups seeking to dismantle the Doctrine of Discovery. We're just the latest to get on a long-standing bandwagon. Indigenous groups have sought to overturn the doctrine since at least 1984. In 2007, the United Nations condemned policies like the Doctrine of Discovery as "racist, scientifically false, legally invalid, morally condemnable and socially unjust."[15] In the last ten years, Christians from all walks of life have made their opposition heard, including the United Methodist Church, the Unitarian Universalist Association, the Episcopal Church, the World Council of Churches, several Quaker meetings, and the United Church of Christ.[16]

You may be thinking to yourself, what good can come of denouncing some ancient documents? I'm with you. Until recently, I've been thinking: sure, apologies can be made. Documents can be denounced. But terrible things still happened, and they can't be erased. What's done is done.

But recently I've come to believe that denouncing the Doctrine of Discovery might help us stop our hardwired habits and break with business as usual. For a society to pursue personal gain at the expense of others and the Earth is to behave like a schoolyard bully; it's a dysfunctional adolescent cultural habit that simply has to stop. It's time to grow up, grow into the people God's been waiting for us to be, and live into a larger sense of "the good life"—good for ourselves, others, and the Earth.

17

REDEFINE THE GOOD LIFE

THOUGHT IT WAS Raul's idea at first. It was 2010 and I'd been in Ecuador for a few months, volunteering with a land-based nonprofit that focused upon sustainable agriculture and community development, when my supervisor Raul Cabrera began to tell me about his vision of *buen vivir*, or "the good way of living." Now, by this time I had tagged along with Raul on rain-soaked motorcycle rides into the jungle, analyzed databases for organic sugarcane inspections, sat in on a few meetings of a banana growers' cooperative, and written a speech for him in English. So I was by no means a newcomer. Perhaps by this time I had earned enough trust and respect that he wanted to share with me his expanded vision of *buen vivir*. Maybe it was just that by this time my Spanish had improved enough that we could converse at a fairly complex level.

Whatever the reason, one day Raul pushed aside his archaic laptop in our bamboo-walled office and began to lay out an inspirational lifeway: *buen vivir* for all. *Buen vivir*, he explained, was a far more expansive social vision than the personalized dream we have in the United States—and in Canada and European countries, for that matter—of life, liberty, and the pursuit of happiness. As he talked, it sounded more and more like the kingdom of God. Instead of focusing upon the individual to the possible neglect of others, a practitioner of *buen vivir* takes all of God's creation into account, pursuing a way of living that is good for the self, for one's human community, and for rest of the natural world around us.

After that conversation, I began hearing Raul speak with a lot of his fellow Ecuadorians about *buen vivir*. In fact, it was often on people's lips in meetings and when talking on the street. When Raul was with indigenous villagers, he would call it *sumak kawsay*—their Quichua term for the same concept. How did this idea spread so fast, I wondered. Was Raul some kind of telepathic prophet?

Little did I know, *buen vivir* was a concept that was captivating the nation, but it didn't start with Raul. It started with their new constitution.

WE THE PEOPLE

We women and men, the sovereign people of Ecuador,

RECOGNIZING our age-old roots, wrought by women and men from various peoples,

CELEBRATING nature, the Pacha Mama (Mother Earth), of which we are a part and which is vital to our existence,

INVOKING the name of God and recognizing our diverse forms of religion and spirituality,

CALLING UPON the wisdom of all the cultures that enrich us as a society,

AS HEIRS to social liberation struggles against all forms of domination and colonialism

AND with a profound commitment to the present and to the
future,

Hereby decide to build a new form of public coexistence, in
diversity and in harmony with nature, to achieve *buen vivir,*
the good way of living, the *sumak kawsay* . . .[1]

So begins the Ecuadoran Constitution, rewritten in 2008.
So begins the imperfect, inspiring story of a country daring
to reimagine itself, acting as a prophetic example to other nations who also seek to part ways with outdated and destructive
business-as-usual policies, and instead find a wilder path into
a better future.

Like leaven in the loaf, *buen vivir* is a hard concept to contain. Once it gains a toehold in a culture's consciousness, it can
be contagious. It's particularly attractive to indigenous communities and land-based peoples; not only did the concept first
originate from the *sumak kawsay* philosophy of the Quichua
of Ecuador, it also resonates deeply with any society that holds
harmonious coexistence with the Earth as a core value. This is
hard to prove, but I sense that it is spreading, community by
community, across many parts of Latin America. Could *buen
vivir* sweep its way here? Which communities in North America
might embrace it first? Might even we privileged Christians let
it invade our hearts?

What would it mean to live the inspiring concept of *buen vivir* on a practical and political level? What kinds of laws would
need to be put in place in the United States and Canada to ensure that citizens and businesses—as they seek the good life for
themselves—would also protect the good life for other humans
and for nature itself?

In the United States today, people have legal rights.
Corporations have legal rights. States have rights. But for *buen*

vivir to become a reality, we'll need to shift our thinking and our laws around a particularly ignored section of our legal code: the rights of nature. For some help with this, let's bring our attention back to a nation the size of a postage stamp, small in square miles but giant in its prophetic vision: Ecuador.

THE RIGHTS OF NATURE

This may be old news to you, but I still reel, even a few years after hearing it: Ecuador was the first country in the world to affirm specific rights of nature in its constitution.[2]

How did such an unprecedented thing happen? Following his election as president, Rafael Correa called for a national referendum to write a new constitution for the country. The 2007 referendum passed with over 80 percent approval; a constitutional assembly was formed and was given six months to craft a new constitution. Eventually, in September 2008, the new constitution was voted into existence, approved by nearly two-thirds of Ecuador's registered voters.

What does it mean to give nature legal rights? Rather than treat nature as property in the eyes of the law, the new constitution holds that nature, in all its myriad forms, has the legal right "to exist, persist, maintain and regenerate its vital cycles." The citizens of Ecuador have the legal authority to enforce these rights on behalf of threatened places and ecosystems. In case this isn't clear, let me be blunt: the ecosystem *itself* can be named as the defendant.[3]

SO FAR . . . SO GOOD?

Ecuador's visionary constitution has now been in place several years. So how has it changed society so far? Has the commitment to *buen vivir* for all made everything good for indigenous folks, even after centuries of repeated exploitation by colonizers following the Doctrine of Discovery?

Of course not. CONAIE, Ecuador's largest confederation of indigenous peoples, makes it clear that their struggle for respect, rights, and justice did not begin and end with the adoption of the new constitution. However, they do believe that proclaiming a national vision of *buen vivir* for all is a historically significant step, and that this constitution provides some new legal tools that are useful in the struggle for a more just and Earth-honoring society.[4]

And how about Ecuador's threatened rain forests and watersheds? Now that nature has been given rights in the constitution, are all vulnerable ecosystems being protected and all damaged areas restored to health? Hardly. Ecuador's implementation of the Rights of Nature has been spotty at best; as you might imagine, it takes tremendous vigilance, funding, staffing, and policing to defend nature from industrial society's long-ingrained corporate habits of careless extraction and pollution.

Perhaps more than pragmatic, Ecuador's constitution is powerfully symbolic. It is one nation among many daring to say enough, daring to break from business as usual. Its constitution opened a doorway for other bold proclamations, for even wilder prophetic imagination, for ever-greater inner authority. Check this out.

BIGGER THAN ECUADOR: THE ETHICS TRIBUNAL

"We will investigate cases of environmental destruction which violate the Rights of Nature." So spoke Ramiro Avila, prosecutor for the Earth, as he opened the world's first Ethics Tribunal on the Rights of Nature in January 2014. He was the chief prosecutor; perpetrators of environmental ruin across the globe were to be the defendants.[5]

Wait a minute. What do these people think they are doing, investigating corporate acts of environmental devastation as if they were genocidal war crimes or something? Who gave them the authority?

"We the people *assume the authority* to conduct an ethics tribunal," Avila stated a moment later in his opening remarks. *Somebody* needs to hold gross environmental criminals responsible, asserted the ten international judges representing seven countries and five continents; this first time around, it might as well be us. Vandana Shiva, internationally renowned author, physicist, and environmental activist, presided over the unprecedented tribunal, which considered nine cases of extreme human-caused environmental damage. Cases investigated included British Petroleum's horrific oil spill in the Gulf of Mexico, Ecuacorriente's open-pit mining in Ecuador's Condor Mountains, the significant injury done to Australia's Great Barrier Reef by coastal coal ports, and damage caused by hydraulic fracking at various locations in the United States. The tribunal intends to be "a permanent platform for hearing and judging cases from around the world."[6]

Will something as lofty as a worldwide "Ethics Tribunal on the Rights of Nature" ever become something real, with teeth, forcing our worst environmental abusers to pay up and restore damaged ecosystems to better health? Or will people in the near future laugh at the fact that, back in 2014, someone was loony enough to dare to assume the title of "prosecutor for the Earth"? It all depends upon how serious we get about treating the Earth as an entity, and how deeply we decide to rewild the law.

REWILDING THE LAW

What if nature had rights? This question was famously raised over forty years ago by a law professor in California as he concluded his lecture. "Yes, rivers, lakes, trees. . . . How could such a posture in law affect a community's view of itself?"

As Cormac Cullinan noted in his 2008 article "If Nature Had Rights," students stared in disbelief at USC professor Christopher Stone when he raised the question: "Professor Christopher Stone may as well have announced that he was an alien life form. Rivers and trees are objects, not subjects, in the eyes of the law and are by definition incapable of holding rights. His speculations created an uproar."[7]

Despite resistance, Stone didn't let go of his mission to rewild the law and give nature legal standing. He found a current legal case, which poignantly raised these issues, and jumped on it. A vulnerable place was being aggressively developed by the Walt Disney Corporation—the Mineral King Valley in the Sierra Nevada Mountains. If the Mineral King Valley itself had been recognized as having rights, it would clearly be considered an "aggrieved party," deserving of some level of restorative compensation; but because the Sierra Club was the bringer of the suit, the valley received no protection, because—even though the valley was being ravaged—the Sierra Club *itself* was not being adversely affected. Using this case study of environmental injustice, Professor Stone wrote an opinion paper titled "Should Trees Have Standing? Toward Legal Rights for Natural Objects." Cullinan sums up the argument this way: "Stone argued that courts should grant legal standing to guardians to represent the rights of nature, in much the same way as guardians are appointed to represent the rights of infants. In order to do so, the law would have to recognize that nature was not just a conglomeration of objects that could be owned, but was a subject that itself had legal rights and the standing to be represented in the courts to enforce those rights."[8]

Supreme Court justice William O. Douglas caught wind of Stone's wild and mind-expanding proposal. Cullinan tells us that "Should Trees Have Standing?" became the basis for Judge Douglas's groundbreaking dissenting judgment in a 1972 case, in which he suggested legal standing be given to inanimate natural objects about to be "despoiled, defaced, or invaded by roads and bulldozers and where injury is the subject of public outrage." I want to repeat this, because even now I find it hard to believe: more than four decades ago, a United States Supreme Court justice was advocating for profound rights of nature. Douglas continued his enlightened legal argument with a persuasive prose that borders on poetry. He begins by naming other inanimate objects that have legal rights:

> A ship has a legal personality, a fiction found useful for maritime purposes. The corporation . . . is an acceptable adversary and large fortunes ride on its cases. . . . So it should be as respects valleys, alpine meadows, rivers, lakes, estuaries, beaches, ridges, groves of trees, swampland, or even air that feels the destructive pressures of modern technology and modern life. The river, for example, is the living symbol of all the life it sustains or nourishes—fish, aquatic insects, water ouzels, otter, fisher, deer, elk, bear, and all other animals, including man, who are dependent on it or who enjoy it for its sight, its sound, or its life. The river as plaintiff speaks for the ecological unit of life that is part of it.[9]

Wild, is it not? The idea of giving nature legal rights may still seem outlandish to you—a proposition only tree huggers would take seriously. In our corporation-controlled culture, you may be so captive to the status quo that you can't imagine a world where coastlines can be treated as legal beings. But we humans will only flourish in the future by changing our legal systems and claiming our identity, and responsibility, as members of a much larger Earth community.

There are wild possibilities in the wind, my friends: a profound rethinking of our legal system that might recognize rights of nature; inspiring constitutional changes in a country far away; and a contagious philosophy called *buen vivir* that promotes a good way of living for the self, the human community, and the larger world. These are global memes, abstract concepts that dwell in the realm of issues and ideology.

Little did I know these incendiary ideas would erupt in my own backyard.

CLOSER TO HOME: COMMUNITY RIGHTS IN MORA COUNTY

In 2013, the county right next door to mine became the first in the United States to ban fracking. That's right: knowing they'd raise eyebrows and rumple corporate suits, the commissioners of Mora County, New Mexico, took authority into their own hands and banned hydraulic fracturing, or "fracking," the nasty, invasive extractive technique that involves shooting a mixture of water, chemicals, and sand deep underground to release oil or natural gas trapped in layers of rock.

As industrial society becomes more desperate for diminishing oil reserves, fracking becomes an option of choice for corporations eager to get their hands on oil. The environmental ruin associated with fracking wasn't a consequence Mora County wanted to accept. Residents of the county have always relied upon agriculture and forestry and prioritized the conservation of both land and traditional culture. Over months of meetings, residents made clear to their commissioners that they wanted to protect their land-based heritage. "If you allow industry to come into your community, it changes the dynamics of the culture," explained county commissioner John Olívas. "I don't think we're ready for that."[10]

My friend Ernie Atencio often gets drawn into situations like this one. He's a rare breed: brown skin in a green movement that is mostly white. As a Hispanic environmentalist in northern New Mexico who cares deeply about protecting both land and culture, he's often at the center of potential conflicts and innovative negotiations. Serving as the head of the Taos Land Trust for several years, he helped protect thousands of acres from development and struck a fine balance between conservation, community needs, and commercial reality.

Ernie's a journalist, too. So when a nearby community in New Mexico became the first county in the whole country to say no to fracking, the *High Country News* sent Ernie over to Mora to investigate. Ernie met with County Commissioner Olívas, the man behind the ban. John Olívas, forty-three, whose family was among the original settlers of the Mora Land Grant in 1835 when it was still part of Mexico, lives in the house his great-grandparents built two hundred years ago. He is also a hunter turned wilderness advocate turned county commissioner, and, like Ernie, he is a brown person in a green movement made up of mostly white folks. As Ernie observes, traditional Hispanics in northern New Mexico often shy away from typical Anglo environmentalism. In the late 1990s, Ernie explains, "environmental activists often came off as villians in racially charged fights over public-lands grazing and community access to firewood."[11] So Olívas sometimes has to step carefully as he does his best to protect the long-term interests of the community he loves.

For his news article, Ernie talked with John Olívas about Mora County's unprecedented decision. Olívas and others in his community are concerned that fracking and other invasive methods of oil-and-gas extraction will use too much water and pollute the life systems that their place-based community depends on to thrive. "We grow our own food," he explained to Ernie. "We burn our own wood. People come to Mora for the landscape and the clean water and the clean air." Fracking would end all that.

As a teen, Olívas would go bowhunting for elk alone in the peaks of the nearby Pecos Wilderness. These rites of passage rooted Olívas in nature and taught him to appreciate the gift and protect the world we've been given. "That's where I think I got into the naturalist part of me," Olívas remembers. "You'd go up there and you'd build a fire, you'd have to get wood, you'd have to do all the essentials of life."[12]

Community-asserting rights certainly raise eyebrows, because for decades our legal system has largely let corporations do what they want, where they want. "A lot of people asked, 'Who in the heck is this small community up in northern New Mexico that's picking a fight with oil and gas?'" Olívas remembers.[13] Mora County made a daring move; like Ecuador, it assumed authority and broke from business as usual.

Will the ban hold? So far—but it hangs by a thread. In October 2014, the ban was upheld, but by a two-to-one margin, and Olívas has been voted out of office for 2015. Lawsuits are pending from both corporations and landowners. Opponents of the ordinance say the ban is unconstitutional because it infringes on individual property rights and restricts the rights that corporations enjoy.[14] "We knew we were going to get sued," Olívas says. People in Mora County knew what they were getting into and plan to fight, with help from larger nonprofits. This is not a battle to enter lightly; experts don't expect the issue to be resolved for five to seven years.[15]

Here's a question for you: Does a community have the right to protect itself and the land it depends upon from permanent damages caused by fracking, even if it defies the desires of profit-seeking individuals or corporations? Does the long-term protection of a place trump the short-term interests of individuals and businesses? What if it was *your* land, *your* water, and *your* air being threatened? These questions are at the heart of the society we need to become, the sense of *buen vivir* we might choose to embrace, the Earth-honoring faith we might choose to adopt.

18

PRACTICE WATERSHED DISCIPLESHIP

WHAT DOES A TRANSFORMATIVE, Earth-honoring
Christianity look like at ground level, lived out in daily
action? Reforms of personal habits—such as recycling
and eating locally and shopping responsibly—are important
steps. But we'll need to embody a much more vibrant Christian
environmental ethic if we are to become the people God's been
yearning for us to be, and address the overwhelming ecological
crisis facing us today. We'll need to do something wild, and take
on the yoke of watershed discipleship.

Watershed discipleship? It's an intriguing, provocative term
that blends two domains rarely joined in our imaginations: one
scientific, the other religious. Yet it's this kind of paradigm—
both data driven and deeply spiritual, ancient and new—that
Christians will need to be part of in the upcoming decades if we
are to play any significant role in our planet's healing.

What is watershed discipleship? It's a movement and a
framework and a practice that is being worked out, on the
ground, in many locations. Activist and theologian Ched Myers
gives the term two meanings, and I've added a third.[1] In a nut-
shell, watershed discipleship can be seen as:

Being disciples during *this watershed moment.* At this crucial turning point in history, our choice is between responsive discipleship and reactive denial. We can't pretend any longer: God's Earth is not just our grab bag and our trash can, to do with however we will. There are consequences to our actions. "The interlocking crises of global warming, diminishing resources, peak 'everything,' and widening ecological degradation compel us to make environmental justice and sustainability integral to *everything* we do as disciples," asserts Myers.[2]

Being disciples within *our watersheds.* Wendell Berry warns us that abstract concepts such as "saving nature," "global thinking," or "creation care" are well intentioned but achieve little unless rooted in *actual landscapes.* The real question, Berry states, "is not how to care for the planet, but how to care for each of the planet's millions of human and natural neighborhoods, each of its millions of small pieces and parcels of land, each one of which is in some precious way different from all the others."[3] Myers suggests that followers of Jesus today must be people of specific places, who root their prayers and practices in actual watersheds of care.

Being disciples of *our watersheds.* Becoming an engaged citizen of a particular place—experiencing its characteristics and being formed by its constraints, its seasons, its bounty, and its boundaries—is the primary task of watershed discipleship. It is the "re-placed" identity we as a species must rediscover if we are to unshackle ourselves from the ecocidal, dis-placed path of empire. More than just memorizing a few facts about our locales, we need to go to school on our surroundings, as the ancients did, and become disciples who learn core life truths from our own home places. We need to take up the yoke of our watershed and treat our region as rabbi.

I realize my attempts to explain watershed discipleship are more *descriptive* than *prescriptive*. That's because watershed discipleship is fluid; it remains a work in progress, an intriguing and powerful concept only discovered and defined as we live it out in our places each day. Here are some thoughts from my practice in northern New Mexico.

REGION AS RABBI

This is the vital adult education of our time—to become "re-placed" in our watersheds. Ched Myers cites Senegalese environmentalist Baba Dioum as saying, "We will not save a place we do not love. We cannot love a place we do not know."[4] To love a place, we must first know it. This means paying attention to it: its seasons, its species, its attributes, its boundaries, and its attitudes.

I took on the yoke of my watershed about five years ago. What could it teach me about how to live as a place-based person? As I learn to re-inhabit the place I live, I see my region as my rabbi in three specific ways: as sustainer, teacher, and corrector.

Try on this idea: my watershed can provide all of my food needs. Sounds crazy? It does to me. Sure, most humans throughout history were sustained by their watersheds, but those were primitive people, right? What about my Italian Parmesan and my Florida orange juice? What about my olive oil and coconut milk?

Can all the items my family loves be sourced in my bioregion? Of course not. But this question leads me to two others: First, what *can* be sourced from our watershed? In the high deserts of New Mexico where I live, the answer is bleak. For us to obtain the foods we love, I'd have to drive hundreds of miles before I found the first orange tree or avocado orchard. This leads me to a second question: To what extent can we become creatures who thrive within the limits of our bioregion? In other words, to what extent can we *adapt*?

Wait—*me*, adapt to my watershed? As an entitled American caught up in affluenza, this idea is not only absurd, it's scandalous. I buy *whatever* I want, *whenever* I want, without a second thought to planetary consequences. Limit my lifestyle? Adjust my appetite? *I'm an American, dammit!*

Yet my watershed, like any good rabbi, corrects my spoiled behavior. Just like in any master-apprentice relationship, my rabbi corrects me as part of my training, just as a master reforms an inappropriate disciple. This is a true conversion, *metanoia*, the same kind of shift that early followers of Jesus underwent. They were taught to walk away from the self-protecting, self-promoting values of empire and instead to care for the poor, love their neighbors, give riskily, pay attention to nature around them, and trust in daily bread. These ancient precepts are central to the Jesus Way; they are equally central to the teachings of my watershed. They cause me to look anew at the two troubling and transformative questions I raised earlier: What *can* my watershed provide? How can I adapt my wants?

AN ECCENTRIC EXPERIMENT

A few years ago, some neighbors and I decided to have some fun with these questions. Instead of bemoaning northern New Mexico's arid high country, we began to explore what food sources *could* thrive in our dry mountain environment. With a perverse joy, we began to break from empire-based thinking and see if we could be happy with what our watershed provided. My ranching friend, Daniel, managed small herds over the years to see which livestock could thrive with minimal inputs while being maximally useful to us. What has he found?

Goats and sheep, we keep. They adapt well to our bioregion, are manageable, and provide milk, cheese, meat, kefir, and yogurt. Yaks? Not so much. After years of experimentation and hard work, Daniel concluded they're more trouble than they're worth. As for vegetables and fruits, we've found success with plenty of the usual fare—carrots, onions, garlic, beets, tomatoes, zucchini, apples, plums, and greens galore. Also, under the guidance of my mentor gardener, Seth, I've adapted my habits and taste buds. I now appreciate hand-ground cornmeal, new types of beans, high-altitude quinoa, plum preserves, wild amaranth and lamb's-quarter, sorrel, kale chips, broccoli leaves, and new varieties of squash and potatoes.

I'm finding many of my current life practices—habits formed unconsciously within a culture of excess—have no part in the life of a watershed disciple, nor of a serious Jesus follower. Even as I adapt, however, a part of me wants to remain an unconscious and self-absorbed consumer. Do you feel it, too? We both know it's easier to remain a spoiled child rather than mature into a responsible adult. Yet in this "watershed" moment in history—with humanity's existence in the balance—it's clear our watersheds call us to do something old-school: *repent*, turn around. To what extent can we thrive within the bounty—and the boundaries—of our bioregions? We'll only know when we start trying.

But what's a demand that is doable? What's a change that is challenging but won't cause our families and our friends to run away in fear? I have an idea.

TOWARD A BIOREGIONAL FOOD COVENANT

If we are to survive much longer as a species, many of us addicted to unbounded affluenza need to make this question central to our lives. As David Orr writes, "It makes far better sense to reshape ourselves to fit a finite planet than to attempt to re-shape the planet to our infinite wants."[5]

How can we, habituated to global gluttony, begin to reshape ourselves as Orr suggests? Let me suggest a practical challenge that might be contagious: the 25/75/100 Bioregional Food Covenant.[6] What's daunting about this is that I've never done it before. What's inspiring about this is that millions of people across the globe are already doing it, whether they're conscious of it or not.

To join, an individual would make this pledge: "By the year 2025, I will source 75 percent of my food from within a hundred miles." Can such a modest personal vow really make a big dif-ference? In the face of the crises we face on a global scale, a one-person vow like this may seem insignificant. But think again: if a critical mass of us joins in, this humble promise could change how humans live on our planet. Let us count the ways.

It enriches local economies. Thousands of families commit-ting to "local for the long term" establish new demand and new markets, creating an incubator for regional companies to grow, sell, and distribute good food within their communities. Hard-earned cash becomes "slow money"—money that circu-lates within the region for a longer period of time. This causes healthier exchange cycles for local goods and services, creating more local food hubs. Right now, there are few local growers and very little local food available in America, because most of us don't demand it.

It corrects our crazy consumption. Sourcing much of our food locally means adapting to our watershed, letting *it* instruct *us* how to be. It means learning to live within healthy natural limits. It means no longer being able to buy *whatever* I want *whenever* I want from *wherever* I want, without a second thought to plan-etary consequences.

It improves individual health. Kale or Krispy Kreme? This is not a fair comparison, but the point is this: when communities encourage one another to eat food produced from the land, better health is likely to develop. Affordable access to farm-fresh food is a promising antidote to many of modern society's illnesses.

It reduces our dependence on petroleum, packaging, and pollution. Currently the majority of mega-chain food travels a thousand miles or more to reach your local grocery store. Massive amounts of petroleum are used to improve soil and to grow, process, store, preserve, package, and deliver food that could be grown and transported within a few miles of home. Reduced travel and storage means reduced packaging and pollution.

It builds basins of relations across race and class. Brock Dolman reminds us that all of us on the planet live in "basins of relations"; everything we do—drive, work, play, go to school, shop, farm, worship, or sleep—occurs within a watershed somewhere.[7] It makes me wonder, what if those who could afford it supported a bioregional food covenant for themselves *and* for another family who wanted to join but couldn't afford it without some assistance? What if congregations or schools or clubs became communities of care and were able to offer this opportunity for *all* their members?

It improves bioregional citizenship. Once we start eating from our bioregion, we start caring about its health—because the water, soil, and air are feeding our food. We see the beautiful complexity of the interconnected living systems required to produce good food. We start organizing in creative and clarifying ways, like the New Mexico Coalition for Community Rights. This group encourages regional groups to adopt community bills of rights like Mora County did, asserting that corporations are not above people and declaring that all citizens of a watershed have an inalienable right to clean air and clean water.

It boosts "community resilience." This is the ability of your home region to thrive in the face of changes and shocks from the outside, as articulated by Transition movement founder Rob Hopkins. A bioregional food covenant supported by community organizations builds local capacity and infrastructure, reduces dependency upon external providers, promotes sustainability, and increases biological diversity.

"By the year 2025, I will source 75 percent of my food from within a hundred miles"; in writing this, I'm making a personal promise. I'm not promising to organize a national movement or maintain a busy website to assist you. But I am promising to change my personal behavior over time. How about you? Right now, as we transition to become watershed people, this is one of the most important things we can do.

ANCIENT VALUES, HIGH-TECH TOOLS: YEAR-ROUND FARMING AT TAOS PUEBLO

Think the local food movement is a fad for elite yuppies and homesteading hipsters? Think again. Meet the Red Willow Growers Cooperative: Taos Pueblo food producers who use cutting-edge technologies to promote the place-based values that have sustained their culture for a thousand years.

The Red Willow Farmers Market is a high-desert haven providing abundant food year-round at 7,100 feet above sea level. Located next to two substantial greenhouses and an educational building on Pueblo lands just minutes from downtown Taos, the market is open Wednesdays year-round and offers grass-fed beef, seasonal produce, eggs, fresh bread, fruits in season, jams, jellies, and soaps. From their rangeland nearby, the Taos Pueblo War Chief's Office provides local buffalo, which is USDA certified, 100 percent grass fed, and sustainably produced. In summer, the farmers' market is both indoor and outdoor, with several vendor tables and an outdoor grill; off-season, it moves inside and is more limited.

The farmers' market operation is impressive by itself. More remarkable are the on-site sustainable greenhouses that grow fresh produce even in deep winter. Angelo McHorse, Red Willow's farm manager, knows the systems well. He needs to. His livelihood—and the well-being of hundreds of other members of his bioregion—depends on it.

This past winter, he took me to the heart of Red Willow's heated greenhouse system. Passing by stacks of locally harvested piñon logs, he swung open the thick round metal door of the GARN biomass heater to reveal a chamber that would soon hold a blazing fire. This high-tech heater is the heart of a complex, sustainable heating system that allows agriculture to thrive even as temperatures plunge. Angelo showed me how the GARN system works: Over three thousand gallons of liquid swirl in a steel chamber surrounding the firebox, getting extremely hot. The superheated liquid then shoots into pipes and travels underground to warm the two greenhouses and two other buildings on site. All the particulates from the piñon fire are burned off as the smoke travels into the second core of the system—a superheated ceramic tube—making the system almost smoke-free.

In search of food sovereignty and regional food security, Red Willow uses high-tech tools to achieve traditional goals. The GARN biomass heater is but one of several innovative systems that make the project a regional model in adaptive, climate change–sustainable farming.

As we walked, Angelo showed me several other sustainable systems: a series of fans that siphon hot air from the top of the greenhouse into an underground piping system in order to prevent ground freezing; cellulose insulation made from news-paper, insulating the market's walk-in cooler; and solar panels providing energy for drip and irrigation systems.

Red Willow's mixture of traditional values and cutting-edge techniques is also influencing younger generations at Taos Pueblo through after-school and summer youth pro-grams started by education director Shawn Duran in 2002. As a twelve-year-old, Angelo McHorse took part in Red Willow's first Sustainability Institute. Now, as farm manager and college graduate, he is deeply grateful for all that has come before him, and feels that he can take the Red Willow project to a new level. "It feels like I'm completing a circle," he says.

My visit to Taos Pueblo left me inspired. This little farm-ers' market is about so much more than local healthy food production. It's also about robust local economic partner-ships, place-based environmentalism, indigenous rights, and community education. More than anything, it is an invi-tation to reinhabitation.

We need hubs like this all over our nation, hubs that retool our food economy. To those of us striving to walk the Jesus Way, my question is this: Why couldn't your local faith com-munity be at the forefront of that movement?

Churches are organized bodies of Spirit-inspired, values-driven people who care for their communities. This is our moment. What if churches saw them themselves primarily as campuses of economic life change, beginning with our own lives? What if thousands of local churches, embodying com-munity resilience, Earth-honoring practices, and compassion-ate connection, were at the forefront of a watershed discipleship movement? What if—instead of dragging our feet and staying immersed in business as usual—churches led outward, energiz-ing a movement that changed how we eat, how we shop, how we farm, how we work, how we use resources, and how we relate to the Earth and each other? If churches did things like this, we might actually carry good news to a culture desperately in need of salt, light, and leaven.

19

REIMAGINE OUR CHURCHES

DON'T HAVE AN EASY relationship with institutional Christianity. All too often, organized religion ends up supporting the warlike tendencies, ravenous greed, and socioeconomic inequities from which Jesus sought to liberate us.

Knowing this, I became a Mennonite almost twenty years ago.

Why? Well, frankly, if you're interested in participating with God's dream to make Earth as heaven, Mennonites are one of the best outfits going. Of course, Mennonite history and practice are fraught with examples of moral weakness and succumbing to the values of the dominant culture. But the opposite is also true: for five hundred years the Mennonite tradition has taken seriously the idea of walking the talk and following a radical Jesus. This has led to all types of embarrassing, empire-defying stances: civil disobedience, refusing to bear arms, intentional simplicity, forgiving murderers, loving enemies, befriending the poor, practicing mutual aid, and engaging deeply in global peacemaking.

And now, add to this list something else: watershed discipleship.

DID NOT OUR HEARTS BURN WITHIN US?

Picture this: July 2013, downtown Phoenix, Arizona. Me at my first national Mennonite convention. During the last hours of the weeklong event, about a dozen of us gathered from across the nation, hastily organizing our own meeting on white plastic chairs in a faceless food court. We came together as Mennonites to see what we could do in the face of environmental devastation and climate change. We came together as North Americans hoping to transform our policies, our perspectives, and our lifestyles. We wanted Mennonites to repent of our culture's ecocidal madness and our churches to engage in watershed discipleship, as followers of a God who loves all of creation.

What began as a hasty assembly evolved into a sacred circle. The Spirit moved strongly among and through us. Together we listened attentively and spoke prophetically. Here we were, at an institutional gathering for an institutional church, and transformation was filling the air. No lie—I was caught up. The potential for a new reality blossomed in my cynical heart. At the end of our meeting, the dozen of us departed to our own scattered parts of the continent, yet we did not feel alone. We now held a common vision: a near future filled with congregations across North America embodying watershed discipleship, changing our society from the inside out.

What do watershed discipleship communities look like? We think they share at least four key traits:

- They practice *bioregional adaptation*, seeking to craft sustainable lifestyles that fit within the gifts and limits of our watersheds.

- They enact *structural mitigation*, resisting ecocidal institutions and policies that threaten the health of our vital life systems.

- They actively support *community-based organizations* and *appropriate technologies* that foster healthy regional economies and provide mutual aid alternatives to dominant culture.

- They embody a *spiritual resilience*, sharing and living a scripturally grounded, community-based, Jesus-following, life-changing, Earth-honoring, despair-erasing Christianity that is light, salt, and leaven, even in the face of hopelessness.

How do we get there from here? How do we, steeped in a displaced and dysfunctional culture, learn to re-place ourselves? How do churches build capacity to become watershed discipleship communities?

RE-PLACING OURSELVES

Albuquerque Mennonite Church did something unusual last year; they became the focus of their own mission. Our own lifestyles in North America are what need changing, AMC realized. *We're* the ones who need to be converted. As we continue to be faithful to God, they asked, how do we live in right relationship with water, land, creatures, and one another? After living so long as un-placed and dis-placed consumers with global appetites and little local awareness, how do we learn to re-place ourselves and become denizens of our specific bioregion—the high desert of northern New Mexico?

As a church body, taking small but concrete steps, they began to respond to these questions. In the early part of 2014, they began with a three-part educational series on "Becoming a People of Place," gaining a scriptural and theological background for Earth justice and reconciliation. Then, in April, they hosted a capacity-building teach-in event, "Re-Placing Ourselves," aimed at increasing their own ability to be watershed disciples. For this event, which attracted more than seventy-five people, they hosted other church communities hailing from up and down the Rio Grande watershed, from up near the headwaters in Alamosa, Colorado, to my community in Taos, down to where the river flows into the gulf near Brownsville, Texas.

In addition to learning, praying, and connecting, the church was *doing*. Members started changing their shopping habits and taste buds, engaging more with local and community-supported agriculture (CSA). Others built hoop houses and are seeking to establish their own CSA. A "pilgrimage" group went to school on their own community to learn about what place-based initiatives and organizations were already established in the area. A "Zero Waste" group—aiming to attain what their name suggests—took a first step by sorting and weighing a week's worth of trash they found the church dumpster, which provided insightful feedback to daycare and congregation alike. A few other intrepid souls organized informational field trips to a nearby recycling plant, a commercial composting facility, and a local water reclamation plant. Three veteran practitioners hosted a composting and vermiculture class at the church, and another member continues to lead a series of "urban home-steader" how-to courses under her business, Old School. In its 2014 annual report, the Zero Waste team states it is now deciding on next steps—whether to concentrate on reducing the church's material waste stream, or to broaden its agenda to include reducing the church's use of energy, water, and toxins.

None of these steps are revolutionary by themselves. Taken as a whole, however, these small actions build upon and re-inforce one another, allowing an Earth-honoring church to act as leaven in the loaf of the dominant culture as we transition into a new era.

AND NOW FOR SOMETHING EDGY:
MENNONITE SUNDAY SCHOOL

Mennonites take their adult education seriously; it's what hooked my wife and I almost two decades ago. In Albuquerque, we joined a small group journeying through a curriculum called *Trek* that focused on the question "What is enough?"

Gathering weekly for soup, we reflected upon what was enough in all aspects of our lives—in categories like financial wealth, prestige, and possessions, but also categories such as free time, happiness, service, and deep relationships. As we reflected, we also made life changes, some minor, some profound. I don't know about you, but I'm not always surrounded by a caring group of friends meeting regularly to raise the question "What is enough?" It gave us a reality check—and an antidote— in a culture always seeking more.

Recently the Mennonites created another curriculum that has hooked me. This one is called *Every Creature Singing*, but don't let its innocent-sounding title fool you. If you let it, it just might change your life.

The curriculum contains a lot of scriptural reflection encouraging creation care, but that kind of study is fairly common and can be done in the safety of the sanctuary or during a comfortable coffee hour. What I like most about *Every Creature Singing* are its "circle questions," referring to the five- and twenty-five-mile "circles of discovery" it suggests you make around your church site and your home places. It is a curriculum of replacement, training you to be an aware and engaged denizen of your own region. It encourages fresh insights about home turf, seeing it with new eyes, with your boots on the ground.[1]

Initially, it asks the kind of fact-finding questions you might expect on a junior high field trip: What river systems, mountain ranges, and open spaces are part of your region?

What plant and animal species live in your ecosystem? In what biome do you dwell, and where else on Earth is this biome found? It also asks some basic economic questions: What do rural areas provide for urban areas? Where do you go for goods and services?

Then it starts getting a bit edgy, raising awareness about the mixed blessing that is our modern techno-industrial society. Where on your map do participants exercise dominion over the environment? Which entities within your region exercise the most decision-making power over the landscape? How do roadways connect certain communities but sever others?

The curriculum gets particularly interesting when it encourages us to look at our locales through a peace-and-justice lens. What forms of environmental damage or potential hazards are nearby? Are there dividing lines in your region regarding race, class, and infrastructure? Can you see any relationships between the location of low-income or minority communities and potential environmental hazards?

As humanity heads into the end of easy oil and the beginnings of a rapidly changing climate, this curriculum encourages us to know some basic transition education: How is your energy generated? If fossil fuels are used, where do they come from? Who are the largest producers of carbon dioxide in your area? Has your local climate changed significantly in recent decades, and how is it expected to change?

Then the curriculum moves to assess your community's preparedness: Where in your region are people planning for adaptation or climate change? Are business or government leaders concerned about this? What organizations are responsible for the environmental health of your area? How can you provide input to these groups?

A final line of inquiry invites us to assess our community's resilience, local health, and relationship to a transnational economy: What kinds of goods and services are actually produced locally? What are the sources of raw materials? What kinds of goods are not produced in our region, and how are they shipped in? Where does our drinking water come from, and where does wastewater go? How much of our food actually comes from our local area? How can we support the farmers nearby who are doing the best job caring for their land and animals?

Will this promising curriculum make any difference? Maybe not. Maybe just a handful of congregations will entertain it, and if they do, they might just stay safe studying Scripture within their sanctuary walls. But maybe some will step out from behind those walls and take a long look outside. Perhaps in these transition times, as dying churches seek to reinvent themselves and seek wiser, more sustainable ways, some will wade into their watersheds and learn again to be simply one part of a rooted and wild web of life.

THE WILDERNESS WAY

The Wilderness Way Community in Portland, Oregon, is not your usual faith community. Like the prophet Jeremiah, they stand at the crossroads of Scripture and nature, asking for the good way, ready to move. They aspire to embody three core values that weave their way through both Scripture and nature: Sabbath, Jubilee, and Shalom, what Jesus called the kingdom of God. In our era of ecological and economic crisis, they are passionate about incubating wild Christian disciples and fearless spiritual leaders who actively engage in the Great Turning, the vital transition work of our time. Journeying together as a faith community, their primary question is this: As followers of Jesus in an overconsuming and Earth-destroying society, how shall we live?

Like many alt-communities, their path of development has not always been easy. The group originated less than ten years ago, yet cofounder Solveig Nilsen-Goodin terms their current configuration a "third generation," since the group has already experienced two significant shifts in membership, and its identity has evolved through these changes. At several times in its young life, the church was on the verge of extinction, yet the vision wouldn't die—it had a life of its own, fueled by the Spirit.

"More than once I was ready to give it up," Solveig told me. "I said, 'God, I don't need to do this.' But new life kept emerging just when I thought we couldn't go on." At a particular low point—just after the other cofounder had moved on—Solveig was overwhelmed with gratitude by the arrival of four high-energy, high-capacity young people who wanted to commit themselves to the group. "It was absolutely providential," she recalls, still amazed. "They brought so much. Their creativity and faithfulness have sustained and shaped us in ways I could never have imagined."

In 2013, the Wilderness Way Community was solid but tiny, with six committed members. But in the last year, it has veritably exploded with new life: last month, seventeen adults and five children participated in a retreat.

SEVEN (ATTEMPTED) PRACTICES

The Wilderness Way Community knows that authentic discipleship is all about how we live. That's why it is a practice-oriented community, a *dojo* in which to practice a way of transformative living. But over the years they've found living transformatively isn't so easy in a conforming world. The seven practices below were developed in the early days of the group, designed as a way to shape their lives intentionally and create a parallel society. For some members, most of the practices were brand new; for others, some of the practices were already part of how they lived their lives.

The group tried to commit to these "sustainability" practices for a while, but then stopped. Why? It was too exhausting. "For three or four years we worked with these, and they were power-ful," confided Solveig. "But after a while, we found them to be, ironically, *un*sustainable, unrealistic. I mean, working on seven different disciplines, all at once? It was just too overwhelming." Members of Wilderness Way were dealing with the kinds of changes that life brings—people moving, children growing up, families needing to tend to their own issues. Simply put, lead-ing an examined life can be exhausting.

Wilderness Way engaged in these practices for a few years, and I include them here because they inspire me.[2] Maybe you, too, will find them inspiring as you seek a better way of living. Maybe someday Solveig and I will be in for a delightful sur-prise, and we'll see wild Christian disciples and fearless spiri-tual leaders living them out in joy.

SEVEN (ATTEMPTED) PRACTICES OF THE WILDERNESS WAY COMMUNITY

1. *Sustainable Life Practice.* We commit to make regular time and space for renewal, including restorative time in nature.

2. *Sustainable Community Practice.* We commit to practice a relational covenant that embodies the values of love, repentance, forgiveness, reconciliation, and peacemaking. (Specifics are laid out in their Shalom Covenant.)

3. *Sustainable Economic Practice.* We commit to continually

name how many financial and material assets are "enough" for ourselves as individuals, households, and as a community; we then share, save, and ask for what we need in accordance with this amount.

4. *Sustainable Food Practice.* We commit to increase the percentage of local, seasonal, organic, and fair-trade food in our daily diets.

5. *Sustainable Energy Practice.* We commit as individuals, households, and as a community to minimize carbon emissions through reduction of energy use and offsets.

6. *Sustainable Consumption Practice.* We commit to continually reduce the amount of "stuff" we accumulate as individuals, households, and as a community.

7. *Sustainable World Practice.* We commit to global transformation by living our values through public witness and action around specific issues about which we feel passionate.

Although the seven sustainability practices proved too daunting for the Wilderness Way Community to embody fully at this time, the group remains passionate and joyful about leading Spirit-filled, practice-centered, values-driven lives. These days, the members of Wilderness Way walk their path of discipleship by living into what they call the "spiritual-social practices of Sabbath, Jubilee, and Shalom."[3]

SABBATH means resisting the pressure to incessantly "do" and "produce" by re-grounding oneself in the beauty, abundance, and trustworthiness of the sacred universe, in order to:

- Restore balance to self and relationships

- Remember who we are and why we are here
- Rekindle creativity and passion for life

JUBILEE means redefining how much is enough in a hyper-consumer society, in order to:

- Restore value to life and relationships in a capitalistic economy
- Release ourselves and others from the burdens of debt, wealth, or poverty
- Reduce the negative ecological impact of our lives on the planet

SHALOM means recognizing the inherent wholeness and unity of all creation, in order to:

- Restore the birthright of all people to live without violence and to be treated with dignity
- Re-establish relationships of forgiveness and healing with others, including the earth and those who may be considered our "enemies"
- Re-create continually the conditions for peace in the midst of world cultures obsessed with war

For Wilderness Way, practice is ongoing and rhythmic. Once a month, as church, the community gathers to reflect upon their discoveries, struggles, and blessings as they try to live an intentional life of Sabbath, Jubilee, and Shalom. Another time each month they are church while hiking and spending time in wild places. Rhythmically, seasonally guided by the twin inspirations of Scripture and nature, this small group strives to become the people God yearns for them to be by walking the Wilderness Way.

CARNIVAL DE RESISTANCE

It was night, the circus tent was steamy, and I was in the middle of a twenty-eight-foot-long whale puppet swimming our way through the wide-eyed crowd. Earlier in tonight's show, when a group of women were dancing ecstatically and waving blue veils to the rhythm of wild drums, I was out of sight offstage, taking my turn on one of the stationary bikes that generated the electricity needed to power the amps. But right now it was my turn to be under the spotlight. Human-sized Raven and Dove had set the week's tone with their prophetic theatre during the Air show yesterday evening. The Fire show was coming tomorrow. Right now, we were still deep in Water.

I suddenly realized: this is church.

If the carnival theatre was church itself, then the carnie campground was communion. The carnival crew—perhaps twenty to thirty of us—dwelled together in the grass and mud for the week, eating and sleeping, praying and singing, practicing and performing as a body of troubadours.

To call our waystation for the week a *campground* is not quite accurate; rather, it became a community and village, an experiential demonstration plot for the kingdom of God. A ring of tents housed us, circled near a hobo-medieval cooking pavilion that used no fossil fuels. The figure who masterminds this petrol-free temporary village is Jon Felton, a man who seems equal parts mechanic, mystic, and musician. His gentle, thoughtful demeanor and captain's hat bring a welcome sense of calm competency and grounded vision to all the idealism and exuberance of the carnival. For every meal during our week together, the kitchen crew heated pots and pans on Jon's twiggy-fire stoves, using local brush and dead tree branches, and we cleaned up by carrying water and using Jon's foot-pump washing stations. Bikes and bare feet were more prevalent than cars. Prayers and song rang out often and enthusiasti-cally. Most of our food was gathered from dumpsters and local farms; each day, miraculous dishes were made from mysteri-ous ingredients—and, somehow, all were fed. Waste, what little there was, was composted and recycled. All of us, under Jon's gentle direction, were encouraged to be responsible citizens and shepherds of this beloved community: to look for what needed doing, and do it.

Tevyn East and Jay Beck, two of the core animators of the Carnival de Resistance, call this kind of experience the "Holy Game." They've mounted three carnivals of this magnitude so far, each one somewhat different than the last. Each time a new carnival experience is initiated, the Holy Game begins. Success is uncertain and results are unknown. What out-comes will happen with all of these untrained people? Will we have enough food, despite the ludicrously small budget? Will it all come together, despite the comically brief amount of rehearsal time? Will the Spirit be present and manifest something altogether unexpected? Will unknown gifts arise and radical grace appear? Each time a carnival is produced, Jon, Jay, Tevyn, and their colleagues set the stage, create the space, open themselves to wild possibility, and then wait upon the Lord. This is church embodied, pure incarnation. As they wrote to me when they sent me an invitation to participate in this year's carnival: "expect for the Spirit to transform us in the process."

What's this carnival about, exactly? That was my burning question before I arrived. I'd been invited to join the troupe for the week's festivities, even though I had no musical talent or theatre experience. I think all they really needed from me was a willingness to work hard, a love of adventure, and a wild desire to jump into new things.

But what was I supposed to *do*? What roles should I take? And what was the Carnival de Resistance trying to accomplish? My head wanted to understand before my body was going to participate. But when I showed up last summer at the Wild Goose Festival in Hot Springs, North Carolina, my questions were not answered immediately. Jay and Tevyn and the rest of the carnival crew gave me warm embraces and wide smiles, but without much explanation we got to work. That first day, as I worked and brought supplies to the grounds, I repeatedly walked by a sign posted at the threshold of the carnival space:

We have to start from where we are.

But can we imagine ways of doing things that keep us
    closer to God's dream for humans and the earth?

And then, as the Spirit begins to work in our imaginations,
    can we put our minds and muscles to the task?

We can.

And thank God for a theology of grace, so we can press
    on in the freedom and joy of humility, despite our
    hypocrisies, our mistakes, our accidental arrogance.

I don't want to wait until I'm sure no one can criticize me.

I want to stumble into Graceland.

Instead of providing me with intellectual information about goals and outcomes, the carnival gave me an experiential invitation, just like the call of Jesus: come and see.

Don't get me wrong about keeping it all mysterious. Tevyn and Jay aren't silent about the reasons why they created Carnival de Resistance; they can spout theology and articulate visionary mission statements with the best of us. They would just rather have you experience it instead of talk about it. "The Carnival is an educational and interactive forum," they state in their program information. "By celebrating the beauty and craft of sustainable options for ecological living, and facilitating rituals for lamenting the harm we have practiced against the Earth and each other, we hope to cultivate reflection and Spirit-led action."

Cultivate seems too mild a term. What they really want to do is what true church should do: interrupt normal consciousness to kickstart awareness and transformation. My job during the days prior to our performances was to build the Clock Tower—a ramshackle, Daliesque tower festooned with multicolored ribbons of cloth and dozens, literally dozens, of crazy timepieces in various states of disrepair. A huge sign hung crookedly across the base asked: "Do you have Time, or does Time have you?"

At certain moments during the carnival midway operating hours—when the milling throng would least expect it—a great bell would sound, and a human-sized cuckoo bird looking like a Mad Hatter would emerge from the massive tower to spout philosophical poetry, providing a raucous disruption. Moments later, the cuckoo-man would return to his lair within the tower, and a degree of normalcy would return to the midway.

The Carnival de Resistance is a liminal space—a threshold between worlds—where one can come to dream, immerse oneself in, learn about, reflect on, and playfully participate in wild-eyed artistic happenings and alternative practices. The immersion zone that is carnival provides shock therapy—immediate bodily experiences that directly jolt us from our captivity to consumer culture, intellectual distancing, alienation from the Earth, unconscious racism, and comfortable oppression.

After simmering in the Carnival de Resistance for a week, I find the experiences of the big top and the wilderness to be eerily parallel. The words of William Stringfellow sum it up well: "biblical people, like circus folk, live typically as sojourners, interrupting time, with few possessions, and in tents, in this world. The church would likely be more faithful if the church were similarly nomadic."[4] The Greek word for church, *ekklesia*, literally means "the assembled ones" or, even better, "the called-out ones." What a fitting term for those who will help us reimagine our churches and the wild calling of Christ.

20

REENViSiON OUR COMMUNiTiES

I WAS BROWSING THROUGH a magazine, early in 2014, when a bold sentence caught my eye: "On a farm in Missouri, a radical experiment in self-sufficiency." But it was the next sentence that stopped me in my tracks: "Marcin Jakubowski has built tractors, a brick press, and other machines from scratch."

The article described Marcin Jakubowski, a Polish-American farmer-engineer with a PhD in fusion physics, as an agrarian romantic for high-tech times who builds industrial machines from basic parts.[1] His life project focuses on designing and building fifty affordable machines, which—together—are able to produce all the basics a small community needs to sustain a comfortable self-reliant existence. The list includes things familiar—tractor, bakery oven, wind turbine—and things more fantastic: for example, a bioplastic extruder that turns plant-based plastic into a wide array of household elements, from window frames to adhesive tape. Another mind-expanding machine in Jakubowski's top fifty is the aluminum extractor, a contraption developed for lunar missions that pulls metal from clay.

CONSTRUCTING A DEMONSTRATION SITE

In our era of transition, this man is reenvisioning what communities should look like, big time. I'm reading in between the lines, but it's obvious that Jakubowski has been asking certain questions for a long time: What do human communities truly need in order to survive and thrive in a sustainable future? How can these things be produced?

I'm guessing that this farmer-inventor would agree with the sentiment behind R.E.M.'s hit song "It's the End of the World as We Know It (And I Feel Fine)."[2] Instead of being depressed or paralyzed about the gradual collapse of contemporary civilization, Jakubowski is catalyzed; in the face of social unraveling, his passion is to complete a demonstration community of radical self-sufficiency that can serve as a template for social rebooting everywhere. The *New Yorker* summarizes his philosophy like this: "Freedom and prosperity lie within the reach of anyone willing to return to the land and make the tools necessary to erect civilization on top of it." As of 2013, Jakubowski had built sixteen of his fifty necessary machines, and was deep into further production.[3]

POEITAI: THOSE WHO MAKE REAL

Marcin Jakubowski is a doer. In Greek, he would be *poeitis*, a "maker," a "doer," "one who makes real." A community of doers would be *poeitai*. Jakubowski's example inspires, challenges, embarrasses, and humbles me, all at the same time. He helps me see a possibility of how much more empowered followers of the Jesus Way can be—and need to be—as we become the people God has been waiting for. I am not universally endorsing Jakubowski's approach; rather, I am in complete awe of his "let's do this thing" attitude. Like many of us who dream about a better world, I tend to be long on ideas but a bit shorter on implementation. The apprentices who show up at his Global Village Construction Set headquarters—a farm and factory in rural Missouri—seem to be a lot like me: most are more about preaching the words than actually producing the works.

Jesus' brother James seems to have been in the same kind of situation—a doer in a community of talkers, striving to create his brother's vision of a parallel society called the kingdom of God. Remember, two thousand years ago this life-changing movement envisioned and embodied by Jesus was in its infancy. Its charismatic founder had just been crucified, and James was the main leader of a community of Spirit-filled Christ-followers in Jerusalem who were doing their best to continue Jesus' legacy, embodying a parallel and transformative society in the shadow of the Roman Empire. Like Marcin Jakubowski, James was surrounded by some action-challenged aspirers to a new way of life who hadn't quite integrated their beliefs and their deeds. Check out what James says: "But prove yourselves doers of the word, and not merely hearers who delude themselves. For if anyone is a hearer of the word and not a doer, he is like a man who looks at his natural face in a mirror; for once he has looked at himself and gone away, he has immediately forgotten what kind of person he was" (James 1:22-24 NASB).

TAKE A LOOK AT LOCALOGY

Jesus' brother James, were he alive today, might be proud of this mission statement: "Our task is to help people move from being passive consumers to active producers in all aspects of their lives." It's the mission of Localogy, a tiny nonprofit organization of which I'm board president. My friend Daniel Hutchison started Localogy in Lama, New Mexico, a tiny canyon community nestled at an elevation of 8,500 feet along the base of the Sangre de Cristo Mountains. Some folks say the Spanish conquistadors named this range the "Blood of Christ" mountains because of the beautiful copper light that illuminates them every sundown, while others say they are so named because the small streams that rush down its canyons are a precious lifeblood—holy water for people living in a dry and fierce land.

Even now, with homes dotting its foothills, Lama Canyon remains a rugged and remote place, only lightly modified by human engineering. As you walk its land, you're more likely to see dogs, horses, or goats than humans. With scattered, humble, earth-built homes and no central water system, the Lama community often seems like another country. It's a fitting home for Localogy, because it's a kind of refuge from technocratic consumer culture—far enough from dominant society to allow perspective, and wild enough to be a place apart.

A LODGING PLACE IN THE WILDERNESS

The prophet Jeremiah was fed up most of the time. Like a lot of us with high expectations of other people, I'm guessing he was a real jerk to the folks around him. He didn't have a lot of patience for a flawed humanity that easily strayed from the good path. In one instance, he reaches his exploding point and exclaims, "Oh, that I had in the desert a lodging place for travelers, so that I might leave my people" (Jeremiah 9:2). Yet although Jeremiah projects the blame upon his people, he also knows he needs to fix himself. Can you identify? Me too. I'm guessing most of us can identify with a man who's both deeply disturbed by—and drawn toward—the dominant culture around him, yet needs a place to escape for a while to clear his soul.

We have a place like that in Lama. My friends and I in Localogy have come to understand that in order to help over-civilized people move from passive consumption to active production they need a place apart, the kind of "wilderness lodge for travelers" that Jeremiah yearned for, removed from dominant society physically, culturally, and spiritually. Our wilderness lodge spaces don't hold much—just a small, wood-heated adobe home and a thirty-foot-diameter yurt without running water, together able to house about six people. But they do the job.

Modern city people usually experience a cultural vacuum when they visit our tiny community of Lama for the first time. They're a little startled: Where are the paved roads and the stop-lights? Where are the shopping centers, movie theaters, and restaurants? Where can I buy a good cup of coffee?

The answer to all of these questions is: *somewhere else.* There is not a lot to purchase in Lama. That does not mean, however, that there is not a lot *here*; open space abounds, and members of our small community are growing their own food, building their own houses, irrigating from the *acequia*, and processing their own wool. There are hundreds of acres of forest and farm-land; there's a thirty-year-old summer camp and an innovative public school; and there's a volunteer fire department and a world-renowned retreat center.

SPECIALIZATION IS FOR INSECTS

In short, Lama is a great place for people to learn how to move from being passive, techno-addicted consumers to active pro-ducers, in many areas of their lives. People often come to this "place apart" to discover how to be a new kind of person and to write a novel, learn an instrument, build a windmill, or learn how to make cheddar cheese. We in Localogy decided a few years ago to run summer internships in the area, help-ing people to become *poeitai*: doers. We're nothing like Martin Jakubowski, with his incredible set of homemade machines to reboot human civilization, but we do our small part to push the human project to its next stage of development. We like incubating modern Renaissance people, doers who are not afraid to try new things and master many skills. We like fostering people who can butcher a sheep and do digital design and repair a motorcycle, and at the end of it all, as Robert Pirsig says in *Zen and the Art of Motorcycle Maintenance*, discover that the motorcycle they've been working on is, in fact, the self.

In this day and age, we can no longer afford to sit back and let other specialists define our planet's future. Like Jesus' brother James, we need to be up and doing, reimagining our communities, engaging the Spirit, and participating in our own fate. Robert A. Heinlein said it best: "A human being should be able to change a diaper, plan an invasion, butcher a hog, conn a ship, design a building, write a sonnet, balance accounts, build a wall, set a bone, comfort the dying, take orders, give orders, cooperate, act alone, solve equations, analyze a new problem, pitch manure, program a computer, cook a tasty meal, fight efficiently, die gallantly. Specialization is for insects."[4]

THE NEW COMMUNITY PROJECT

The New Community Project (NCP) doesn't kid around. Well, they do, but not about their mission. Situated in the town of Harrisonburg, in Virginia's Shenandoah Valley, they aspire to do exactly what their name suggests: embody a new kind of community. This community exists as a living laboratory, a demonstration site, promoting peace and cooperation through works of justice, creation care, and experiential learning.

NCP Harrisonburg's vision is as audacious and expansive as its founder and animator, Tom Benevento. They seek transformation and healing at all levels—the interpersonal and the planetary, the spiritual and the political, the economic and the ecological, the neighborhood and the national. The New

Community Project is all about creating and embodying sustainable systems that care both for their place on Earth and for underserved populations, including homeless and immigrant populations who live in their area. At their main community house, residents are a mix of young, eager idealists and weathered older folks overcoming addictions, all striving to live better together in their precious place.

When I first met Tom, he was pulling up to the community house on his bike, immediately greeting a small gang of residents who were preparing to continue work on an outdoor cob oven. I'm not sure which of Tom's traits I find most appealing: his articulate passion, his vibrant youthfulness, his wide-ranging intellect, or his sincere humility and desire to learn from anyone, anytime. Understand, this is a distinguished, silver-haired man who could easily be in charge of a corporation; but he just seems to want to spend his time doing something more worthwhile, like shifting Harrisonburg—and perhaps the rest of America—into a new way of living. The man is a fount of energy; around him, it seems like anything is possible. In fact, most things *are* possible for the New Community Project; in a very short span of time, a host of initiatives and start-up projects have erupted into mature, sustainable systems. A neglected block of old, dilapidated homes in a part of town historically called "the Wasteland" now forms a thriving source of community strength. Like master weavers, Tom and the NCP team bring together many separate entities— granting agencies, loan officers, city councils, neighborhood advocacy groups, the housing authority, visionary young adults, immigrants wanting gardens, addicts desiring a new chance— and integrate them in one big visionary fabric that reinvents the downtown community. I like how Tom puts it: "We seek to create space for resurrection and reciprocity where we can make whole that which is broken or wasted, animate a society in which it's easier to be good, and divest from destructive systems and create new ones to which people can say yes."

Gardens and bicycles are in the lifeblood of NCP, literally and metaphorically. Two community homestead gardens were initiated by NCP more than five years ago in areas across town, providing low-resource families and immigrant populations places to plant and harvest. Another large garden sources the Muddy Bike Urban Market Garden, a business venture employing NCP people and folks off the street to deliver produce by bicycle to local restaurants, a grocery store, and nearby public schools. Though initiated with grant support, this start-up venture became self-funded by its fourth year. A new partnership with the Salvation Army is in the works to establish a neighborhood orchard. Everyday Bikes, a community bicycle shop started in 2008 with a grant from the Voluntary Gas Tax, has operated for years largely through the devoted efforts of Daniel, a long-term NCP member. This bike shop serves the needs of low-resourced individuals and runs primarily on funds earned from the shop products. Daniel, Tom, and other NCP folks were crucial to the visioning and creation of the Northend Greenway, a multiuse bicycle/pedestrian path and greenbelt serving the north end of Harrisonburg.

The members of New Community Project continue to learn and adapt as they seek a better world. For example, instead of simply providing abundant food, they now center on food justice—a big-picture vision of diverse communities exercising their right to grow, sell, and eat food that is fresh, nutritious, affordable, culturally appropriate, and grown locally with care for the well-being of the land, workers, and animals.[5] Hearing this vision for Harrisonburg, I couldn't help but think of Raul

Cabrera in Ecuador, sharing the nation's constitutional vision of *buen vivir* for all.

NEW HOPE ON MAIN STREET

NCP's Hospitality House and Sustainable Living Center, located on Main Street in Harrisonburg, is thriving. The house was obtained through a joint partnership with community nonprofits and the Harrisonburg Redevelopment and Housing Authority. The center's purpose is to help people gain new skills and training so they may leave homelessness behind and start new lives. Just in case you find this mission too narrow, don't be worried; the center is also all about intentional living, hosting demonstrations for Harrisonburg residents to learn about sustainable living practices, and is an incubation center for projects throughout the city.

During my visit, it felt like the NCP residential community ran like a hybrid between a summer camp, college dorm, and monastery. The day began with optional prayer or meditation, followed by breakfast. The community then laid out its day together: individual crew leaders described projects to be done; residents selected activities they would do; special events were announced, updates were given, and unique needs addressed; and then people got to work. *Bread labor*—an age-old monastic term NCP uses to describe practical chores like food growing, construction, wood chopping, bike maintenance, and cottage enterprises—is usually done in three-hour blocks in the morning or afternoon, interspersed with lunch and singing and followed by free time, dinner, and special community events. Four square matches happen every Thursday and sometimes get quite rowdy. "I am still determined to win," Tom tells me, and I can't quite tell if he's serious.

NCP's combination of shared purpose, passionate playful spirit, and creative mindfulness is hard to resist. Even though the community works very hard, labor stops seven times a day when the bell of mindfulness is rung. For sixty seconds, all work ceases. "The bell is central to our understanding of sustainability," explains Tom. "As we learn to stop and slow down, our hope is that we can better be in the present moment and experience the beauty that is right in front of us."

NCP seems to embody a rare blend of boundaries and possibility. Because of its diverse constituency, full occupancy, and mission to end addiction, the community house needs some pretty direct house rules: rules banning alcohol, drugs, weapons, and violent behavior; rules for designated smoking areas and locked prescription medication; rules regarding common spaces, quiet times, visitors, and sleepover guests.

Yet right next to the house rules are expectations for creation care. The New Community Project expects all its members, from any background, to uphold a culture-shifting commitment to sustainable living. NCP's written commitment to creation care reads: "NCP is moving towards a carbon-zero environment by limiting its waste production, recycling and salvaging materials, and creating closed-loop systems. Limited use of electronics is expected in the common areas of the house. Residents of the NCP house must be willing to make changes to their lives and habits to increase the well-being of our world as well as increase the well-being of our own spirits."

Visionary, vulnerable, passionate, and imperfect, New Community Project is an experiment in living, an active research and development site for humans transitioning to a new way of living, in which the Earth is not to be treated as an object and the Other is not to be treated as an enemy.

By no means is it smooth or easy; in fact, my visit was interrupted when my host was called away for an intervention with another community member. But it is filled with light, life, and exciting possibility. NCP Harrisonburg seems like a flagship for all of our communities-in-transition, charting the waters and showing us better ways to live together in the precious places we call home.

21

RESTORE OUR HOME

A **DUBIOUS ACQUISITION**," a friend muttered about the old adobe hacienda we had just acquired in early 2014. After living in the mountains of Lama fourteen years, five of them in our yurt, we had decided to relocate to Taos because our son was starting high school downtown. We were looking for an earthen home that could be an anchor for an intentional community. It needed to be inexpensive and centrally located, built of natural materials with lots of room for improvement. We finally found such a place and jumped at the option. "A unique opportunity," a realtor had commented—a little too brightly for my liking. "Tons of potential!"

Little did I know then how important this home's story would become to my journey of re-placement.

The house had been on and off the market for years, unsellable. It was far too vast for anyone wanting a cozy family home and far too handmade for anyone looking for a mansion. Its recent history was not good. The place had been neglected for some time, and after being purchased as a foreclosure in 2009, had not been substantially improved. At the time we encountered the house in late 2013, it was unoccupied. In room after room, garish blues, attacking oranges, and electric greens assaulted the eyes. "Who would paint their house like this?" we couldn't help but wonder. My friend said, "It feels like I just walked through four different houses."

A dubious acquisition, indeed. Yet something enticed. Beneath the gawdy veneer were hidden good bones and a rich history, I just knew it. Underneath the cheap and superficial trappings was a deep and rooted sense of place. Someone had once taken great care of this home, I realized. Someone had cared about materials and detail and quality. It was worth a second look.

BENEATH THE SURFACE

When we returned a second time, we dug beneath the surface tackiness to find its original nature. When we returned a third time, we brought a plumber, an electrician, a roofer, and a builder. I challenged each to tell me why this house was a bad idea. And when we returned a fourth time, we kindled flames in the fireplaces and spent the night in sleeping bags, wandering the rooms in firelight, imagining its first inhabitants and listening to its noises. The next day took a deeper look.

Our patience paid off. Under bad paint we found eternal adobe bricks, handmade on site from local earth. Covered by a depressing dark stain, the ceiling was made of massive hand-peeled *vigas* and beautiful *latillas* harvested from Taos Canyon. Inset next to cheesy lamp fixtures in the thick walls we discovered deep *nichos* awaiting saints, books, and candles.[1] Under cracking parquet flooring hid hardwood planks, locally milled. Next to a newer section of cheap drywall stood two massive wooden posts, brought eighty years ago from Taos Pueblo. Side by side with inexpensive kitchen cabinets we uncovered intricately carved drawers and lintels, designed by a sure hand.

But *whose* sure hand? Who had built this impossible house, with ten rooms and seven fireplaces? Early documents named a man called Udell. As we spent our first night in the home, we read by candlelight a handwritten note from the builder's daughter. She had grown up in this house eighty years ago, and in her old age had written about her father and her life under this roof, memories to share with whomever might live here after.

A MAN AND HIS LABOR

We discovered that Isaac Udell first came to Taos in 1924. He was a chiropractor by training, but was grandfathered into the medical profession in 1930. Udell became a birth specialist—a midwife—and drove long distances on rough rural roads to meet those who needed his services. Taos was a different world then, far more elemental than it is now: sparsely settled by Pueblo peoples and descendants of the conquistadores, the region was mostly earth and sky. Electricity didn't come to the area until 1928, and paved roads wouldn't arrive for another few decades. "Doc" Udell delivered 3,300 babies during his time in Taos, and for his services would often get paid in apples or meat rather than American currency.

His daughter, in her letter, recalled being a small girl while her father and brothers built the house around her. They made adobes on the spot, and when the first room was complete they all moved in for their first winter. She remembers her father adding on every summer; he was up early many mornings, building by himself. He had two sawhorses, and the family took turns peeling roof beams with a sharp drawknife.

Step by step, room by room, Udell built his house by hand. His daughter remembered that he gathered rocks for the foundation one load at a time, mixed cement in a wheelbarrow one bag at a time, and mixed the mud one batch at a time, adding straw until it was perfect. He dug the well by hand and planted saplings, thin as a pencil. All timbers came from Taos Canyon. The massive wooden posts with the holes in them that frame the walls in one room were gateposts from Taos Pueblo, probably received in a trade for medical services.

Reading the letter by firelight, wandering through the rooms of this hand-built house, I realized something. The posts, the beams, the walls, the sacred *nichos*, and beautiful carvings—this wasn't just a house. This was a work of soul made of earth, a body of art planted in one place. We hadn't just bought a house; we'd inherited a legacy.

Like the adobes themselves, hidden under layers of time and decades of neglect, Doc Udell's story had been waiting, patiently, to come to light. Buried under layers of neglected history, the legacy of the master craftsperson who constructed my adobe home has been revealing itself to me. Like Marcin Jakubowski and Robert A. Heinlein, Isaac Udell must have thought specialization was for insects. I've discovered he was a true Renaissance man; not only was he a chiropractor, midwife, and builder, he was also a talented sculptor, painter, and writer. A Taos folk historian recalled the doctor as a man who valued a few useful possessions: he owned his own home, two chairs, three pairs of boots, an eight-year-old car, and a hunting rifle. She concluded, "He also owned his own soul."[2]

His was a consciously crafted life of authenticity and creativity, uniquely integrated with the people and the place of Taos. As a transplant to this area, it's the kind of life I strive to live: a life of service and relationship, of creativity and compassion, of embodied respect for local earth, culture, and people. But let's be clear: like me, and perhaps like you, Udell was a transplant, a newcomer to an area and a culture he chose to call home.

I want to take his specific story and relate it to our larger story today: In our modern society of rootlessness and globalism, how can displaced people re-place themselves? We were all native once, at home in some place. How can modern settlers learn how to become re-placed again, creatures of a culture and a bioregion, and learn lifeways from those who came before? Is it even possible? In my mind, it *has* to be possible, because this is the only hope we moderns have. If we are to become the people God yearns for us to be, we need to learn to coexist as interdependent creatures of a place—not extracting and exploiting and importing from every corner of the globe to satisfy our appetites, not modifying everything to fit our whims. It seems like Doc Udell did a pretty good job fitting himself to the local culture and landscape rather than modifying the indigenous to fit to him. I cannot be sure, but I believe he was welcomed and received warmly by the native folks of Taos Pueblo. From an old, obscure magazine I discovered, I do know his character aligned deeply with that of Taos: "The reality of Taos puzzles and offends those visitors who look only for the values of industrialism and modern technology. The visitor often . . . feels that the world of Taos is out of the running, is archaic, is foolish nonsense. It is the intuitive person who gets inside Taos, understands it, and learns to love it as well as fear it. Such a person is Doc Udell."[3]

A HUMAN RE-PLACED

"I am come home."[4]

These words written by Udell about his connection to Taos were no false boast. He was a man married to place. Eighty years ago, even as he built his home by hand, he built his home with words:

Taos—a town of mud houses, houses whose mud is trampled by big-jointed bare feet and waded into form by young brown hands or wrinkled old ones. . . . Houses they are of earth, yet more than earth, houses of the core. Houses which shall one day be sifted back to center—back through the rumbling bowels of the earth . . . back to that pure state to complete the cycle, the highest not the last, for in again reaching the center, purified, they shall have but come to the beginning. Man here has served his mud house, has been served by it. He has been the conductor and the conducted.[5]

In my new old adobe, I read these words by firelight. I touch the massive traditional roof beams he set above me, the foot-thick walls of mud he formed at my side. Will I ever be able to live in a way that embodies Udell's words, "I am come home"? Will you? I think of the man writing his words, building with earth, adapting to place, serving the people, living with the land, and creating his paintings in these very rooms. In all these things, he poured out from his creative well his deep appreciation of Taos and his deep respect for the existing culture. The house has been neglected, yes, but its spirit is strong, and as I reflect on Udell's legacy I hear a voice whisper: *Restore my home.*

Legends tell us that, nearly a thousand years ago, a young Italian named Francis was in the crumbling Chapel of San Damiano in Assisi, war-troubled, world-weary, and uncertain how to proceed in his life, when he heard God's voice speak clearly: "Francis, rebuild my church, which you can see has fallen into ruin." Looking around at the condition of the dilapidated little chapel, Francis took this command literally, and began restoring the church, stone by stone. From that starting point, he began to understand God's directive to include also the spiritual rebuilding of the larger church.

I wonder, how is God calling to us today? Could God be whispering, "Restore my home"? Even as I restore Udell's adobe back to vibrant life, even as we modern people today build our personal homes out of more sustainable materials, can we come to realize that our true calling is much bigger—about renewing and restoring our relationship to our larger home, the sacred Earth, the place God has chosen to pitch his tent, to be his dwelling place?

My friend Stephanie came by yesterday to plug in her electric car. She lived next door to us in Lama, and we shared a washing machine when we lived in the yurt. Now that we live in the center of Taos, twenty miles away, we've become her way station. She can do errands and bring her kid to gymnastics, and then visit with us and top off her battery in case it's a bit low. Out here in our little mountain town, electric cars are still oddities. Convenient charging stations and smooth, level roads are rare or nonexistent. But Stephanie's household and mine are partners, taking small steps together to help restore our relationship to our Earth home, so we get creative.

When she arrives, I drag her 220-volt extension cord through my house and plug it into the outlet for our clothes dryer, which we rarely use due to the abundance of Taos sun that strikes our backyard clothesline. This time when she visited we updated each other on our latest findings. She had discovered a farm in our region that sold flour from wheat they had grown and ground, and I told her about the barley I'd planted this winter so that we could provide our own fodder for our milk goats instead of importing so much hay from farther away.

Stephanie's household and mine are walking together on a journey of rewilding and restoration. It's slow, and we stumble, but we help one another on the path. Inspired by the ancient biblical example of Ruth, we're beginning to live into what it means to say your way is my way. Inspired by modern examples of the Transition movement and the New Community Project, we—like Doc Udell before us—are taking a few of our own steps on the path of energy descent and community resilience. We are learning to live a bit more within our niche as citizens of our watershed.

Like many of my friends in Taos, Stephanie is intelligent, passionate, creative, and totally suspicious of organized religion. She left institutional Christianity a long time ago—it was far more hurtful than helpful to her as she was growing up—but she likes the way my wife and I are trying to follow Jesus. She's part of the loosely affiliated band we call TiLT, the Taos Initiative for Life Together. Some of us label ourselves as Christian, others do not, but we all strive to reimagine and rewild the good life in America, starting with our own. We're inconsistent and distracted with other concerns, but we often find ourselves growing food together, raising goats together, educating children together, wandering the mountains together, resisting empire together. We run camps and start schools and lead treks and build greenhouses and mentor apprentices and manage nonprofits and conspire to change our lives together, journeying and dreaming of a wilder way.

As we go about our daily lives here in Taos, trying to restore right relation with our Earth home, I often find myself humming a hymn I learned from my friends of Wilderness Way in Portland: "Can we be manna for each other? Can we be manna, manna? Everything I need is right in front of me. Everything I need is right in front of me."

STUMBLING TOWARD BETHLEHEM

A ND SO WE COME to the close of this book. My prayer, of course, is that it might urge all of us toward transformative Spirit-led action, and help us to become the prophetic people God yearns for us to be. I pray the message of this book might, in its own way, stir up a little holy discontent in the vein of this inspiring hymn: "Spirit, spirit of gentleness / blow through the wilderness, calling and free / Spirit, spirit of restlessness, stir me from placidness / Wind, wind on the sea."[1]

My prayer, however, might be a bit grandiose. It is only a book—a stack of words—and a flawed one at that. Did it provide enough inspiration? Did it include enough concrete examples? Did it go deep enough? Probably not, on all three counts. As I wrote, I listened to God as best I could, but this manuscript is at best a sketch, an invitation, a beginning step as we stumble forward together into times of wild transition. I cannot tell you how to rewild. Only you can take your next unfamiliar step. As a parting encouragement, I want to share some recent unfamiliar and stumbling steps of my own.

WALKING THE WATERSHED WAY

Last month I was licensed by Mennonites in our Mountain States region to be an educator, organizer, and capacity-builder for watershed discipleship in New Mexico and Colorado. What does that mean? I'm not sure, exactly, but I plan to find out. My first step will be to visit with existing groups in the larger region to find out what they are already doing and to highlight some of their place-based practices that they might want to share with others.

Next, I want to encourage groups and congregations in our Mountain States region to enter into a ten-year exploration with us, an invitation to life change that we're calling "Walk the Watershed Way." How can we each, in our own context, free ourselves from harmful lifeways and transition into a better future together by altering habits, innovating systems, and living lighter on the Earth? We're living into this question in 2015 by initiating a decadelong period of shared exploration, initiating and observing significant change in our own lives and in our communities. Each year, participating communities will craft an annual reflection and then share it with other communities, describing the best practices, struggles, questions, and surprises that emerged for them during the year. Peer communities will help develop measurable next steps and guiding questions, and together we'll head into the next cycle.

Why did we choose ten years? Three reasons. First, it's a time frame that encourages continued attention and accountability. Our Earth is going to undergo significant change in the next ten years. As we participate in this change and check in with each other each year, we want to think and act patiently like trees, but probably not so patiently as tectonic plates. We need to have a healthy sense of informed accountability within community, because our planet's health will be changing and we need to stay vigilant.

Second, a ten-year time frame gives a sense of practical urgency dosed with a healthy forgiveness. It makes us plan, prioritize, and prepare without feeling defeated. The kind of structural changes we need to make—in areas such as food sourcing, housing, energy, transportation, and community economics—are not going to happen overnight, or even in a year. Ten years seems like a daunting but doable time frame that honors the significant transition work ahead of us yet gives us breathing room. It allows us to make mistakes and learn from them.

Third, ten years from 2015 is 2025, which marks the five hundredth anniversary of Anabaptism. Five hundred years ago, a little after Martin Luther tacked his protests on the door of a Catholic church, the forebears of the Mennonites and Amish broke the law and scandalized Catholicism by baptizing one another and forgiving one another's sins without needing professional priests to do it for them. *Anabaptist* means *rebaptizer*, and these brave folk had the wild idea that true discipleship was about adult choice making, not about being saved through institutional allegiance and infant baptism. Five hundred years after these transformative actions, it seems fitting to have a reckoning and ask, what are we doing today that is transformative? What adult choices are we making now that are transforming today's institutions of conformity?

Where will this exploration of the Watershed Way lead each of us over the next decade? I'm guessing that no two communities will follow the same path. Some may be inspired by the example of Albuquerque Mennonite and turn collective will toward goals of drought-resistant xeriscaping, zero waste, and incubating community-supported agriculture. For other groups located in dense urban areas, walking the Watershed Way could turn both prophetic and political—in Detroit, for example, some faith communities are resisting powerful interests that willingly accept unpaid water bills by corporations but turn off the taps of the poor. Others, like Stephanie's family and mine, might enter into bioregional food covenants to see how we can adapt to what is available in our area.

I am both a Mennonite and an environmentalist. But where I live in northern New Mexico, the Watershed Way is deeper than either of those traditions. I'll be joining an ancient river, not creating something new. Over the next decade, I'll be learning from my neighbors at Taos Pueblo how they have been able to walk the Watershed Way in this bioregion for thousands of years. I'll be learning from traditional Hispanic farmers and ranchers how they have been practicing the Watershed Way here these past five centuries. I'm guessing that, where you live, you have mentors and guides, too.

Watershed living is one path of rewilding, one I am currently pursuing. For me, as a "half-done" Christian, it is not an intellectual exercise; it is experiential and transformational education, a learning-by-doing that results in liberated lifeways and systemic change. As I said earlier, you must be the one to choose your next unfamiliar step. Whatever path you choose to rewild the Way, I believe that it must be personal *and* political, social *and* spiritual, encouraging initiatives that are both individual *and* communal. What will it be for you, in your place, in your situation?

This book is no how-to manual, but it may have given you inspiration to see how the Spirit is stirring you from placidness in your own place. Perhaps you'll encourage your church to "go green" with solar panels *and* encourage your electric company to provide cleaner energy to the community. Perhaps you'll harvest roof rainwater *and* advocate for clean water laws. Maybe you'll get a few folks to commit to a bicycle-based lifestyle *and* fight against fracking. Or maybe you'll grow more of your own food *and* support local food hubs connecting producers to consumers and helping low-income people get healthy, fresh food. Maybe you'll travel light and get lost in the woods for weeks at a time, finding out you need a lot less from industrial society than you thought.

We're heading into transition times, my friends, an unknown wilderness for which there are no maps, only sketches. God is doing something new, and the Spirit is troubling the waters. As Ched Myers observes, whenever the Holy Spirit is poured out in human history, "traditions and institutions will be disrupted and disturbed." Our untamed God "is not a domesticated deity . . . but the one who seeks to liberate us from our enslaved condition."[2]

In a wilderness time like ours, we need a wilderness guide. The Greeks had a word for this: *hodēgos*, meaning a leader for the journey or a guide for the way. It comes from two other words: *hodos*, a noun describing a road, a way, or a journey; and *hēgeomai*, a verb that means "I lead" or "I think." *Hodēgos*, then, means a conductor, both literally and figuratively—a wilderness guide, or a mentor on a spiritual path. When Jeremiah advised his people, "Stand at the crossroads and look," I think he was acting as both.

In Jesus, we have the ultimate *hodēgos*, the eternal guide for wilderness times. He not only knows the way, he is the Way, and he calls us to follow along unfamiliar paths. By following his call, we'll be joining countless other disciples before us who have left empire behind for a wilder way, trusting in the words God loves to say: Be not afraid, for I am with you always, to the ends of the Earth.

ACKNOWLEDGMENTS

THANKS TO Valerie Weaver-Zercher, who—for some wild reason—found me in the midst of the unknown masses, tapped me on the e-shoulder, and suggested that I write this book. To Valerie and the rest of the team at Herald Press, particularly Amy Gingerich, Ben Penner, Merrill Miller, Jerilyn Schrock, and Dorothy Hartman: if it weren't for your encouragement, brave imagination, thoughtful questioning, wise editing, compelling design, savvy marketing, and consistent championing, this book would not exist. Many thanks to all the early reviewers of this manuscript, or sections of it, who made this a better work, especially Vickie Machado, Dave Pritchett, Julie Battenfield, Jennifer Davis Sensenig, and Luke Gascho.

Thanks to those who first sent me on the path of wildness and wilderness: Joe Yuska, Kelly Stevens, Kim Stafford, Tom Kittleman, Kate Gunness Williams, Ken Thompson, Kurt Hahn, Paul Petzoldt. Thanks to early mates John Gastil, Dan Jacobson, Chris Adams, Doug Caum, and Scott Laidlaw, who helped me see that life is an adventure.

Gratitude to those who first woke me to Sanctuary and social justice: John Fife, Jim Corbett, Jean Peacock, Rick Ufford-Chase,

Randy Claxton, and the beloved community at Southside Presbyterian Church in Tucson. Gratitude to those in Ecuador who have provided their friendship, food, shelter, guidance, passion, and opportunity, including the communities of Arte del Mundo, CRACYP, San Luis de Pambil, and Piedra Blanca.

Deep thanks to those who teach me how to be a good, earthy Mennonite, both relational and radical: Anita Amstutz; Ken, Leona, and Andrew Gingerich; Clayton Roberts; Herm Weaver; Joanna Shenk; Jaime Lazaro; Elaine Enns; Mark Van Steenwyk; Donna Detweiler; Jeff Books; Chuck Hosking; and the community of Albuquerque Mennonite. Thanks to my brother, Scott, for keeping me grounded and honest. And a special wave to my tramping teacher, Dimitri Kadiev, somewhere on the road with a paintbrush and a smile.

Much appreciation to all my guides and friends in Taos who deeply walk their own Watershed Way. I especially want to acknowledge Dr. John "Bud" Wilson and his late wife, Barbara; Stephanie Owens; Daniel Hutchison; Daniel Carmona; Roberta Salazar; Chris Pieper; Seth Blowers; Tony Duran; and Ernie Atencio.

Thanks to several communities who through their presence help me see and write about what more is possible: the New Community Project, Bartimaeus Cooperative, Lama Foundation, Wilderness Way, Carnival de Resistance, Possibility Alliance, and the Center for Action and Contemplation.

Special acknowledgments to Richard Rohr and Ched Myers—mentors, allies, and friends—who have shaped my soul with their words and deeds.

Most importantly, gratitude to my family for all the endless reading, listening, suggestions, and support you've given as I have grown as a writer and a person. Your patience and perspectives have been of incredible help. Thanks for believing in me.

NOTES

Prologue

1. Caroline Fraser, *Rewilding the World* (New York: Metropolitan Books, Harry Holt and Co., 2009), 8–9.

2. Ibid., 10. Fraser reports: Only one thousand protected areas existed in 1962, representing 3 percent of the Earth's surface. Now there are over one thousand protected areas worldwide, expanding conservation to more than 12 percent.

Chapter 1

1. Faith Citlak and Huseyin Bingul, *Rumi and His Sufi Path of Love* (Somerset, NJ: Tughra Books, 2007), 81.

2. Gilbert K. Chesterton, *What's Wrong with the World* (New York: Dodd, Mead & Co., 1912), 48.

3. Malcolm Muggeridge, *A Third Testament* (Maryknoll, NY: Orbis Books, 2004), 88.

4. John Dominic Crossan, *God and Empire* (New York: HarperCollins, 2006), 116.

5. Also can be translated "in your midst," "within you," and "among you."

6. Crossan, *God and Empire*, 117.

7. Theodicy—or the problem of evil—was a passion of Irenaeus, as well as modern religious philosopher John Hick. To explore more of Irenaeus's views—and the views of others—on this topic, I suggest two sources: Hick's *Evil and the God of Love* (Basingstoke: Macmillan, 2007), and Hick's essay "An Irenaean Theodicy," in *Encountering Evil: Live Options in Theodicy*, ed. Stephen T. Davis (Edinburgh: John Knox Press, 1981).

8. Richard J. Foster, *Streams of Living Water: Essential Practices from the Six Great Traditions of Christian Faith* (New York: HarperCollins, 1998), 197.

9. Thomas Merton wrote these words in August 1967 as part of a message from contemplatives to the world, as requested by a Cisterican abbot and Pope Paul

VI. This text is included in a number of Merton compilations, including *Hidden Ground of Love: Letters of Religious Experience and Social Concerns* (New York: HarperCollins, 1990).

[10] For PBS's identification, diagnosis, and treatment of affluenza, see "Affluenza," http://www.pbs.org/kcts/affluenza/.

[11] For a great primer on the subject, see John de Graaf, David Wann, and Thomas H. Naylor, *Affluenza: The All-Consuming Epidemic*, 2nd ed. (San Francisco: Berrett-Koehler Publishers, 2005).

[12] Joanna Macy and Chris Johnstone, *Active Hope* (Novato, CA: New World Library, 2013), 113.

[13] Jonathan Turley, "'I'm Outta Here': Wealthy Texas Teen Kills Four People, Seriously Injures Others, In DUI Case," December 12, 2013, http://jonathanturley .org/2013/12/12/im-outta-here-wealthy-texas-teen-kills-four-people-seriously-injures-others-in-dui-case-given-probation-and-no-jail-time/.

[14] Madison Gray, "The Affluenza Defense: Judge Rules Rich Kid's Rich Kid-ness Makes Him Not Liable for Deadly Drunk Driving Accident," *Time*, December 12, 2013, http://newsfeed.time.com/2013/12/12/the-affluenza-defense-judge-rules-rich-kids-rich-kid-ness-makes-him-not-liable-for-deadly-drunk-driving-accident/.

[15] Turley, "'I'm Outta Here.'"

[16] Gray, "The Affluenza Defense."

[17] Patrik Jonsson, "Rich Kid Gets Probation for Drunk-Driving Deaths," *Christian Science Monitor*, December 12, 2013, http://www.csmonitor.com/USA/ Justice/2013/1212/Rich-kid-gets-probation-for-drunk-driving-deaths.-His-defense-Affluenza.-video.

[18] Turley, "'I'm Outta Here.'"

Chapter 2

[1] DuPont's official slogan from 1935 to 1982 was "Better things for better living . . . through chemistry."

[2] Anna McCarthy, *The Citizen Machine: Governing by Television in 1950s America* (New York: The New Press, 2010), 50.

[3] Jim Corbett, *Goatwalking* (New York: Penguin, 1991), 4.

[4] Matthew Colwell, *Sabbath Economics: Household Practices* (Washington, DC: Tell the Word, 2001), 52.

[5] Delores S. Williams, *Sisters in the Wilderness: The Challenge of Womanist God-Talk* (Maryknoll, NY: Orbis Books, 2013), 110. The lyrics cited come from William Francis Allen, Charles Pickard Ware, and Lucy McKim Garrison, *Slave Songs of the United States* (New York: Dover Publications, 1995), 14. *Slave Songs of the United States* was first published in 1867.

[6] Ibid., 112.

[7] From the title of the book by Lynn Truss, *Eats, Shoots & Leaves* (New York: Gotham, 2006).

[8] The exodus story views the entire desert experience as a proving ground. One

location on the journey, Massah, is mentioned four times in Old Testament texts, and literally means "the place of testing." See Exodus 17:7 and Deuteronomy 6:16; 9:22; and 33:8.

9 Fraser, *Rewilding the World*, 4.

Chapter 3

1 James Douglass, *Lightning East to West: Jesus, Gandhi, and the Nuclear Age* (Eugene, OR: Wipf and Stock, 2006), 1. One of the most thought-provoking books I've had the honor to read.

2 Thomas Merton, *Wisdom of the Desert* (New York: New Directions, 1970), 5.

3 Ibid., 11.

4 Ched Myers, *The Biblical Vision of Sabbath Economics* (Washington, DC: Tell the Word Press, 2001), 16.

5 Merton, *Wisdom of the Desert*, 5–6.

6 Madison Kahn, "Divine Intervention," *Boston Magazine* (September 2013), www.bostonmagazine.com/news/article/2013/08/27/tim-dechristopher-divine-intervention/.

7 All quotations and information in this section regarding Tim DeChristopher are from an interview by Terry Tempest Williams, "What Love Looks Like," *Orion Magazine* (December 2011), orionmagazine.org/article/what-love-looks-like/.

8 In addition to many Web resources, see Shimon Gibson, *The Cave of John the Baptist* (New York: Doubleday), 2004. Also: Shimon Gibson and James Tabor, "John the Baptist's Cave: The Case in Favor," *Biblical Archaeology Review* 31, no. 3 (May–June 2005): 36–41.

Chapter 4

1 Martin Luther King Jr., "Remaining Awake through a Great Revolution" (commencement address, Oberlin College, Oberlin, OH, June 1965).

2 Ibid.

3 From Drew Dellinger's poem "Hieroglyphic Stairway." If this excerpt intrigues you, you can get the full poem at http://drewdellinger.org/pages/products/342/hieroglyphic-stairway_-poetry-poster-(digital-download).

4 Delivered at the National Cathedral, Washington, D.C., on March 31, 1968. Congressional Record, April 9, 1968.

5 Leviticus 26:12; Ezekiel 36:28; Jeremiah 30:22.

Chapter 5

1 Joseph Rawson Lumby, *The Acts of the Apostles* (Cambridge: The University Press, 1891), 233.

2 According to biblical scholar Henry T. Sell, retrieved from http://biblehub.com/library/sell/bible_studies_in_the_life_of_paul/study_iii_first_missionary_journey.htm/.

3 N. T. Wright, "Paul, Arabia and Elijah," *Journal of Biblical Literature*, 115, no. 4 (Winter 1996), 683–92.

Chapter 6

1. Richard Rohr, "Nature and the Soul," *Radical Grace* 24, no. 3 (Summer 2011).

2. This quote permeates Outward Bound literature and can be found at http://www .kurthahn.org/quotes/quotes.html.

3. Walt Whitman, "#82, Song of the Open Road," *Leaves of Grass.* The first edition was published in 1855, but Whitman spent much of his later life writing and rewriting it, resulting in many different versions over four decades, each so different that they range from a mere dozen to four hundred poems.

4. This quote is also a mainstay in Outward Bound literature and can be found at http://www.kurthahn.org/quotes/quotes.html.

5. Golo Mann, "Kurt Hahn," *Encounter* 46, no. 3 (March 1976): 84. Also available online at http://www.unz.org/Pub/Encounter-1976mar-00084.

6. Michael Knoll, "Schulreform through Experiential Therapy: Kurt Hahn—An Efficacious Educator," Catholic University, Eichstaett, Germany (2011), 6.

7. Robert Skidelsky, "A Respectful Farewell," *Encounter* 46, no. 3 (March 1976), 87. Also available online at http://www.unz.org/Pub/Encounter-1976mar-00087.

8. Ibid.

9. Ibid., 89–90.

Chapter 7

1. Bill McKibben, *Eaarth* (New York: St. Martin's Griffin Press, 2011), 100.

2. Donald D. Palmer, *Kierkegaard for Beginners* (New York: Writers and Readers Publishing, 1996), 100–103.

3. Slavoj Žižek and Glyn Daly, *Conversations with Žižek* (Cambridge: Polity Press, 2004), 54.

4. Lev Grossman and Matt Vella, "iNeed?" *Time* 184, no. 11 (September 2014), 42.

5. Ibid.

6. Ibid., 47.

7. Ibid., 44.

8. Ibid., 47.

9. Ibid., 45.

10. Malcolm Muggeridge, *A Third Testament* (Maryknoll, NY: Orbis Books, 2004), 81.

11. Ibid.

12. Ibid., 82.

13. Ibid.

Chapter 8

1. Melanie Jae Martin, "Newly Released: Tim DeChristopher Finds a Movement Transformed by His Courage," *Yes! Magazine*, May 23, 2013, http://www .yesmagazine.org/planet/tim-dechristopher-peaceful-uprising-movement- transformed-courage/.

2 Samantha Herndon, "Bidder 70: The Tim DeChristopher Story," *YES! Magazine*, Fall 2012.

3 Sarah Gelder, "The Boomers 'Failed' Us: Climate Activist Tim DeChristopher on Anger, Love, and Sacrifice," *Yes! Magazine*, Summer 2014.

4 Madison Kahn, "Divine Intervention," *Boston Magazine*, September 2013, www.bostonmagazine.com/news/article/2013/08/27/tim-dechristopher-divine-intervention/.

5 Melanie Jae Martin, "Newly Released"; and Jeff Goodell, "A Rosa Parks Moment: Climate Activist Tim DeChristopher Sentenced to Prison," *Rolling Stone*, July 27, 2011, http://www.rollingstone.com/politics/news/a-rosa-parks-moment-climate-activist-tim-dechristopher-sentenced-to-prison-20110727.

6 Ric Hudgens, "Tim DeChristopher's Unreasonable Morality" October 18, 2013, http://rdhudgens.blogspot.com/2013/10/tim-dechristophers-unreasonable-morality.html; and Herndon, "Bidder 70."

7 Gelder, "The Boomers 'Failed' Us."

8 Amy Goodman interview, "Released from Prison, Climate Activist Tim DeChristopher on Civil Disobedience and Building Movements," *Democracy Now*, NPR Radio, May 17, 2013, http://www.democracynow.org/2013/5/17/released_from_prison_climate_activist_tim.

9 Gelder, "The Boomers 'Failed' Us."

10 Ibid.

11 Martin, "Newly Released."

12 Jim Catano, "Returned 'Missionary' Tim DeChristopher: Activist Returns from Jail More Devoted to Cause," *Salt Lake City Weekly*, April 24, 2013, http://www.cityweekly.net/utah/returned-missionary-tim-dechristopher/Content?oid=2287471.

13 Gelder, "The Boomers 'Failed' Us."

Chapter 9

1 Wendell Berry, "The Futility of Global Thinking," in *Learning to Listen to the Land*, ed. Bill Willers (Washington, DC: Island Press, 1991), 154.

2 Ched Myers, "Repentance as Recovery: What the Church Can Learn from the Twelve Steps," *The Living Pulpit* (July–September 2004).

3 Jon Gertner, "We're Running Out of Water," *Fast Company* (December 2014–January 2015), 40.

4 Myers, "Repentance as Recovery."

5 Merton, *Wisdom of the Desert*, 24.

6 This paraphrase of Jesus' words and actions refers to John 8:10-11.

7 Rohr's and Sweeney's related comments following this footnote can be found in Richard Rohr, "Daily Meditation," Center for Action and Contemplation, December 2, 2014. They can be also found online at http://stjohnsquamish.ca/richard-rohr-death-heaven/.

Chapter 10

1. James Strong, *Strong's Expanded Exhaustive Concordance of the Bible* (Nashville: Thomas Nelson, 2009), s.v. Greek "*memyēmai*" of Philippians 4:12, http://biblehub.com/greek/3453.htm.
2. Frederick Brenk, "Old Wineskins Recycled," in *Relighting the Souls: Studies in Plutarch, in Greek Literature, Religion, Philosophy, and in the New Testament Background*, ed. Frederick E. Brenk (Stuttgart, Germany: Steiner, 1998), 347.
3. Ibid., 345.
4. Ibid., 347.
5. Ibid., 348.
6. Origen, *On Prayer*, chapter 17.
7. For a summary of this historical event, as well as its German sources, see http://en.wikipedia.org/wiki/Epiousios.
8. James Strong, *Strong's Expanded Exhaustive Concordance of the Bible* (Nashville: Thomas Nelson, 2009), s.v. Hebrew "*lechem*," http://biblehub.com/hebrew/3899.htm.
9. N. T. Wright, "The Lord's Prayer as a Paradigm of Christian Prayer," in *Into God's Presence: Prayer in the New Testament*, ed. R. L. Longenecker (Grand Rapids, MI: Eerdmans, 2001), 132–54.
10. Ibid., 152.

Chapter 11

1. James Strong, *Strong's Expanded Exhaustive Concordance of the Bible* (Nashville: Thomas Nelson, 2009), s.v. Hebrew "*anav*," http://biblehub.com/hebrew/6035.htm.
2. Thich Nhat Hanh, *Being Peace* (Berkeley: Parallax Press, 2005), 56.

Chapter 12

1. John Dominic Crossan, *God and Empire* (New York: HarperCollins, 2006), 122.
2. Ibid.
3. Herndon, "Bidder 70."
4. Terry Tempest Williams, "What Love Looks Like: An Interview with Tim DeChristopher," *Orion Magazine* (January–February 2012), https://orionmagazine.org/article/what-love-looks-like/.
5. Ibid.
6. Ibid.
7. Ibid.
8. Herndon, "Bidder 70."
9. Williams, "What Love Looks Like."

Chapter 13

1. Rebecca Solnit, *A Paradise Built in Hell: The Extraordinary Communities That Arise in Disaster* (New York: Viking, 2009), 4–5.

2 Macy and Johnstone, *Active Hope*, 125.

3 Ibid., 126.

4 D. L. Mayfield, "The Persecution Is Already Here," *Geez* 36 (Winter 2014), 11.

5 Roy Scranton, "Learning How to Die in the Anthropocene," *New York Times*, November 10, 2013, http://opinionator.blogs.nytimes.com/2013/11/10/learning-how-to-die-in-the-anthropocene/.

6 Ibid. Scranton says this advice comes from Yamamoto Tsunetomo's eighteenth-century manual *Hagakure*.

7 Ibid.

8 Ibid.

9 "The Dark Mountain Manifesto," http://dark-mountain.net/about/manifesto/.

10 Ibid.

11 Ibid.

12 Ibid.

Chapter 14

1 Mark Scandrette, *Practicing the Way of Jesus: Life Together in the Kingdom of Love* (Downers Grove, IL: InterVarsity Press, 2011), 11–12.

2 Wikipedia reports this passage occurs near the beginning of Murray's *The Scottish Himalayan Expedition* (1951).

3 Joanna Macy, *World as Lover, World as Self* (Berkeley, CA: Parallax Press, 2007), 150.

Chapter 15

1 Doris Janzen Longacre, *Living More with Less* (Scottdale, PA: Herald Press, 1980), 15.

2 Ibid., 53.

3 Doris Janzen Longacre, *Living More with Less,* 30th anniv. ed. (Scottdale, PA: Herald Press, 2010).

4 Derrick Jensen, "Forget Shorter Showers," *Orion Magazine,* (June–July 2009), https://orionmagazine.org/article/forget-shorter-showers/.

5 Ibid.

6 Ibid.

7 Joanna Macy, http://www.joannamacy.net/three-dimensions-of-the-great-turning.html.

8 Bill Plotkin, *Nature and the Human Soul* (Novato, CA: New World Library, 2008), 4.

9 Ibid., 4–7

10 Ibid., 7.

11 Ric Hudgens, "The Land Shall Have Its Rest," *Geez* 26 (Summer 2012), http://www.geezmagazine.org/magazine/article/the-land-will-have-its-rest/.

12 Ibid.

13 Tim Gorringe and Rosie Beckham, *Transition Movement for Churches* (London: Canterbury Press, 2013), 2–3.

14 Ibid.

15 Ibid., 4.

16 Rob Hopkins, *The Transition Handbook: From Oil Dependence to Local Resilience* (White River Junction, VT: Chelsea Green Publishing, 2008), 94.

17 Ibid.

18 Ibid., 98.

19 Gorringe and Beckham, *Transition Movement for Churches*, 11.

20 Ibid., 13.

21 Ibid., 34.

Chapter 16

1 Rabbi Saul Berman, "Jewish Environmental Values—The Dynamic Tension Between Nature and Human Needs," http://www.jewishvirtuallibrary.org/jsource/Environment/berman.html.

2 The four different translations of Genesis 2:15 presented are, in order, from the New American Standard Bible, the International Standard Version, the NET Bible, and Young's Literal Translation.

3 These translations come from the New Living Translation and the Holman Christian Standard Bible, respectively.

4 A very incomplete list: *of* the land is found in the NIV; *for* the land in Webster's Bible Translation; and *to* the land in Young's Literal Translation.

5 Kim Stafford, *Having Everything Right* (New York: Penguin, 1986), 3.

6 Ibid.

7 Franz Boas, "Geographical Names of the Kwakiutl Indians," *Columbia University Contributions to Anthropology*, No 20 (New York: Columbia University Press, 1934).

8 Stafford, *Having Everything Right*, 3–4.

9 Ibid., 4.

10 Ibid., 6.

11 Cited from curricular material provided by the Anti-Defamation League, http://archive.adl.org/education/curriculum_connections/doctrine_of_discovery.html.

12 Ibid.

13 City of Sherrill v. Oneida Indian Nation of New York, 2005.

14 Renee K. Gadoua, "Nuns Blast Catholic Church's 'Doctrine Of Discovery' That Justified Indigenous Oppression," Religious News Service, September 10, 2014, www.huffingtonpost.com/2014/09/10/catholic-church-doctrine-of-discovery_n_5793840.html.

15 Ibid.

16 Ibid.

Chapter 17

1 English translation of the Constitution of the Republic of Ecuador, as published in Georgetown University's Political Database of the Americas, http://pdba.georgetown.edu/Constitutions/Ecuador/english08.html.

2 Ibid.

3 "Ecuador Adopts Rights of Nature in Constitution," http://therightsofnature.org/ecuador-rights/.

4 Mario Melo, "Good Living and Nature in Ecuador's Constitution," http://therightsofnature.org/good-living-ecuador-2008/.

5 "International Rights of Nature Tribunal—Quito," http://therightsofnature.org/rights-of-nature-tribunal/.

6 "2014 Global Rights of Nature Summit Outcomes," http://therightsofnature.org/ron-summit-outcomes/.

7 Cormac Cullinan, "If Nature Had Rights," *Orion Magazine* (January–February 2008), https://orionmagazine.org/article/if-nature-had-rights/.

8 Ibid.

9 William O. Douglas's dissenting opinion in the case Sierra Club v. Morton can be found at http://faculty.cua.edu/pennington/Law508/DouglasDissent.htm.

10 Ernie Atencio, "The Man Behind a New Mexico County's Fracking Ban," *High Country News*, June 24, 2014, http://www.hcn.org/issues/46.11/the-man-behind-a-new-mexico-countys-fracking-ban.

11 Ibid.

12 Ibid.

13 Ibid.

14 Mark Oswald, "Mora County Fracking Ban Stays, For Now," *Albuquerque Journal*, October 14, 2014, http://www.abqjournal.com/479944/news/mora-county-fracking-ban-stays-for-now.html.

15 Atencio, "The Man Behind a New Mexico County's Fracking Ban."

Chapter 18

1 For the foundational thoughts of Ched Myers, as well as others' contributions to this growing and fluid movement, see www.watersheddiscipleship.org.

2 Ibid.

3 Wendell Berry, "The Futility of Global Thinking," in *Listening to the Land*, ed. W. B. Willers (Washington, DC: Island Press, 1991), 153.

4 watersheddiscipleship.org.

5 David W. Orr, *Earth in Mind: On Education, Environment, and the Human Prospect*, 10th anniv. ed. (Washington, DC: Island Press, 2004), 9.

6 See www.bioregionalfoodcovenant.org.

7 More about Dolman's concept of "basins of relations" can be found at http://oaec.org/our-work/projects-and-partnerships/water-institute/.

Chapter 19

[1] *Every Creature Singing* can be found at http://www.mennocreationcare.org/every-creature-singing.

[2] "Sustainability Practices," Wilderness Way Community website, http://www.wildernesswaypdx.org/resources/practices.

[3] "Core Values of WWC," Wilderness Way Community website, http://www.wildernesswaypdx.org/home/commonpractices.

[4] William Stringfellow, *Keeper of the Word: Selected Writings by William Stringfellow*, ed. Bill Wylie Kellerman (Grand Rapids, MI: Eerdmans, 1994), 53.

Chapter 20

[1] Emily Eakin, "The Civilization Kit," *The New Yorker*, December 23, 2013, http://www.newyorker.com/magazine/2013/12/23/the-civilization-kit.

[2] From the R.E.M. album *Document*, I.R.S. Records, 1987.

[3] Eakin, "The Civilization Kit."

[4] Robert A. Heinlein, *Time Enough for Love* (New York: G. P. Putnam's Sons, 1973), 248.

[5] As communicated to me in personal correspondence with NCP member Jonathan McRay, January 2015.

Chapter 21

[1] *Latillas*, from the Spanish word *lata*, or "stick," are thin, peeled saplings laid between *vigas*, or beams. *Nichos* are display places in a wall that show its depth and provide a place to put objects.

[2] Tricia Hurst, "The Legendary Characters of Taos," *New Mexico Magazine* (October 1977).

[3] Comments by editor John R. Milton from Isaac L. Udell, "In the Dust of the Valley," *South Dakota Review* 7, no. 1 (Spring 1969): 123.

[4] Isaac L. Udell, "In the Dust of the Valley," 18.

[5] Ibid.

Epilogue

[1] James K. Manley, "Spirit," http://www.hymnary.org/tune/spirit_manley.

[2] Ched Myers, *The Biblical Vision of Sabbath Economics*, 50.

THE AUTHOR

WHEN HE'S not rewilding Christianity, Todd Wynward spends his time reinventing public education and re-imagining the American way of life, starting with his own. He is crazy in love with his wife and son, and most of the time with his dog, too. He has been engaged in experiential education and social change movements for twenty years, and has spent more than a thousand nights outside. Wynward is cofounder of a wilderness-based public charter school, leads backpacking and river trips for adult seekers, and is an animating force behind TiLT, an intentional life-change movement in Taos, New Mexico. Richard Rohr calls his novel, *The Secrets of Leaven*, "a spiritual roller-coaster that skewers everything we think we know about organized religion, social change, and human potential." Recently he was licensed by the Mountain States Mennonite Conference and Albuquerque Mennonite Church to be an educator and capacity builder for watershed discipleship in the region. Further writings and doings can be found at www.rewildingtheway.com and www.TaosTiLT.org, or find Todd Wynward's author page on Facebook.